Was Baseball Really Invented In Maine?

A Lively Look
at the History of Professional Baseball
in Maine and at Every Mainer Who's
Ever Played in the Majors

Was Baseball Really Invented In Maine?

by Will Anderson

Will Anderson, Publisher
7 Bramhall Terrace
Portland, Maine 04103

Other Books by the Author
Beer, New England, 1988
New England Roadside Delights, 1989

Library of Congress Catalogue Card Number 91-90687

Anderson, Will 1940-
1. Baseball 2. Maine

ISBN 0-9601056-5-4

Studio photography by A. & J. DuBois Commercial Photography, Lewiston, Maine
Designed and typeset by PrintMedia, Portland, Maine
Color separations by Graphic Color Service, Fairfield, Maine
Printed by Spectrum Printing and Graphics, Lewiston, Maine

Text stock: 70 lb. Warrenflo, S.D. Warren Co., Westbrook, Maine
Cover stock: 12-point Lusterkote, S.D. Warren Co., Westbrook, Maine

Cover design: Mitchell Fernie, PrintMedia

Cover graphics, clockwise from upper left:
August, 1988 photo, vendor Matt Sherm at The Ballpark, Old Orchard Beach
Circa 1947 photo, Portland Pilot pitcher Charlie Dyke and unidentified fan, Portland Stadium, Portland
Lewiston's Bill Carrigan as depicted on a 1912 Hassan Cigarettes' card
Porter's Harry Lord as depicted on a 1909 Sweet Caporal Cigarettes' card
Circa 1964 photo, Cherryfield's Carlton Willey with the Mets
1987 Maine Guides' schedule
1985 photo, Auburn's Bert Roberge fires one in for the Expos

Table of Contents

Acknowledgments

Without the help of a lot of wonderful people WAS BASEBALL REALLY INVENTED IN MAINE? would most likely still be, as the saying goes, somewhere out in the centerfield bleachers. Thanks to:

Anne Ball, Portland Public Library, Portland, Maine   Marilyn Bennett, *The Piscataquis Observer,* Dover-Foxcroft, Maine
Gloria Bishop, Portland, Maine   Cliff Blake, South Portland, Maine
Ralph Botting, Mission Viejo, California   Dick Bresciani, Boston Red Sox, Boston, Massachusetts
Bill Carrigan, Jr., Auburn, Maine   Jane Carter, Portland, Maine
Emily Clark, Chicago Historical Society, Chicago, Illinois   Donald R. Close, Portland Public Library, Portland, Maine
Agatha and Bobby Coombs, Ogunquit, Maine   Karen Coombs, Westbrook, Maine
Anne Cough, Maine State Library, Portland, Maine   Gretchen Curtis, National Baseball Library, Cooperstown, New York
Paul D'Alessandro, Portland Public Library, Portland, Maine   Bob Davis, Portland, Maine
Bill Deane, National Baseball Library, Cooperstown, New York
Anna Delaware, Scarborough Historical Society, Scarborough, Maine
August Flaherty, Portland Public Library, Portland, Maine   Grady Fox, Breckenridge Library, Breckenridge, Texas
Rita Gorham, Portland Public Library, Portland, Maine   Larry Gowell, Lewiston, Maine
Joe Gromelski, Lewiston, Maine   John Ham, Falmouth, Maine
Roy Heisler, Vinalhaven Historical Society, Vinalhaven, Maine   Augie Helms, Union, New Jersey
Hale Joy, Ellsworth, Maine   Ben Keating, Maine State Library, Augusta, Maine
Patricia Kelly, National Baseball Library, Cooperstown, New York
Tom Knight, Borough of Brooklyn Baseball Historian, Brooklyn, New York
Veve Lele, Georgetown University, Washington, D.C.   Patience-Anne Lenk, Colby College, Waterville, Maine
Corky Lippert, California Angels, Anaheim, California   Eileen MacAdam, Portland Public Library, Portland, Maine
Debbie Matson, Boston Red Sox, Boston, Massachusetts   Don MacWilliams, Portland, Maine
Sheila McKenna, Maine State Library, Augusta, Maine   Arnold McKenney, Auburn, Maine
Sonny Noel, South Portland, Maine   Barbara O'Donnell, Aroostook County Historical and Art Museum, Houlton, Maine
Andrew, Jason, and Sharon Packer, Auburn, Maine   Tom Renino, Portland Public Library, Portland, Maine
Bert Roberge, Auburn, Maine   Glover Robinson, East Rochester, New Hampshire
Marjorie and Robin Rominger, Breckenridge, Texas   Muriel Sanford, University of Maine, Orono, Maine
Cindy Scott, Rochester Public Library, Rochester, New Hampshire   Karen Shafts, Boston Public Library, Boston, Massachusetts
E. Shorey, *The Bridgton News,* Bridgton, Maine   Arlene M. Stone, East Rochester, New Hampshire
Suzanne Sullivan, Goodall Memorial Library, Sanford, Maine   Stan Thomas, Redmond, Washington
Ron and Robin Tingley, Riverside, California   Kris Toothaker, Bowdoin College, Brunswick, Maine
Debra VanLaningham, St. Louis Cardinals, St. Louis, Missouri   Mary Anne Wallace, Westbrook College, Portland, Maine
Ed Walton, Bridgeport, Connecticut   Nela (Mrs. Bill) Weir, Anaheim, California
Beverly Wescott, *Morning Sentinel,* Waterville, Maine   Carlton Willey, Cherryfield, Maine
Claudua Zaher, Cincinnati Historical Society, Cincinnati, Ohio
Abigail Ewing Zelz, Bangor Historical Society, Bangor, Maine

Special Thanks To

Laura (Mrs. Del) Bissonette, Winthrop, Maine, for the loan of photographs.

Tom Hug, Lorain, Ohio, for the loan of graphic material and for invaluable research on the naming of the Cleveland Indians.

Leroy Rand, South Portland, Maine, and the Maine Baseball Hall of Fame, for the loan of photographs and for general input.

Clyde Sukeforth, Waldoboro, Maine, for the loan of photographs.

Kim Barry, Dawn Patterson, and Liz Valliere of Print Media for their care and concern.

Preface

I am privileged to write this book.
I spent the first ten years of my life in Yonkers, New York, just north of the Bronx line. It was a hotbed of baseball enthusiasm. We'd play hardball or, more often, stickball every day from late March until late autumn. And when we weren't playing ball, we were busy - very busy - collecting baseball cards.

At age ten my family and I moved to Ardsley, about fifteen miles further north. My mother and father thought it would be a "better environment" for my sister and me. But it was the suburbs. It was dull. Nobody ever heard of stickball, and even rounding up enough players to shag flies was difficult.

Still I persevered. Somehow I got my allotment of baseball. My parents, while hardly big fans of our National Pastime, didn't discourage my love of the game. In fact, my mother often told the tale of how her father, Patrick Phelan, fresh from County Laois in Ireland, would labor six days in a Brooklyn, New York furniture factory . . . and then on the seventh day - after church, of course - would take his family to Ebbets Field. "He felt," my mother used to say, "that it would help make us American." He was right.

There is a beauty and a rhythm to baseball that seems almost like a ballet . . . a ballet set in a diamond. It's a ballet with over a century of folklore woven into every game. And over a century of batting averages and earned run averages and stolen bases that allow - better yet, encourage - grandparents and parents and sons and daughters to debate the merits of a Ty Cobb vs. a Stan Musial vs. a Wade Boggs. It is a sunny day holding down third base or relaxing in the stands. It is checking a box score to see how a favorite player has done. It is lining a single up the middle. It is baseball. And there is nothing else quite like it in the world.

I am also privileged to live in Maine. I am "from away." Yonkers and Ardsley are not Maine. It is possible, though, that I appreciate the wonder and beauty of Maine more - or, certainly, differently - because I am a native of elsewhere. This book is my way of showing my feelings for my adopted state.

I have very much enjoyed researching and writing WAS BASEBALL REALLY INVENTED IN MAINE? I very much hope that you enjoy reading it.

Will Anderson

Portland, Maine
November 21, 1991

Dedication

WAS BASEBALL REALLY INVENTED IN MAINE? is dedicated to everyone who's ever enjoyed the game of baseball, either as a player or as a spectator. It is especially dedicated to my southern Maine Singles' Network comrades . . . with whom I've spent so many wondrous hours playing softball by the sea.

Singles' Network Softball Gathering
Fort Williams Park, Cape Elizabeth, June 1991

BASEBALL AND MAINE

No, baseball was not invented in Maine. In fact, baseball wasn't invented anywhere: the game we know today evolved from a number of British games, with rounders having the most influence.

But baseball and its predecessors have been played here a long, long time.

Beginning in the late 1700s, town ball and "one old cat," both variations of cricket and rounders, were popular throughout New England. In 1828, just eight years after Maine gained statehood, a Portland newspaper made reference to boys playing at "bat-and-ball."

In June of 1846 the first "modern" game of baseball - with a diamond and rules not awfully dissimilar from today - was played. And, notwithstanding the wonderful legends that surround Cooperstown, New York, it was played in Hoboken, New Jersey.

It took awhile, but this modern game - and its popularity - moved steadily north. By 1858 we know it had arrived in Maine . . . because an article in the September 11th issue of *The Portland Daily Advertiser* heralded the fact that the Portland Base Ball Club had ventured to Boston to play the Tri-Mountain Base Ball Club of that city. The game was played September 9th on the Boston Common.

We Win

What is especially heartwarming about the article is that it reports that the Portland club not only played the Tri-Mountains . . . but beat them. The score was 47 to 42. It was a score representative of baseball's early days. Fielders wore no gloves; pitchers tossed the ball underhanded (i.e., they really did "pitch"); and batters could signal where they wanted the ball pitched. There was plenty of action, resulting in scores that appeared more as if the two teams were having a go at football rather than baseball.

The First Game in Maine?

The first *documented* game of baseball (it should be noted that newspapers of the day did not exactly have "sports pages"; in fact they were basically advertising vehicles) to actually be played in Maine took place on October 10, 1860. Although a time of year now generally set aside for World Series' games, that October saw the Sunrise Club of Brunswick host the senior class team of Bowdoin at the Topsham Fair Grounds.

With the outcome again a scorer's delight, the Sunrise squad triumphed 46 to 42. The club's outburst of 12 runs in the fifth inning was the big difference. Remarkably, a box score published in the October 12th issue of *The Brunswick Telegraph* looks very much like the box scores of the 1990s, over 130 years later.

A Media Event in Portland

The game that appears to have really gotten the grand old game going in

Maine, though, was another almost four years in coming. When it arrived, however, it was not just a game. It was a media event. It was a contest between Bowdoin and the sophomore class team of Harvard.

Played on July 4, 1864 in Portland, it was trumpeted by the press throughout the state from June 20th on. *The Bangor Daily Whig and Courier, The Brunswick Telegraph, The Lewiston Daily Evening Journal*, and Portland's *Daily Eastern Argus* all carried, some with more than one announcement, the news that Bowdoin and the boys from Cambridge were going to square off on the Fourth. Typical of the announcements was this one, from the "Local Intelligence" section of the June 28th *Argus:*

> Base Ball - It seems that the most skillful ball players of Harvard and Bowdoin Colleges are to contest in the match game to be played in this city on the Fourth of July. The citizens are to offer a purse of $75, "just to make it interesting." Two hundred students are expected to be present from Harvard and a still larger number from Bowdoin. The Harvard boys are the challengers.

One final announcement followed, on the 4th itself, that "The match game of Base Ball between Harvard Sophomores and Bowdoin nines will be played on the Trotting Park near Camp Berry this afternoon at 3 o'clock."

Alas, the game did not fare well for the Bowdoin nine. Just organized that very spring, they were no match for the Harvards. As reported in the July 6th *Argus:*

> HARVARD AND BOWDOIN AT BASE BALL
> The first nine of the Sophomore class of Harvard University and the first nine of Bowdoin College indulged in a contest for muscular superiority and skill by a game of base ball near this city on the Fourth. Although the result was by no means close the match was well contested. The Bowdoin boys, notwithstanding they were soon left far behind, played with pluck and spirit to the end. The Harvard boys won chiefly by their rapid pitching and skillful catching. The Bowdoin students have been accustomed to playing with a slow pitch, and when the ball came to them as if sped from a parrot gun, it completely upset their calculations.

There was more. Lots more. The write-up was remarkably extensive. And it proved, in another way, that not all that much has

Special Meeting.

The Members of the Queen City Base Ball Club are hereby notified to meet at their Hall Wednesday evening, June 12th, at 7½ o'clock. All are hereby requested to be present, as important business will be brought before the meeting.
Per order of Com.
junell 2t°

Bangor Base Ball Club.

There will be a meeting of the Club at the usual place, on FRIDAY, May 29th, at 9 P. M. Members are urgently requested to be present.
Per Order. W. E. BROWN,
may 29 Sect'y.

A pair of baseball club announcements from *The Bangor Daily Whig and Courier*. The Queen City notice is from June of 1867; the Bangor Base Ball Club's from May of 1868.

When the Pennesseewassees Played the Crescents

By the second half of the 1860s a Maine Base Ball Association had been organized, and an annual tournament was held to determine the state's very best. Teams such as the Augusta Cushnocs, Portland Eons, Lewiston Androscoggins, Bowdoins, Newport Unas, Bangor Penobscots, Saccarappa Crescents, and Norway Pennesseewassees competed for first (a silver ball), second ($50.00) or third ($25.00) prizes.

It is worthy of note that, after an 1868 match in which the Pennesseewassees (referred to in the write-up as "the P-and-the-rest-of-its") bested Saccarappa 26-5, the *Whig and Courier* opined that "The Crescents ought to have known better than to have attacked such a name as that!"

It is also worthy of note that, in 1869, a sporting periodical out of Boston known as the *National Chronicle* chastised one of its own state teams for melting down - and cashing in on - its first-place silver ball, while commending Maine's victorious team for not doing the same.

changed; good pitching and a solid defense generally still wins. Not that Harvard hurling was invincible. Bowdoin scored 13 runs in their nine innings. The problem was that Harvard scored 40 in theirs.

What was more important - much more important - than the game's outcome was that it attracted attention. Less than a week later, on the 12th, the *Argus* reported that the game had "aroused the interest of our young men in this fine sport." It was further reported that a number of the city's populace had met on the Arsenel grounds and organized a club.

The success of the Bowdoin-Harvard game did more than attract the attention of the area's young men. It attracted, as well, the interest of the City of Portland's governing fathers: the next year, 1865, they included baseball in the city's official 4th of July Celebration. Any club in the state could participate. A prize of $50.00 was to be awarded to the best team, with $25.00 going to the second best. Three teams from Portland, plus Bowdoin (from Brunswick) entered . . . and this time Bowdoin reigned supreme. They topped the Eon Club, 34-31.

Portland was not alone; baseball became a highlight of Independence Day festivities throughout much of Maine.

The Grandest Fourth of Them All

The grandest Fourth of July of them all had to be July 4, 1876. Our Centennial. America was one hundred years old! Was baseball included in the festivities? You bet it was!

From far and wide throughout the state came reports of a grand and glorious Fourth . . . with a ballgame - or even a pair of them - generally a key ingredient in the celebration. *The Bangor Daily Whig and Courier,* in its coverage of the day's events headlined "WELL DONE, BANGOR," declared that "The most exciting spectacle of the entire celebration was the game of base ball between the Mutuals of St. John and the Orients of this city." A large part of the excitement most likely stemmed from a great comeback staged by the home team: down 11-1 at an early point in the game, the Orients came back to take the game - and the silver ball, of course - by a margin of 18-16.

In Lewiston/Auburn it was reported that over 50,000 people took part in the day's merrymaking. Two ballgames, one in the morning and one in the afternoon, added to the splendor of it all.

Baseball was a part of what was billed as "The Grandest Demonstration Ever Witnessed in the Town" in Machias, while Rockland's program of "bells, salutes, procession, trial of engines, sailing and rowing regatta, tub and foot races, and other diversions, ending with an oration by Prof. A.A. Woodbridge," was dampened - if you'll pardon the pun - by its ballgame between the Rockland Dirigos and a picked nine being broken up by a heavy rainstorm.

Not to be outdone, of course, Portland staged its own day of days. The press reported that "The principal streets at an early hour were thronged with people in holiday attire, and the numbers were constantly increased by the arrival of trains coming in laden with celebrators from the surrounding country." Featuring several parades and processions, a rowing regatta, band concerts, a grand sailing regatta, an historical pageant, the ringing of bells for an hour, and the salute of guns - three times, once to honor the original thirteen states, once to honor the twenty-four states which made up the union at the end of its first half-century, and once to pay tribute to the thirty-six states then in existence - the "celebrators" were further

Greetings

Time was when everybody sent postcards . . . and most everybody collected them, too. Here is a sampling of postcard art from Independence Days of long ago.

On Deck

The term "on deck" - meaning the batter who's up next - was born in Maine. In Belfast. Baseball historian Ed Walton, in his book THE LANGUAGE OF BASEBALL, reports that in an exhibition game between the Boston Red Stockings and a Belfast nine on August 6, 1872, the field announcer shouted his proclamations to the crowd for the Red Stockings as "Wright at bat, Leonard and Barnes next." But when the home team was up he added a bit of a nautical flair: he announced "Moody at bat, Boardman on deck." The Bostons liked the term and brought it back to the Hub. It has been a part of baseball's lexicon ever since.

treated to a pair of baseball matches. At 9:00 AM, on the Western Promenade, the Portland Dirigos took on, and beat, the Portland Juniors for a purse of $50.00. At 2:30 the Resolutes and the Dry Goods, both also of Portland, fought it out for a purse of $125.00, no small amount in those days. Shortened by rain, the game went to the Resolutes by a score of 10-1.

Augusta, alas, reported that "The Centennial Birthday of the United States was quietly observed in this city." *The Daily Kennebec Journal* for the 4th, in fact, included but one reference to baseball in capitaland. On page three was a public notice from one B.F. Harris, Superintendent of Public Buildings, expounding that "all persons are forbidden to play 'Ball' on the State Grounds." Could this have been the derivation of the word "spoilsport"?

The 1880s

By 1880 major league baseball was fast becoming firmly entrenched in the minds and hearts of much of America, Maine most certainly included. In those halcyon days before radio and television, it was fully up to the press to keep the fans informed. Closest to the action, among the state's host of newspapers, was the *Daily Eastern Argus*, as yet Portland's paper of the day. The *Argus* had begun to include - under the heading "Sporting Matters" - a more or less complete rundown of major league standings, replete with commentary. It was at best a once-a-week affair, usually appearing on Saturday or the following Monday. But it was informative. And candid. Here are a pair of examples from 1880:

> During the past week the weak nines have bettered their positions. It will be noticed that all the clubs which bring up the rear have advanced a few per cent since we published the last schedule. Boston gave the Chicagos a surprise and demonstrated that the latter nine were not quite as invincible as they were considered. (June 5)

> The games the past week have resulted favorably for Boston, Buffalo, Chicago and Troy. Poor Cincinnati meets with its usual success, receiving defeats from every nine it plays with. The Chicagos still continue in their successful career, and it looks as though the question was settled as to who will fly the pennant next season. (June 12)

And fly the pennant Chicago did. Known as the Cubs today, Chicago's National League entry was then known as the White Stockings. They finished well atop the eight-team loop, not in the least because of the splendid success of Hartland, Maine's very own George Gore. Nicknamed "Piano Legs," Gore played a very respectable centerfield for the White Stockings, and batted a robust .360 . . . good enough to lead the league in hitting. A distant second was teammate Cap Anson, with a .337 mark. Third was first-baseman Roger Connor, of the Troy Trojans, with .332. (Both Anson and Connor are, incidentally, enshrined in the Hall of Fame. Piano Legs is not.).

"Worsted"

What I, at least, most appreciate about the "Sporting Matters" news and views of baseball is the descriptive nature of the words chosen. Some may consider it stilted, even flowery. I consider it wonderful. For example, when the Belfasts - a powerhouse representing, of course, the city of the same name - played the Portlands in August of 1884 it was written that their pitcher "was a puzzler, his swift drop demoralizing the base hits." Belfast, which outscored Portland 6-1, had a third inning which was described as "prolific in runs." In spite of the loss for the home team, though, the paper could and did report that "The ladies were quite numerous in the grand stand yesterday, and their fair faces and bright colors attracted admiring comments."

Teams did not lose; they were "worsted." When a team was hitting well it was stated that it "took kindly" to the opposing pitcher's efforts. When a team had difficulty scoring it was because "the necessary hit or error would not occur." Enthusiasm on the part of the players was worthy of praise. The Belfast nine, for example, was characterized as a team that "play ball with an apparent love for the game, which may account for their good success." Goading - in a genteel fashion, of course - was not above the "Sporting Matters" staff. After a loss to a team called the Shoe and Leather Nine, the Portland club could read that some of its members "do not put enough life in their playing." The paper's advice: "Move about lively, boys, and try for everything. It adds interest to the game."

But the *Daily Eastern Argus* was, after all, a Portland newspaper. When, later in the season, the Portlands rebounded to top Belfast 11-6, the paper's headline was slightly less than genteel. It read "Ha! Ha!! We're tickled."

The year 1884 was an especially rewarding one for Portland-area baseball enthusiasts. Not one, not two, but six major league teams came to town to put on exhibition games before delighted audiences. To be sure, big leaguers had come to Maine before. The champion Boston Red Stockings had barnstormed the state in the early 1870s, and the Cincinnati Red Stockings, in the National League's inaugural year of 1876, had trounced the Portland Resolutes in a game in Portland. But never had there been such an outpouring as in 1884.

Starting it all off was a game between the Boston Nationals (known then as the Red Stockings; later to be known as the Braves) and the Portlands played on July 22nd. Newspaper accounts reported "an immense audience gathered to witness the Boston's method of manipulating the bat and ball." They were not disappointed: the Boston nine clobbered the local squad. When all the talleying was done the score was 29-3. Portland had the 3. "The detailed score," as the account concluded, "will give an idea of how

When Chicago Ruled the Baseball World

From 1880 through 1886, the Chicago White Stockings - the predecessors of today's Cubs - dominated the National League, capturing five out of a possible seven pennants. Patrolling centerfield for all seven of those seasons - and batting over .300 in six of them - was Hartland, Maine's George Gore.

Team portrait, 1881 Chicago White Stockings

LADIES' BASE BALL
Walking Shoes.
Grand Thing for the Sea-shore.
PINAFORE SLIPPERS, STRAP SLIPPERS
Opera Slippers, Opera Newport Ties, Opera Sandal Button Shoes, Cloth Top Button Boots,
GENTS' FINE SUMMER SHOES.
Straw and Manilla Hats.
HAMMOCKS,
From $1.00 Upwards.
F. A. CURTIS,
2 Kenduskeag Bridge.
July1

"Base Ball Walking Shoes"
What do these shoes, advertised in the July 3, 1880 issue of *The Bangor Daily Whig and Courier*, have to do with baseball? Nothing. And that's the charm of the ad. Baseball was catching on. To associate with it was beginning to be in fashion.

much running the Bostons did around the bases, and how industriously the home out fielders hunted leather."

Undaunted, the Portlands took on the Providence Grays - the team that was to top the National League that year - slightly less than a month later, on August 18th. The outcome was little changed: the Grays won handily, 20-1. Portland catcher Callahan averted a shutout by "lifting the sphere over the left field fence" in the fifth inning. Graciously, the *Daily Eastern Argus* noted that "the (Portland) boys were too well aware of the superiority of their opponents; were too anxious to do well, and therefore were unable to do decently."

The parade of big league teams continued. For the rest of the season, however, they played among themselves rather than feast on the Portlands. On August 25th, Providence and Boston - in the midst of their battle for the flag that Providence eventually won; Boston finishing second - returned, playing before a packed crowd of 4,000 at Presumpscot Park. The Grays' famed Charles "Old Hoss" Radbourn (who won a never-to-be-approached sixty games that season!) "rested" his arm: he played centerfield for the first six innings, not coming to the mound until the seventh. Even then he did not do well . . . but it was clearly Boston's day anyway. They won 9-0.

On September 6th, a Boston team of a different league - the Union Association, a major league that existed only the year of 1884 - visited Portland. The Boston Unions entertained the Pittsburgh (nee Chicago) Unions. This was not nearly the draw that the Red Stockings vs. the Grays had been, but still a good crowd made their way to Presumpscot Park. They were treated to a dandy of a game, a 5-5 ten-inning tie. The game was made all the more intriguing by the strong hurling of Frederick "Dupee" Shaw, the Boston's one-armed pitching ace.

Last in the parade to Portland in 1884 was Buffalo vs. Cleveland, then both full-fledged National League clubs, on September 8th. Playing on the Portland Ball Grounds, the teams put on quite a show. "Several difficult flies were captured and pretty double plays accomplished," waxed the *Daily Eastern Argus*. In a seesaw contest, Cleveland finally took the lead in the eighth inning, and held on to win, 7-6. Half of Buffalo's runs were scored by their firstbaseman, future Hall of Famer Big Dan Brouthers. The *Daily Eastern Argus*, perhaps with an eye to the ever-increasing female fans attending the games, elected as how Big Dan had "an almost perfect physique."

Big Dan Brouthers in a circa 1883 view

"Almost Perfect Physique"

When future Hall of Famer Dan Brouthers and his Buffalo National League contingent visited Portland for an exhibition game against Cleveland in September of 1884, the city's newspaper, the *Daily Eastern Argus*, marveled at his "almost perfect physique." The Clevelands marveled at his playing ability: he recorded fifteen putouts at first base and tallied three of the seven runs in a 7-6 Buffalo victory.

Enter the Eastern New England League

Professional baseball came to Maine in a different way in 1885. Both Portland and Biddeford gained their very own minor league teams. Together they made up 40% - two of the five entries - in the Eastern New England League. The other three were Brockton, Haverhill, and Lawrence, all in Massachusetts. A sixth club, representing Gloucester, dropped out at the very last minute, leaving resultant scheduling problems.

Both Maine teams, unfortunately, had more than scheduling problems. The teams started out on a positive note. They were outfitted in the snappiest of uniforms. The Biddeford club's was described as gray ("Providence gray") with navy blue trimming and a huge letter "B" on the breast of the shirt. Navy blue jerseys and "the league style of caps" rounded things out nicely. Portland's was even more jaunty: a white college coat, white pants, dark wine-colored jersey, stockings and belt. The cap was also white, with wine-colored trimming. Snappy-looking as they were, however, both clubs were far from powerhouse squads. Both got off on a losing foot, dropping their first three in a row. Portland's first win came against Lawrence, May 12th, before 900 or so fans at the Portland Grounds. Biddeford's first came May 15th . . . against Portland. Less than fully charitable in defeat, the *Daily Eastern Argus* called the umpire "a dough-head," commented that Long, Portland's thirdbaseman, "played a miserable game. It gives one the shivers to see a grounder go towards him," and closed with the observation that the home team pitcher, who was wild, "was rattled in the same old way." But the baseball crew at the *Argus* could be upbeat, too. And they had fun. When a Portland pitcher named Watson (first names were rarely included in the press of the day) beat Haverhill the headline read "Watson's Whizzing Whirlers Worst the Wary Whackers." *The Biddeford Journal* got in on the fun, too. After an *Argus* writer, in early July with Portland in dead last place, reflected that the only thing to do was "to abandon all hope of the pennant," tbe *Journal* responded "Didn't suppose you had any to abandon."

Biddeford, itself, gave up completely on July 18th. Suffering with a 14-20 mark and a lack of fan support, the Reserves (that was the team's nickname; Portland's team appears not to have had one) disbanded.

The league muddled through to the end of the season. A team representing Newburyport (Massachusetts) played out the remainder of the Reserves' schedule. Lawrence ended the year playing most of its home games in Manchester, New Hampshire. Portland, financially at least, did acceptably well. The payroll for its entire team (which was actually only eleven men at the time) was given as $1,800 a month in mid-season. Admission to games was 25¢. Brockton and Lawrence ended in a disputed first-place finish. In a three-game playoff Lawrence won. Portland, with a 34-46 mark, was fourth, ahead of only the come-lately Newburyports. The *Argus* wrapped it all up in its own inimitable style on September 1st: "Thus closed the career of the Portland nine of 1885, and doubtless the majority of them will not be seen here again - as ball players. Doubtless some of the fair sex will feel a fluttering of the heart at the thought of the absence of particular ones, but it will soon cease."

"The Championship of New England"

A new league was formed in 1886. It was the New England League, and was composed of Portland, Brockton, Haverhill,

Lynn, Lawrence, and a team representing Boston named the Blues.

New league. New team. New results. This year the Portlands were the talk of the town. They surged into first place on August 9th - "Which Shows What Perseverance and Pluck Can Do" headlined the *Argus* sports column - and remained there, winning the pennant by a wide margin over Haverhill ("Broken-hearted Haverhill": again the *Argus*). It's no wonder: while none of them are in the Hall of Fame or are household names today, every member of the 1886 Portland starting team eventually made it to the majors.

Heavy hitters included firstbaseman Lewis "Jumbo" Schoeneck, centerfielder Ted Scheffler, catcher Tom O'Rourke, and thirdbaseman Gil Hatfield. Pitching in right field at the end of the season was a "local" Lewiston player named Pat O'Connell. The real find, however, was truly local - he was from the Munjoy Hill section of Portland - 19-year-old southpaw hurler Michael "Kid" Madden. Given a trial by manager Harry Spence (himself soon to be in the bigs) early in the season, he proved to be a real ace of the staff. Madden even topped the Boston Red Stockings when they ventured to Portland for an exhibition game on October 12th. The "Kid" pitched "with the coolness of a veteran" *(Daily Argus)*, holding the National Leaguers to nine hits and four runs. Portland bats picked up an even dozen hits, enough for seven runs and a clear victory.

A second game was played between the two teams the next day, with the score ending in a 7-7 tie.

Said the *Argus:* "If the two games with the Bostons can be taken as a criterion, the natural inference is that the Portlands can justly lay claim to the championship of New England."

The Kid from Munjoy Hill

Looking for all the world as if he were about to bowl a candlepin string, this is Michael "Kid" Madden as depicted on an Old Judge Cigarettes' card. The earliest baseball cards were issued by cigarette - not bubble gum - firms. This one dates to 1888, just one year after a Richmond, Virginia tobacco company named Allen & Gitner introduced the world's first such cards.

***The* Box Score**

Game of October 12, 1886, between the Portland club of the New England League and the Boston Red Stockings of the National League.

PORTLANDS

	AB.	R.	1B.	TB.	PO.	A.	E.
Galligan, lf	5	1	0	0	2	0	0
Kearns, 2b	5	0	0	0	2	5	1
Wheelock, ss	5	2	2	2	0	4	0
Hatfield, 3b	5	3	3	4	3	3	0
Scheffler, of	4	1	2	3	0	0	0
O'Rourke, c	1	0	0	0	0	0	0
Reilly, c	3	0	0	0	0	1	0
O'Connell, rf	4	0	3	4	0	0	0
Schoeneck, 1b	4	0	1	1	20	0	0
Madden, p	4	0	1	1	0	6	0
Totals	40	7	12	15	27	19	1

BOSTONS

	AB.	R.	1B.	TB.	PO.	A.	E.
Hornung, lf	4	2	2	2	2	0	0
Sutton, ss	4	0	0	0	2	6	3
Gore, rf	4	1	2	3	0	0	1
Allen, 2b	4	0	1	1	1	2	0
Buffington, 1b	4	0	1	1	16	1	0
Stemmyer, p	4	0	1	1	0	7	0
Johnston, cf	4	0	0	0	1	0	0
Daily, 3b	3	1	1	4	1	3	1
Gunning, c	3	0	1	1	4	2	0;
Totals	34	4	9	13	27	21	6

(Note: "1B" meant number of hits; "TB" meant total bases)

How often does a Maine team defeat a major league team? And one representing Boston at that! What's, perhaps, even more rewarding is that three Mainers played in the game. Hartland's George Gore, playing right field for the Red Stockings, whacked a single and a double. His rightfield counterpart for Portland, Lewiston native Pat O'Connell, whacked two singles and a double. And Portland's Michael "Kid" Madden . . . well, he allowed nine scattered hits and handily prevailed over the mighty National Leaguers.

Gore would play fourteen seasons in the majors, retiring with a very creditable .301 lifetime batting average in 1892.

O'Connell would play in the majors for a brief period in 1890.

Madden would play in the majors for a solid five seasons, commencing the very next year when he won 22 games for the Red Stockings . . . the very team he so handily beat on October 12, 1886.

> **"It is said that the grass is so high in the Lynns' outfield that a circle has to be mowed around the fielders' position to enable them to be seen."**
>
> ***Portland Evening Express***
> **June 28, 1888**

Two in a Row?

It looked for all the world as if a second-in-a-row pennant would fly over Portland in 1887. Again the only Maine entry in a seemingly-strong eight-team loop that also included Lowell, Lawrence, Lynn, Salem, Haverhill, Manchester and the Boston Blues, the team started like a house afire. It won 17 of its first 20, 22 of its first 25, 30 of its first 40. A May 12th article in the *Argus* boasted that "The Portlands are so tired (from) running around the bases that they have to go to bed at 8 o'clock to get rested."

Last place Salem and the Boston Blues both dropped out of the league in July. Portland kept on winning. Late in the season, however, they began to falter. Their hitting prowess continued but their pitching, always suspect, got worse. The result: a very tight - and disputed - finish with Lowell and Portland neck and neck. The league's directors decided the only way to settle things was via a five-game playoff between the two teams. When it ended, sad to say, Lowell was the winner. The Portland club had to be content with a second-place mark.

In 1888 the New England League fielded six teams: Salem, Lynn, Lowell, Worcester, Manchester and, of course, Portland. This year, however, the team's "strategy" appeared to be the exact opposite of the year before: start super weak. Plagued by bad breaks and lifeless hitting, the club dropped 14 of its first 15 games. The *Argus*, in a June 4th article on the team and its weaknesses, summed up: "We want nearly a whole new club badly, men who can hit the ball preferred."

There was to be no such luck. In fact, within a week, Portland would have no team at all. A victim of cold weather, poor attendance, and a miserable record (5-28), the club disbanded on June 11th. It could have at least one consolation: it was the last of the original New England League teams to fold.

As it turned out, 1888 was to be it for both Portland professional baseball *and* the New England League for the next several years. Both would go into hibernation until 1891.

The Summer of '91

The summer of 1891 was - and wasn't - a big one for Lewiston. It was big in that "The Spindle City" gained its first professional team. It wasn't in that the league in which it played was mired in tarnish.

The league was again the New England League, reorganized and reborn. It began, on April 30th, with six teams: Portland, Lynn, Worcester, Lowell, Salem, and Manchester.

Portland jumped off to an early lead by taking ten games in a row in early May. A month later, in early June, it was announced that Lewiston and Woonsocket (Rhode Island) were being added to the league. Both, having little time to get a team together, were weak. Both lost their first nine games, sometimes by rather embarrassing scores (Portland beat Lewiston 25-0, for example: "A regular slaughter," the *Argus* sadly observed.).

But it had to happen. The two Johnny-come-latelies had to play one another. And one of them had to win! It happened on June 23rd. The winner - scoring a run in the seventh to break a 5-5 deadlock - was, of course, Lewiston.

It would be nice to be able to report that the Lewiston nine went on to win their next 84 straight games, clinching the flag by a landslide. However, it didn't exactly work out that way. No, the Lewiston nine went on to win but another eight games (which was still one more than Woonsocket). But, then again, none of the other teams were to win that many more, either. In mid-July, Salem, then Lynn, then Lowell, all dropped out of the league. Financial woe brought on by poor attendance was the cause. Several other teams were reportedly shaky. The end came in early August. Portland, with a 46-23 record, won the league title, such as it was. You have to give Woonsocket credit, though: although they finished dead last with an 8-29 mark, the team's owners had the moxie to wire the Portlands suggesting that, since they were the only two teams in the league that were financially stable, they should play a best-of-five series to determine the championship. Nothing, not surprisingly, came of it.

The New England League fared better in 1892. Eight teams started the season. Five finished. But they did finish, making it through to September. Portland and Lewiston were two of the finishing five . . . and Portland almost took the flag again. Woonsocket, they of last place the year before, got hot in late August, passed Portland, and won the league title. Lewiston finished a strong third. That the city (of Lewiston) was pleased with the showing of her "boys" was evident from words expressed in *The Evening Journal* (Lewiston's daily newspaper) of September 12th: "They (the players) have been courteous, sober, industrious, honest ball players. Through them, no discredit has been cast upon the game. They have eliminated all elements of the bum and the tough from base ball in this city." No mean words, these . . . especially when it is realized that it was in this very same decade (in 1897) that *The New York Times* termed ballplayers "degenerates."

The next season, 1893, was not unlike 1892. A Maine team - in this case, Lewiston - held first place for much of the season, only to lose it at the end. This year it was the Fall Rivers who were crowned champs. Lewiston finished second; Portland third.

Life in the New England League was further enriched in 1894. Bangor joined the loop! *The* (Lewiston) *Evening Journal* welcomed them with a hearty "Bangor has our permission to beat every other club than Lewiston." Again, however, it was the Fall River team to watch for. They jumped off to an early lead and never looked back. (Their secret to success: they claimed to be "all teetotalers."). After Fall River in the standings came Haverhill, then Portland, Lewiston, and Bangor all bunched together. Bringing up the rear were Pawtucket and Brockton.

The Ultimate

If 1894 was a good year for Maine baseball fans - with three teams in the New England League - 1895 was the ultimate. The Kennebecs, representing Augusta/ Hallowell/Gardiner, were admitted as well. The league was now 50% teams representing Maine, 50% teams representing "away." Unfortunately, however, none of the Maine contingent could muster up much competition versus the yet-again victorious Fall Rivers. It was, in fact, almost a foregone conclusion that they - the Fall River nine - would once again reign supreme. On Opening Day, April 27th, *The* (Lewiston) *Evening Journal* conceded that "Lewiston does not expect and hardly dares hope to win at Fall River." The paper then went on to strongly suggest that their Portland counterparts would fare no better that day: "Portland will not win at New Bedford unless the New Bedford men all drop dead."

Ever witty, *The Evening Journal* seemed to rise to new glory in 1895. (Even ninety-six years later it's still fun to read!). After a 27-3 shellacking at the hands of Pawtucket, the *Journal's* scribe wrote it off with a glib "Nowadays we are ready for anything and any score of less than three figures (say 99 to 1) will not surprise us. However, any score of over 100 to 1 will be equivalent to a reprimand. If we are beaten worse than that the team will be severely talked-to by the Grand Lecturer."

On the occasion of another loss, it was reflected that "There is one advantage in a team like Lewiston - they don't get hurt running around the bases." And, late in the season, when the home team had succeeded in topping Bangor 15-5, it was lauded as especially sweet "just to reduce

Continued on page 18

"That Man Lajoie"

The man who tore up the New England League in 1896 was Fall River's Napoleon Lajoie. Observed *The Bangor Daily Whig and Courier* in mid-June: "That man Lajoie, of Fall River, is fast enough for any league." With a New England League average of .429, the Philadelphia Phillies obviously agreed. They called him up late in the season. Twenty-one years and 3,251 hits later, Nappy retired . . . to eventual enshrinement in the Hall of Fame and everlasting glory as one of the game's true greats.

Base Ball

In the 1890s - when the *Bangor Daily News* was holding a Most Popular Player contest - "base ball" was almost universally spelled as two words. It would generally remain as such until 1915 or so when, with America's penchant for shortening things, spelling the "Grand Old Game" as one word became the norm . . .

"Base Ball" ads and announcements from various Maine publications, 1887-1922

PUBLISHERS

BANGOR DAILY NEWS

BANGOR, ME.

Please credit

With one vote for the complete Clothing outfit offered by you to the member of '94 Bangor Base Ball Team who receives the largest number of votes during the Base Ball season.

1894

THE ACADEMY BELL.

F. P. BENNETT,

Apothecary & Stationer.

—· BASE BALL GOODS ·—

A full supply waiting to be ordered to the field of action.

Call on us when you may, you will always find us ready and willing to serve you. Remember where to find us:

PONDICHERRY SQUARE,

BRIDGTON, MAINE.

1887

D. & M. and SPAULDING
BASE BALL GOODS

Tennis Goods

Iver Johnson and Crosby Bicycles

Bicycle Tires and Sundries

DISCOUNT TO STUDENTS

THE S. L. CROSBY COMPANY

146 and 150 EXCHANGE STREET

1916

BASE BALL AND TENNIS GOODS
LORING SHORT & HARMON
PORTLAND, MAINE

1911

Base Ball Goods

1908

For the——

NORWAY HIGH

RAH! RAH! RAH!

At——

Kimball's Noyes Drug Store

Norway, Maine

BASE BALL!

BATES vs. MAINE.

LEAGUE GAME PLAYED ON THE NEW GARCELON FIELD.

SATURDAY, MAY 20th.

Admission 25 Cents.

LADIES FREE. GRAND STAND, 15 CENTS.

Game Called at 3 P. M. may17d3t.

1899

Waterboro Town Report

SPORTING GOODS

AND

SPECIALTIES

Base Balls
Catcher Mits
Baseman Mits
Fielders Gloves
Coaster Carts
Couch Hammocks

Bicycles
Velocipedes
Sweaters
Masks
Bats

The James Bailey Co.

264 MIDDLE STREET

PORTLAND, MAINE

1922

. . . although the two-word version still had its believers well into the 1920s and even into the 1930s.

the overwhelming pride of the citizens of Sawdustville." (An obvious, if not flattering, reference to Bangor's claim to fame as "The Lumber City.").

"We Wuz Robbed"

The season of 1896 was the one that almost was for Bangor. Led by the pitching of Willard Mains ("The Windham Wonder": so-called because he was from North Windham, Maine) and the heavy hitting (.317; 113 runs scored) of Bangor-born John Sharrott - both of whom would later have meaningful stints in the majors - the Bangors looked as if they had the league crown sewn up. They easily outdistanced intrastate rivals Augusta, Lewiston, and Portland, and interstate Brockton, New Bedford, and Pawtucket. Only perennially strong Fall River had a chance to upset the applecart. In an almost neck-and-neck finish it appeared as if Bangor were number one. But wait. The Fall River crew claimed they'd won three games not previously reported. The league bought it . . . and once again Fall River was crowned the New England League leader. If it sounds as if Bangor was robbed, that's about how the team and its fans felt about it, too.

"The Chief" and Bangor Baseball by Night

If ever there were a year that could have really put Maine on the baseball map it was 1897.

First, one of the game's first real superstars/gate attractions appeared on the big league scene. He was Louis Francis Sockalexis. And he was from Old Town, Maine.

A standout at Holy Cross, Sockalexis was signed by Cleveland, then in the National League. For the first half of 1897 "The Chief of Sockem" was nothing short of amazing. He batted almost .400 and seemed to be able to run faster, throw further, and hit harder than anyone else in the league. The fans loved to watch him play. But then "demon rum" stepped in. The amazing feats began to dwindle. Within three years the Chief, sad to say, was out of the majors. The career that could have been was never to happen.

Secondly in 1897, Bangor almost was thirty-three years ahead of the times: it was on the verge of seeing baseball played under the lights when its entry in the Maine State League folded prematurely.

"So Many Remarkable Accomplishments"
Louis Sockalexis as sketched for the *Cleveland Plain Dealer*, August 17, 1897. Said future Hall of Famer Hughie Jennings: "At no time has a player crowded so many remarkable accomplishments into such a short period of time."

The New England League had, temporarily at least, abandoned northern New England. All six of its teams for 1897 were in Massachusetts and Rhode Island. The Maine State League was accordingly organized. Maine would have its own league!

Teams representing Augusta, Bangor, Belfast, Lewiston, Portland, and Rockland started play in late May. Augusta jumped off to an early lead. *The Daily Kennebec Journal* showed its delight in a June 1st tribute: "Doesn't it seem nice to be all alone at the top of the list, with no one in sight that we care a snap for." Augusta was not to be atop for long, however. Portland caught up in early June and held first place for the remainder of the season. The problem was that the season was far shorter than planned. Teams, lead by Bangor, started dropping out from early June on. The root of the matter was not an unusual one: bad weather kept attendance - and gate receipts - low. What was left of the league came to a grinding halt in early July. Had Bangor hung in there until the end it is very probable that the course of the game would have been changed. In the June 2nd issue of *The Bangor Daily Whig and Courier* it was reported that "Manager Toole (Bangor's manager) has about completed arrangements whereby he will play a series of games early in July by electric light." Night baseball was about to come to Bangor. And the world. Instead the Bangor team disbanded, the

Advertisement, *The Daily Kennebec Journal*, June 8, 1897

AUGUSTA
vs. BELFAST
Trotting Park Augusta
Tuesday at 3.30.
Two games, Wednesday with BELFAST at 10 A. M. and 3.30 P. M.
Admission......................25 Cents
Ladies..........................15 Cents
June7d3t

great Maplewood Park (the home of the Bangor nine) experiment was forgotten, and the world had to wait over three more decades - until Des Moines of the Western League installed lights in its park in the summer of 1930 - to enjoy baseball by electric light.

With the failure of the Maine State League, professional ball disappeared from Maine for the next several years. In 1901, however, the New England League once more ventured north. Again, four of the starting eight teams were from Down East: Augusta, Bangor, Lewiston, and Portland. The usual shiftings occured: Augusta dropped out, the Bangor team shifted to Brockton, Brockton dropped out, etc., etc. To enliven interest in his team, Lewiston manager Fred Doe promised to jump in the canal - "with his best clothes on" - if his team lost to Portland. (They did . . . but there's no evidence he did.). In fact, in a down-to-the-wire race between Portland

N. E. League Standing.

	Won.	Lost.	Played.	Per ct Won.
Portland	51	36	87	.586
Manchester	47	38	85	.553
Lowell	47	44	91	.516
Haverhill	43	48	91	.473
Nashua	39	47	86	.453
Lewiston	40	50	90	.444

Lewiston on Top at Last.

They Did Have Their Fun

No, this is not a misprint. It's the way the New England League standings appeared in *The Lewiston Evening Journal* of September 2, 1901. If you're going to be in the basement (actually the paper cheated a little: Lewiston was actually slightly ahead of Nashua, safely ensconced in fifth place) . . . you may as well have some fun about it. Right? Right!

and Manchester (New Hampshire), the Lewistons greatly helped Portland win it by topping Manchester twice in the last week of play. "We couldn't stand to have the pennant leave the dear old State," explained *The Evening Journal*.

From 1902 until 1907 there was no professional baseball played in Maine. But that didn't mean that Mainers weren't still playing the Grand Old Game. In the world's first World Series, between the Pirates and the Red Sox (then generally known as the Pilgrims), a Mainer was at that most pivotal of positions - shortstop - for the Sox. Born in Biddeford, raised in Sanford, Freddy Parent was only 5′5½″ tall, but he was a key to the American League champs' victorious season, batting a solid .304, with 83 runs scored, 80 batted in. Triples were Parent's forte. He whacked 17 of them during the regular season. During the Series - won by Boston five games to three - he added three more, scoring eight runs in the eight-game history-making event. Obviously proud, the *Portland Evening Express* observed "that we are fellow citizens, and here in Portland, we are almost neighbors, of the cleverest of shortstops, quiet, diminutive, good natured but industrious Fred Parent." As to the outcome of the Series itself, the paper seemed to have less conviction: "We here in Maine are pleased as a whole, chiefly because Boston is nearer to us than is Pittsburgh and another reason is that we have a Maine boy in the infield."

The years 1907 and 1908 saw a flurry of minor league activity throughout Maine. The Maine State League set up again. Various teams (Augusta, Waterville, and Manchester, New Hampshire were all in the loop for a period of time) floated in and out in 1907. When it ended, Bangor took home the honors. In second were the Biddeford Orphans, followed by the Portland Blue Sox and Pine Tree (South Portland). Helping the Bangor cause was

Freddy Parent as he appeared in his victorious team's 1903 composite photo. The "B A" stood for "Boston Americans" . . . as there was then a Boston National League club, too.

The World's First World Series

The world's first World Series, played in 1903, featured Maine's Freddy Parent at shortstop for the winning Bostons . . . and featured frenzy on the part of the Boston fans. In fact, "fans," generally thought to be derived from "fanatics," was never a more apt term. The Boston faithful swarmed over fences to get into the game, had to be contained behind ropes to allow play and, most of all, sang an almost constant array of songs calculated to drive the opposing Pittsburgh Pirates to distraction and to defeat. It worked. The team that four years later would adopt the name "Red Sox" took the Series five games to three. A key part of the victory was the play of Freddy. The diminutive shortstop clearly outplayed his Pirate counterpart - the legendary Honus Wagner - in the field, and clearly outhit him, too . . . socking .281 (including three triples) to Honus' .222.

The most ardent of the Boston faithful - shown here in various stages of cheering their team on to victory on October 13th - were known as the Royal Rooters, and were led by a local saloonkeeper by the name of M.T. "Nuf Said" McGreevy.

Rooter's Souvenir

BOSTON - PITTSBURG

Oct., 1903. M. T. McGreevy

No. 1.

Boston, Pittsburg,
Who are we?
We are the rooters for 19–3.
We will win,
Go tell your pa,
We Beaneaters, Beaneaters,
Rah! Rah! Rah!

No. 2.

Five games, Five games,
We want five,
We are here and all alive;
Biff! Bang! Bang, Bang, Bang!
Zim! Zam! Zam, Zam, Zam!

No. 3.

In the good old summer time,
Our Boston Base Ball Nine
Beat the teams—east and west,
Now they're first in line.
The Pittsburgs they are after us,
O me! O me! O my!
We'll do them as we did the rest
In the good old summer time.

3rd Base. 14 **Nuffsaid.**

"Finest Grounds in State"

Almost completely forgotten now, the Pine Tree Grounds adorned the Mill Creek section of South Portland for many seasons in the earliest years of this century, providing the scene for countless crackerjack minor league and semi-professional games. The Grounds were billed as being the finest in the state, had a grandstand with a seating capacity of over 500, were ten minutes from Monument Square by trolley, and especially courted the ladies. One 1905 ad told the tale of a man who came home from work one afternoon to find his wife gone. A note was pinned to the table cover. A thousand thoughts raced through his head. Had she taken ill? Had she run away? Had she eloped with another man? Finally he steeled himself and opened the note. It read:

> **"Gone to the Ball Game at PINE TREE PARK. You know that Wednesday is Ladies' Day, and all the neighbors are going, and I just could not stay at home."**

Scorecard from 1906

Advertising woodcut from 1905

" 'It wasn't like this in the olden days,' goes the refrain of a familiar song, and ball players are mighty glad - when the saying is applied to the matter of base ball salaries. Some of the stars on the diamond today draw princely stipends every couple of weeks or so, and are cared for in the very best possible manner."

From an article entitled "BALL PLAYERS GET BETTER MONEY NOW," *Portland Evening Express*, May 7, 1909

Fred "Biddo" Iott ("the one and only 'Biddo' Iott, the great Aroostook player, known far and wide as a heavy hitter and all 'round expert at the game": *The Bangor News*), a Houlton native who'd played here and there and everywhere, even seeing service in the American League with Cleveland.

To 1908 goes the "honor" of being Maine's most confused season . . . with respect to its organized ball configuration, anyway. A brand new league, the Atlantic League, got rolling in early May. Sort of a condensed New England League, it fielded teams in Lewiston, Portland, Attleboro, Massachusetts, and Newport and Pawtucket, Rhode Island. But it didn't field them for long: by late May the fledgling league had folded. Both Lewiston and Portland then hitched up again with the Maine State League, which, conveniently, didn't begin play until June 10th. In the MSL this year were Bangor, Pine Tree, and, of course, the back-in-the-fold Lewiston and Portland teams. In early July Biddeford and York Beach joined in, both teams being admitted with an assigned 7-7 record in order to have an equal shot at the league pennant.

Nothing was to remain settled for long in 1908, however. Attendance - or, rather, lack of it - was the usual problem. (Biddeford team management suggested having Thursday afternoons declared a holiday, so that all the stores would close and the clerks could attend the game.). Pine Tree was dropped by the league. York Beach dropped out of its own accord. The Lewiston team was transferred to Augusta. With four teams left, a hotly contested race developed between Bangor and Portland for the crown. Portland, with a late surge, was certain to be the winner . . . but then, in the last week of play, its team disbanded. Bangor claimed victory, declaring that Portland belonged in "the lemon class." Portland, as well, claimed victory, saying there was no way they could have lost, and chiding Bangor - which kept on with its remaining games against Augusta - as playing in the "Bangor-Augusta League."

In 1909 a pair of four-team leagues provided sport for much of the state. In the south the Portland Blue Sox and the Pine Tree Capers (playing at Pine Tree Park in South Portland) joined with Dover and Somersworth, New Hampshire to form the Twin State League. The league lasted from late May until late June. Meanwhile, the north saw the Northern Maine League. Commonly referred to as "The Potato League," it consisted of Bangor (transferred to Caribou in August), Houlton, Old Town, and the league champ, Millinocket.

The Main Maine Team

It was quite a year, that 1910. President "Big Bill" Taft lauded baseball at the start of the season. "The game of baseball is a clean, straight game, and summons to its presence everybody who enjoys clean, straight athletics," said Bill.

And . . . the Chicago White Sox had, at one time or another during the year, five (that's five!) Mainers on their squad. You'd think that alone would have been enough to ensure a triumphant season, with a pennant flying high on the south side of the Windy City!

But it wasn't. The team still bore their 1906 tag "Hitless Wonders" - although there was far less wonder than when the team had won the flag, and then the World Series against the cross-town Cubs, four years earlier. They would finish sixth in 1910, ahead of only the lowly Senators and the even more lowly ("First in booze, first in shoes . . . and last in the American League") St. Louis Browns.

The first Mainer to make his White Sox debut in 1910 - in center field on Opening Day - was Freddy Parent, the same Freddy Parent who'd starred for the Red Sox as their shortstop in the first-ever World Series in 1903. Traded to the White Sox after the 1907 season, Freddy had a poor season (.207 batting average in 118 games at short) in 1908, and a pretty good one (.261 average with 32 stolen bases in 136 games at short and the outfield) in 1909. The season of 1910 would be his last complete one in the majors, and it would not be a good one: a .178 average in 81 games as a part-time outfielder, part-time infielder.

Next in order of appearance - batting clean-up and playing center field against the Browns on April 21st - was 27-year-old Roland "Cuke" Barrows. Born in Gray, reared in Westbrook, "Cuke" ran wild with the New Bedford Whalers in the New England League in 1909, but was given limited opportunity to show his stuff with the Chisox in any of the four years, 1909 to 1912, that he was up with them. Playing in but six games in 1910, he had four hits in twenty at bats.

Irv "Cy the Second" Young had won twenty games in his rookie year for the Boston Nationals back in 1905. A native of Columbia Falls, he had the misfortune to always play for mediocre clubs. The 1910 White Sox were no exception. For them he won but four games that year . . . but all four games were shutouts. It was the only sure way to avoid a loss!

In August the White Sox traded for Harry Lord, a stellar performer for the Red Sox since 1907. Installed at third, the Porter native was a solid addition, batting .297 in the season's remaining 44 games.

Last to make his debut was Bangor's Bobby Messinger. After a less-than-fully robust .170 in 31 games with the Sox in 1909, Messinger was farmed out. Recalled late in 1910, he batted a major league career high of .231 (six hits and seven runs scored in 26 official at bats) while appearing in nine games in the outfield.

The highlight of it all - from a decidedly Maine point of view! - came on October 11th when four Mainers took the field for the White Sox in a game against Cleveland. All four did well, too. Irv Young allowed just five hits in four innings. Harry Lord went three for four. Freddy Parent went one for three. Bobby Messinger went one (a triple) for four.

It was quite a year, that 1910.

They All Wore White Sox

Harry Lord, shown here on what is known in baseball card lingo as a Turkey Red, came over from the Red Sox to the White Sox in August, 1910. The Porter, Maine thirdsacker batted .297 for the Chisox; was a part of that historic day - October 11, 1910 - when *four* Mainers took to the field for the Sox in a single game.

T-3 card - better known as a Turkey Red - from 1911. These cards were large - they measured 5¾″ x 8″ - and they were beautiful.

FANS—LOOK HERE—FANS

AMERICAN LEAGUE STARS

VS.

ALL LEAGUERS

Friday, October 21

2.00 P. M. at

Pine Tree Park

The Maine Central Railroad Co.

WILL SELL

EXCURSION TICKETS

Friday by any train reaching Portland before two o'clock p. m. Electric cars from Union Station direct to Ball Grounds. Room for thousands. Don't miss it. The Biggest Game ever played in Maine.

SEE

BIG ED. WALSH

the great Spitball Artist of the Chicago White Sox.

LORD, CARRIGAN, PARENT, COLLINS, GESSLER

and others. In fact one brilliant array of base ball stars who will fight this game for blood.

Take Morning Trains to Portland Friday. Return that night or following day if preferred. If stormy Friday game will be played Saturday

ADMISSION, - 50 cents

ALL UP! ALL UP!! ALL UP!!!

Reserved Seats at Loring, Short & Harmon's

Maine Central Railroad broadside, 1910

"The Biggest Game Ever Played in Maine"

It was billed as "The Biggest Game ever played in Maine," and it was a major event, indeed. It was the American League Stars vs. the All-Maine Minor League Stars. Played at the Pine Tree Grounds in South Portland on October 21, 1910, it brought to southern Maine Big Ed Walsh, Doc Gessler, Freddy Parent, Harry Lord, and, as Portland's *Evening Express* nicely put it, "a dozen more twinklers of the baseball firmament." The American League Stars won, 3-2, in a ten-inning thriller, but doubtless no one really cared what the game's output was: they were there for the spectacle.

A Grand Opening for Fenway

After two postponements due to inclement weather, that park of parks - Fenway Park - celebrated its Grand Opening before 27,000 delighted spectators on April 20, 1912. It's especially appropriate that the team the Red Sox played - and beat - was that team from New York, the Yankees. The score was 7-6.

Twenty-five players, in all, took part. Five of them were from California, three apiece were from Illinois and Pennsylvania. "The Grey Eagle," Sox star centerfielder Tris Speaker, hailed from Hubbard, Texas. One player - pinchhitter Olaf Henriksen - was a native of Denmark. Closer to home, three of the participants in what has turned out to be an historic occasion were native New Englanders. And one of these was from Maine: Bill "Rough" Carrigan, the pride of Lewiston, caught the end of the game for Boston. Within a year he would be managing the club . . . and would eventually, in 1915 and 1916, lead them to two World Championships in a row. (Quick, name another Red Sox manager who's guided the Sox to even *one* World Championship in a row in the past seven decades . . .).

The Return of Maine to the New England League

Minor league activity started up once more in Maine in 1913. Portland built a brand new stadium, named it Bayside Park, and was again invited to become part of the New England League. An estimated 9,000 enthusiasts turned out to celebrate the dedication of the park - and to welcome organized baseball back to the state - on May 8th. The Portland *Eastern Daily Argus* described Bayside Park as "a home for the national game of which any city might justly feel proud." The team was owned and managed by

Continued on page 30

He Was There

The pride of Lewiston, Bill "Rough" Carrigan, was there the day they opened Fenway Park on April 20, 1912. Within a year he would be the club's manager.

Bill Carrigan as depicted in a supplement to the *Boston Sunday Post*, 1909

The Birth of a Team Nickname

In January of 1915 there occurred an event that has a bearing on baseball to this day. A club was named in honor of an individual. In the earlier days of the game this was not all that unusual. The Braves were once known as the Doves, in honor of owner George S. Dovey. Brooklyn's entry in the National League was long known as the Robins, a tribute to their rotund manager, Wilbert "Uncle Robbie" Robinson. Teams were sometimes even nicknamed for products. The Brooklyn representative in the Federal League was often called the Tip Tops, the team's owners being the Ward Brothers of Ward's Tip Top Bread fame and fortune. And Colonel Jacob Ruppert wanted to change the name of the Yankees to the Knickerbockers - his brewery's best seller was Ruppert Knickerbocker Beer - but was denied permission by the other club owners in the American League.

The club featured here was - and is - Cleveland. Organized in 1879 and originally in the National League, the city's baseball team was variously known as the Spiders (there was an abundance of tall and skinny players on the squad!), the Forest Citys, the Blues, the Bluebirds, and the Broncos. A charter member of the American League in 1901, the team was generally referred to as the Naps from 1903 through 1914. It was another case of a name that honored a person. Napoleon (often called Nap or Nappy) Lajoie was the grandest player of his day, and he played for Cleveland for all of those twelve years (plus 1902 as well). On January 5, 1915, however, "The Woonsocket Wonder" (yet another tag) was sold to the Athletics. No longer should the team be called the Naps.

What to do? Well, Charles W. Somers, the team's owner, solved the dilemma by appointing a committee of local sports writers to come up with a new name. Fans were encouraged to send in their suggestions. Names came pouring in. There was the Leafs, Barons, Hustlers, Youngsters, Foresters, Kids, Grays, Bears, Lions, Climbers, Bruins, Blues, Royals (Kansas City, are you listening?), Minors, Tip Tops, Buckeyes, Settlers, Lakedgers, Vels, Originals, and Terriers, among many others. One fan suggested the Some Hams . . . a not-very-flattering merger of the first four letters of the owner Somer's name and the last three of manager Joe Birmingham's. Another wrote they should be called the Scraps: "That's all that's left of 'em." And mindful of the team's horrendous 51-102 last-place finish in 1914, one E.H. Kramer suggested they be labelled the Sleepers.

The name chosen was, of course, the Indians, a suggestion from a long-forgotten fan who wanted to pay tribute to none

other than Old Town's Louis Sockalexis. Actually, though, the idea was far from brand new. When "The Chief" was pelting the ball for the Clevelanders - then officially known as the Spiders - in 1897, the nickname Indians was sometimes also used by both fans and the Cleveland daily newspapers of the day. "The Indians Have Good Practice" read a Cleveland *Plain Dealer* subhead of April 6th. "The Indians Play a Tie Game with Indianapolis" read another on April 16th.

With Sockalexis' fall from stardom as 1897 wore on, however, the name was used less and less, until it was finally not used at all. Its rebirth in 1915 was based as much on practicality as sentiment: the team was dreadful, and the Committee wanted a name that, as *The Cleveland Press* readily admitted: "couldn't be converted into a joke." "They won't be able to poke fun at the Indians," reflected a club vice president. But they did. Commented *The Press*, "Now that the Naps have been renicknamed the Indians, we hope they will become very Indian-like and wake up." A further quip followed: "Wait until they begin to lose and see how soon the fans will dub them the Squaws."

The Committee's selection of the name was thought to be temporary. Announced on January 16th, the very next day the *Plain Dealer* made it clear: "The nickname, however, is but temporarily bestowed, as the club may so conduct itself during the present season as to earn some other cognomen which may be more appropriate."

The team did manage to "conduct itself" upward in 1915. It moved out of the cellar, ahead of the team its former namesake - Nap Lajoie - had been sold to, the Athletics. The name stuck, and is today still with us: the only major league club to be named after a human being. Louis Sockalexis would be proud.

"You Wukoig!"

When the Cleveland *Plain Dealer*, in its edition of January 17, 1915, announced the choice of the new name for the city's baseball team, it did it with panache . . . and an abundance of cartoon art. While such art would almost certainly be considered in poor taste today, it was perfectly acceptable in 1915. Regardless of nickname - or what language their fans used to cheer on the team - Cleveland's entry in the American League has generally been less than a powerhouse. The team has won but three pennants - in 1920, 1948, and 1954 - in the ninety-one seasons since its inception in 1901.

Hugh Duffy, whose batting mark of .438 for the Boston Red Stockings in 1894 still stands as the all-time single season high. Nicknamed the "Duffs" or the "Duffyites," the team more than held its own against the other seven teams - all representing Massachusetts - in the league. The Duffs hung in there in third or fourth place all through May, June, July, and early August. They moved up to second in mid-August, fell back to third, and, at the very end of the season, moved up to second again . . . where they finished, behind only the Lowell Grays.

Meanwhile, further down east, the New Brunswick and Maine League started up, with teams representing Bangor, Calais-St. Stephens (replaced by St. Croix in July), Fredericton, and St. John. Beset by poor attendance, the league did not last out the season. The loss of the New Brunswick alliance was at least partially compensated for by the addition, in 1914, of Lewiston to the New England League. The team took as its nickname the Cupids.

All the World Loves a Lover

When it re-entered the New England League for the season of 1914, the Lewiston team took as its nickname one of the *loveliest* (sorry, I just couldn't resist) choices around . . . the Cupids. While the *Lewiston Journal* wrote that the choice was apropos because "all the girls here are sure to fall in love with our players," the idea for the name really came from the fact that the team's owner, Joseph W. Burns, was nicknamed "Cupid."

The Team's owner, Joseph W. Burns, was nicknamed Cupid, which prompted the *Lewiston Journal* to suggest it. But they had other reasons, too, as promulgated in a March 6th editorial: "Cupid suggests beauty, and we understand that our players have some of the handsomest phizzes in the biz. Cupid was the god of love - why not, when all the girls here are sure to fall in love with our players. The name lends itself to all sorts of humorous suggestions. It is short, easily spoken, easily written, falls trippingly from the tongue." The city's fans liked it. Cupids it was!

League play was strong: neither Maine entry was able to do much against the clubs from Massachusetts. In the eight-team loop, the Duffs took third, while the Cupids finished fifth. The Lawrence Pirates took the crown (whereupon the team name was changed to the Lawrence Champs!).

Things were different in 1915. Hugh Duffy's boys got off to a good start, engaged in a seesaw battle with Lawrence for most of the summer, grabbed the lead in mid-August, built a commanding lead, and clinched the pennant by defeating the Cupids (who came in sixth) 3-2 at Bayside Park on August 31st. Stars of the team included centerfielder Joe Burns (who has a lifetime major league batting average of .429 . . . but with only 14 at bats), firstbaseman John Dowell, rightfielder Pete Clemons, shortstop Walt Lonergan (who'd spent some time with the Red Sox in 1911), and catcher Jack Hayden (who'd also spent some time with Boston, hitting a solid .280 in 322 at bats in 1906).

Portland almost made it two in a row in 1916. Playing in a new ten-team league called the Eastern League (no relation to today's league of the same name) that spread as far south and west as Bridgeport, Connecticut, the Duffs were in a thriller

Portland Liked Hugh, Too

Hugh Duffy - whose .438 batting average in 1894 is still the highest ever recorded - owned and managed the Portland team in the New England League from 1913 through 1916. In 1915, the year the Duffs took the NEL crown, Hugh was especially laudatory with respect to Portland and the city's fans, calling it "the finest minor league city I ever saw."

Hugh Duffy, in cartoon form, escorting Miss Pennant around Portland, August, 1915

BOOST BASEBALL!
BOOST PORTLAND!
BOOST THE DUFFS!

Portland *Daily Eastern Argus* ad, July, 1916

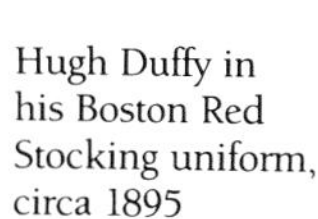

Hugh Duffy in his Boston Red Stocking uniform, circa 1895

with New London, Connecticut from the opening pitch. The Millionaires (also known as the Planters in deference to their owner, millionaire sportsman Morton F. Plant of New London) held the lead until July 23rd. On that day, three days after the Portland-South Portland Million Dollar Bridge was opened, Portland took over and was on top until the very last day in August, when New London again surged to number one. That's the way it ended. An interesting sidebar - to show that things have changed - was the league vote, on May 15th, to allow each team to carry fourteen players instead of thirteen. The reason given: "the teams would be unable to get along with only four pitchers during the hot weather when they are playing off doubleheaders."

Screenland Comes to Portland

Before 1917 could roll around there were rumors that Hugh Duffy was going to pack up the team and move it elsewhere. Instead, Hugh just packed himself up. He moved on to be baseball coach at Harvard, selling the club he'd owned and managed for four years to a group headed by showman Hiram Abrams. Abrams was big on spectacle. For the team's "Getaway Day," as Opening Day was known in those days, he arranged for such screen notables as Fatty Arbuckle, Norma Talmadge, Jesse Lasky, Adolph Zukor, and Marcus Loew to be on hand for the

cover, *The American Boy* magazine, May, 1910

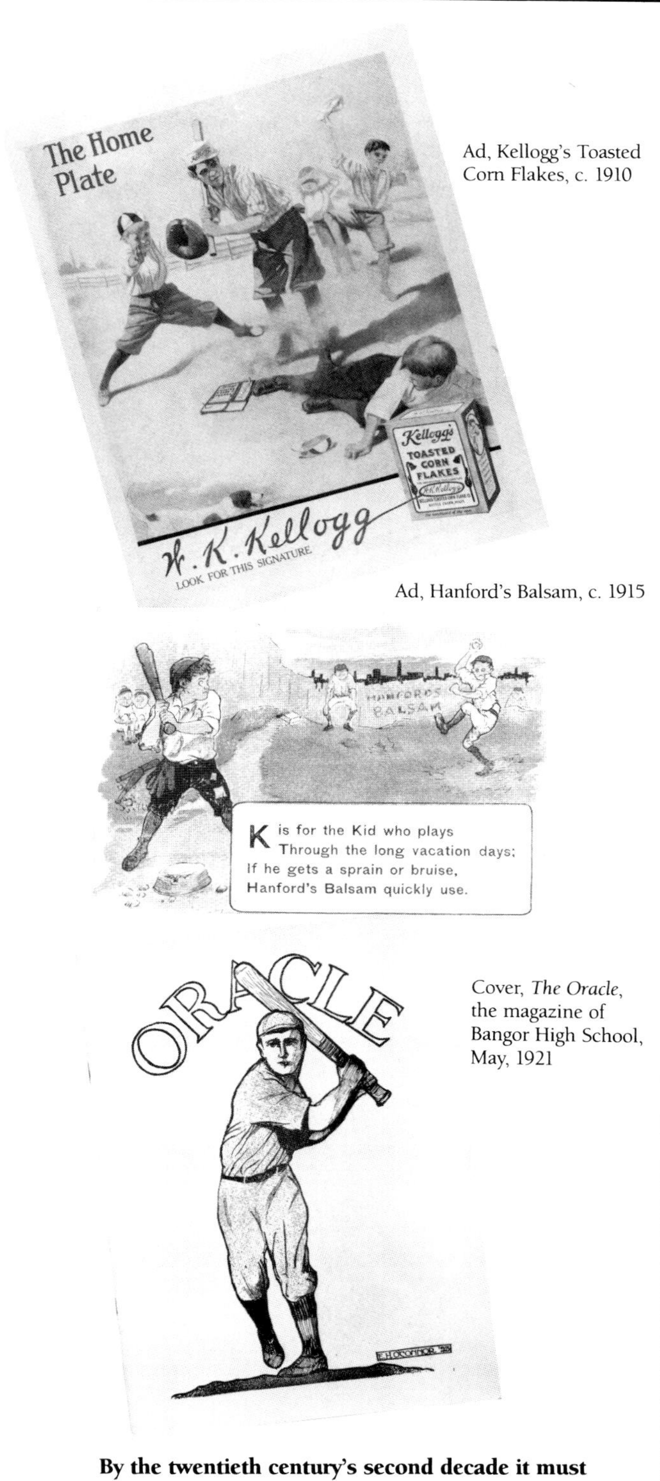

Ad, Kellogg's Toasted Corn Flakes, c. 1910

Ad, Hanford's Balsam, c. 1915

Cover, *The Oracle*, the magazine of Bangor High School, May, 1921

By the twentieth century's second decade it must have seemed as if every boy in Maine - and across the rest of America, too - was playing baseball. And when he wasn't playing baseball . . .

festivities at Bayside Park. Fatty, then America's reigning movie comedian and fresh from his latest success in *A Reckless Romeo*, was an especial hit. As the *Daily Eastern Argus* headlined: "5,000 See Movie Stars and Go Away Happy." Portland lost the game, but who cared? Continued the *Argus:* "We'll get that back before the season closes, but we may not have another chance to breathe the same air as the real 'Fatty,' or gaze on the lissome figure of Norma in the flesh."

Hoopla aside, however, the team just didn't have it. It sank into the second division almost immediately, and remained there all season long. What to call the team was a problem, too. With Hugh Duffy gone it wouldn't have been right to continue with the Duffs' tag. "The Portland Movies," in obvious deference to the Getaway Day celebration, was used occasionally. More often the team was just called "Garrity's boys" or "Garrity's crew," in tribute to new manager Mike Garrity. Toward the end of the season "Paramounts" caught on, but it made little difference to the team's standing in the league. By whatever name, Portland was destined for second division honors. It eventually settled in sixth place, far beneath the frontrunning New Haven Murlins.

After the 1917 season the Portland Eastern League franchise was shifted to Providence, Rhode Island. There was no professional ball in Maine in 1918.

Lewiston - With a Little Help from Lowell - Wins It

The season of 1919 was another one of those crazy ones in the life of minor league activity. It worked out well for Lewiston, though . . . with a little help from Lowell. A "rejuvenated" New England League began play on May 23rd. It

Continued on page 36

. . . he was reading about it. Scores upon scores of baseball books, stories, dime novels, etc., were published, every year, about the sport that had truly become our National Pastime.

Embodying all that was virtuous in these publications was that ultimate hero, Frank Merriwell (who would later, when he had grown "old," be replaced by his younger brother, Dick Merriwell). Created in 1896, Frank (for the admirable trait of the same name) Merriwell (a combining of "merry" and "well"), appeared in the magazine *Tip Top Weekly* for almost two full decades, until 1914. Every word of every story - averaging 20,000 words each, for a grand total of something like 20,000,000 words - was penned by a man from Maine (and mostly *in* Maine, too). His nom de plume was Burt L. Standish; his real name was Gilbert Patten. Born in Corinna in 1866, his own life story had very definite dime novel overtones to it. He ran away from home at age sixteen; worked in a machine shop in Biddeford for six months; returned home; hammered out two short stories in four days; received a check for $6.00 for them; never stopped writing from then on.

Patten's stories, beginning in 1896, featured the adventures of either Frank or Dick, both lads who were "All American" in every respect: intelligent, fearless, well-educated, handsome, gentlemanly and, of course, athletic. "These stories are rich in fun and thrills in all branches of sports and athletics. They are extremely high in moral tone, and cannot fail to be of immense benefit to every boy who reads them," promised Street & Smith, publisher of *Tip Top*. And while the lads starred - first at Fardale Academy and then at Yale - in all sorts of sports, it was at baseball that they may have starred the most. Patten (who managed a semi-pro team in Camden, Maine in 1890 and 1891), portrayed both of the Merriwells as pitchers. To Frank he gifted a "double shoot," a pitch that curved first in one direction and then in the other. To Dick he went one step further, endowing him with a "jump ball" . . . a pitch that leaped a full foot in the air just as the batter began to swing. Try hitting that, Jose Canseco!

Top to bottom: an illustration from a 1912 book by Lester Chadwick entitled BASEBALL JOE OF THE SILVER STARS; the cover of Zane Grey's 1909 THE SHORT-STOP; an illustration from RIVAL PITCHERS OF OAKDALE, a 1911 saga from the pen of Morgan Scott.

Although best known for his westerns, Zane Grey devoted a fair share of his early writing efforts to baseball. A standout player during his college days at the University of Pennsylvania, Grey even played some minor league ball. He is known for his quote: "Every boy likes baseball, and if he doesn't he's not a boy."

cover, *Tip Top Weekly* magazine, June 15, 1907

was a six-team affair, with two of the six in Maine. Portland, managed by former Red Sox infielder Heinie Wagner, was called the Wagners or, ugh, the Heinieites. (Later in the season that would change to the Blue Socks/Sox.). Lewiston, managed by fellow former Red Sox infielder Freddy Parent, was nicknamed the Red Sox. Renewing their traditional rivalry, the two battled back and forth for the league lead all through June. By early July, though, Portland was well ahead, trailed by Lowell and Lewiston.

Then on July 12th, the bottom fell out of the league. Lawrence, Lewiston, and Lowell all dropped out. In a complicated maneuver, however, the Lowell team - and its won-lost record - was transferred to Lewiston, and the league continued on with four teams: Portland, Fitchburg, Haverhill, and, as referred to by the *Lewiston Evening Journal*, the "Lewiston-ized Lowell team." The change in uniform acted as an elixir for the former Lowells. They caught up with and inched past the Blue Sox. In spite of a heated pennant race, though, the New England League was its wobbly old self. On August 1st it was announced that the games of August 2nd would end the season. On that day the Red Sox and the Blue Sox fought it out in a doubleheader in Portland.

The Blue Sox needed to take both to win. They almost did it. They won the opener, and had a 1-0 lead after seven in the second. The Red Sox came back with one in the eighth, and one in the ninth. Lewiston won it. "Thus," mused the *Evening Journal*, "ended the league in a fighting finish that makes baseball the all-world game."

The 1920s

The first half of the 1920s was a bleak period insofar as Maine baseball was concerned. There was no minor league ball, and Mainers in the majors were scarce. Very scarce. Clarence "Climax" Blethen, of Dover-Foxcroft, twirled 17⅔ innings for the Red Sox in 1923 (he would later hurl another two innings for the Dodgers six years later, in 1929), posting a 7.13 ERA and a 0-0 record. Ellsworth's Curt Fullerton also pitched for the Red Sox in the early 1920s. While nowadays folks in New England bemoan the fact that the Bosox never "take it all," in the 1920s the complaint was that they never took anything at all. It was true. In the nine years from 1921 through 1929, the Sox won 519 games while losing 857. They finished last - worse even than those perennial cellar-dwellers the Browns and the Senators - seven times. A "Decade of Despair," Ellery H. Clark called it in his book, RED SOX FOREVER. With both a lackluster offense and defense behind him, Fullerton, a starter in 42 games from 1921 to 1925, did not fare well. He posted a 10-37 record, including an especially depressing 2-15 mark in 1923.

The baseball picture improved for Maine in 1926. Making his first appearance in the majors - in a most modest way: he was 0-1 as a pinchhitter for the Reds late in the season - was Clyde Sukeforth. A Washington, Maine native, "Sukey" would be a part of the big league scene for the next five decades . . . and play a significant role in two of baseball's most historic moments. For more on Clyde and his many, many contributions to the game please see pages 119-125.

The year also saw the beginning of the next-to-last great hurrah of the New England League. With both Lewiston and Portland included, the league was off and running again . . . and would do so until 1930. Lewiston's team was named the Twins, logical in that they represented the Twin Cities of Lewiston and Auburn. Portland's name was the Eskimos . . . the result of a name-the-team contest held by

The Augusta Millionaires

Five major leaguers are included in this 1922 team photo of the Augusta Millionaires. Front row center, in white, is Ben Houser (born in Pennsylvania but closely associated with Maine baseball for many years), who had played with the Athletics and the Braves from 1910-1912. To Ben's immediate left is Sid Graves (born in Massachusetts), who would do a little outfielding for the Braves in 1927. Second from the left in the top row is Old Town's George "Squanto" Wilson, who had been up briefly with the Tigers in 1911 and the Red Sox in 1914. To Squanto's left is Sukey - Clyde Sukeforth - who would spend all or part of ten seasons in the bigs with the Reds and the Dodgers. And, second from the right in the top row, is Augusta's own Don Brennan, later to enjoy some good seasons on the mound for the Yankees, Reds, and Giants.

The Millionaires were a strong semi-pro outfit all during the 1920s. The team was reborn from 1948 to 1953 and contributed such players as Ted Lepcio, Harry Agganis, and Haywood Sullivan to the majors.

the *Portland Press Herald* and the *Evening Express*. The winner, one Wendell Little, came up with the moniker after becoming chilled on a particularly raw March day. Reasoned he: "This is the farthest north state in the Union, and if there's any place colder, the Eskimos can have it."

From their opening loss to Haverhill ("Eskimos Sock Apple Hard But Haverhill Grabs Bacon": *Evening Express*) right through to the end of the season the Eskimos were weak. They finished seventh, ahead of only the Nashua Millionaires. The Twins, lead by the hitting of former Bowdoin star Asa Small and the mound work of Augusta's Don Brennan (who, as we shall see, was later to be the first Mainer to pitch in a World Series), did better. They finished a most respectable third. Season highlights included Baseball Commissioner Judge Kenesaw Mountain Landis being on hand for both the Twins' and the Eskimos' home openers, and the invasion of Bayside Park by George Sisler and his St. Louis Brownies for an exhibition game against the Eskies on August 19th.

Portland Wins Half a Pennant

In 1927, the year the Bambino was letting loose with his 60 home runs, the New England League experimented with a split season. One winner was to be crowned for the first half; another, presumably different, winner would be crowned for the second. The two would then meet in a best-of-seven "Little World Series."

Both Lewiston, which finished second, and Portland, which finished third, played well in the first half. But not well enough. There was no stopping the Lynn Papooses. The second half was a different story, however. Portland, managed by all-time former Red Sox great Duffy Lewis, gave notice they were the team to beat by knocking off arch-rival Lewiston ("the

"Big Ball Game"

In the good old days, ball games were quite often "big ball games." This is an advertising fan heralding the coming of one such event as a part of Piscataquis County's Monson Fair.

Androscoggin Apple Assaulters," as the *Portland Press Herald* chided the Twins) in a July 4th doubleheader that launched the second half. The Lewismen (as in Duffy *Lewis*) fought a seesaw battle with both Salem and Nashua for the better part of July and August. Suddenly, though, Lynn got hot. Super hot. They won sixteen in a row. The race went down to the very last day of the season. With Lynn sweeping a pair from Salem, Portland had to take at least one game of a doubleheader from the Twins, who finished sixth, to clinch the flag. The first game, played in Lewiston in the morning, saw the Twins win, 4-1. In the second game, played in Portland in the afternoon, the Lewismen came through, winning 6-1 before a crowd of 3,554. That set the stage for the Little World Series. The high drama, however, was over. The Papooses swept in four straight. Even the *Maine Sunday Telegram*, while referring to the team from Massachusetts as "Luck-Laden Lynn," did have to concede that the Papooses were the better team.

The league continued with its split-season arrangement in 1928. The biggest drawback: it allowed both Maine entries to finish out of the running twice instead of just once. Duffy Lewis came back to handle the reins of the Portland club - now called the Mariners - while Lewiston hired fan-favorite Jesse "The Old Crab" Burkett to do the honors. Jesse, who possessed a .341 lifetime batting average and was elected to the Hall of Fame in 1946, would exchange repartee with most anyone: opposing players, umpires, the folks in the stands. The fans loved it.

The season began on a soggy note. After but four days of play it rained for nine straight afternoons. Frank Bushey, scheduled and rescheduled to pitch for the Mariners each of those nine straight afternoons, thereafter became known as "Rainy Day" Bushey. Rain or shine, neither

Lewiston schedule for 1926, and Lewiston and Auburn score card from 1929. "Baseball," it's interesting to note, was still spelled as two words on the earlier piece of memorabilia.

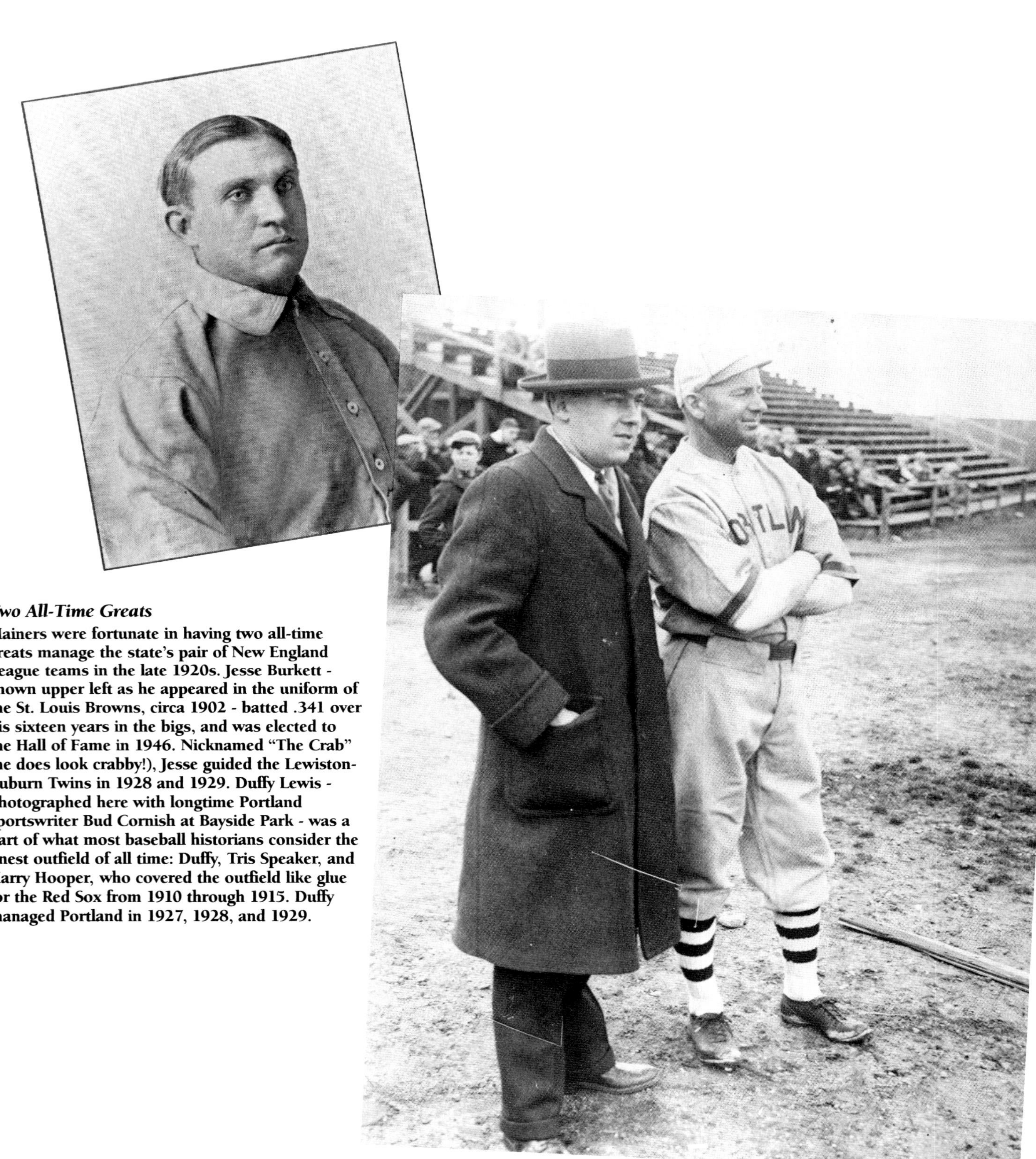

Two All-Time Greats

Mainers were fortunate in having two all-time greats manage the state's pair of New England League teams in the late 1920s. Jesse Burkett - shown upper left as he appeared in the uniform of the St. Louis Browns, circa 1902 - batted .341 over his sixteen years in the bigs, and was elected to the Hall of Fame in 1946. Nicknamed "The Crab" (he does look crabby!), Jesse guided the Lewiston-Auburn Twins in 1928 and 1929. Duffy Lewis - photographed here with longtime Portland sportswriter Bud Cornish at Bayside Park - was a part of what most baseball historians consider the finest outfield of all time: Duffy, Tris Speaker, and Harry Hooper, who covered the outfield like glue for the Red Sox from 1910 through 1915. Duffy managed Portland in 1927, 1928, and 1929.

the Twins nor the Mariners were ever in the running in the first half. Lewiston finished a distant third, Portland a more distant fifth, in the eight-team league. In the second half Jesse got his team off to a good start. They won nine of their first fifteen. Then they began to slide. Portland slid the whole way. When it was all over, the Twins were in fourth with a 31-30 mark. The Mariners finished dead last. They were 22-44, which means, quite simply, that for every game the team won it lost two. Dismal indeed.

In what was to be the last complete season for the New England League for the next seventeen years, 1929 was not unlike 1928 insofar as the two teams representing Maine were concerned. The Mariners were still the Mariners and they were still managed by Duffy Lewis. The Twins were still the Twins and they were still managed by Jesse Burkett. And neither team set the league afire. In the first half, Portland came in fourth, Lewiston fifth. In the second half, the two traded places: Lewiston was fourth, Portland fifth. If it was any consolation, two of the loop's top three hitters played for the Maine twosome. Portland's Rusty Saunders, who'd seen a handful of games with Connie Mack's Athletic's in 1927, was tops with a hefty .399, while Herb Rauding of the Twins came in third with a solid .359.

For the year 1930 Portland took yet another nickname. They were the Hustlers. Lewiston remained the Twins. The league got off to a wobbly start. There was talk of adding St. John, New Brunswick. Manchester was uncertain. As late as April 24th it was admitted that plans for the season were "still somewhat up in the air." Finally, on May 21st, the circuit got going, but with only six teams. Within less than a month that number would drop to four as Lewiston and Nashua dropped out. Play continued among the remaining foursome, and Portland teamed up with one of them in what was, perhaps, the weirdest game in the league's history. On June 1st the Hustlers met the Salem Witches in Salem in a game marked by weather so windy the pitchers had little control over where their pitches went. Before it was mercifully called after seven innings, the game saw 25 walks (and 31 runs, with the Witches scoring 21 of them). Three weeks later, on June 22nd, the league itself came to a halt. Not until 1946 would professional baseball be again played in Maine.

The Year of the Hitter

If 1930 was known locally as the year organized ball went into hibernation, nationally it was of far greater import. It was The Year of the Hitter. The Great Depression was upon us. The powers that be in baseball decided that more hits and runs were the best way to ensure that folks would continue to come out to the ballpark. The most logical way to provide those extra hits and runs? Liven up the ball. Add more "juice" to it.

The result was pure heaven for hitters, terror in the afternoon for pitchers. Especially was this true in the National League. Some statistics:

> Every single starter for the champion Cardinals batted over .300, plus they had subs who weighed in at .366, .374, and .396.
>
> Fireballer Dazzy Vance was the sole ERA qualifier with an average of less than 3.76.
>
> The Phillies averaged almost 6 runs per game and had three regulars who hit over .340, yet finished deep in the basement.
>
> Bill Terry of the giants hit .401. No National Leaguer has reached that magic mark since. "Memphis Bill" also pounded out 254 hits, the all-time league high.
>
> The Cubs' Hack Wilson set the all-time league record for homers (56) and the

major league record for RBIs (an astounding 190!).

Six of the eight clubs batted over .300 . . . and the *entire league* averaged .303. (Heck, no *team* in the Senior Circuit has even batted .300 in the 61 seasons since.).

Staggering!

Joining in the barrage was - of course - a Mainer. Adelphia Louis ("Del") Bissonette, born and raised in Winthrop and a graduate of Portland's Westbrook Seminary high school (where he batted .600 his senior year!), was undeniably the greatest ballplayer to ever come out of Maine. Had it not been for injuries (for Del's complete story please see pages 79-88) there is no telling what he might have accomplished. As it was, he played four complete seasons in the majors, all with the Brooklyn Robins (Dodgers). His 1930 stats were especially impressive. Playing first base and batting cleanup in a line-up that included Babe Herman, Glenn Wright, and Al Lopez, "The Winthrop Wonder" clouted .336, scored 102 runs, and knocked in 113 more. Normally, of course, an average of .336 would place its owner at the top of the heap or at least close to it. In 1930 that was hardly the case: Del's average was good enough for a tie (with future Hall of Famer Chick Hafey) for 19th place. Nevertheless, it was one wonderful year for Del, and was especially gratifying in that he helped propel the Robins into the first division - and an honest-to-goodness pennant race! - for the first time since 1924.

Sluggin' 'Em Out

Hack Wilson, left, and Bill Terry set records in 1930 that still stand today. Hack's 56 home runs in a single season tops the National League, while his 190 RBIs is the all-time mark for both leagues. Bill Terry pounded out 254 hits - an amount never surpassed in the Senior Circuit - en route to a .401 batting average. He is the last player to bat .400 in the NL.

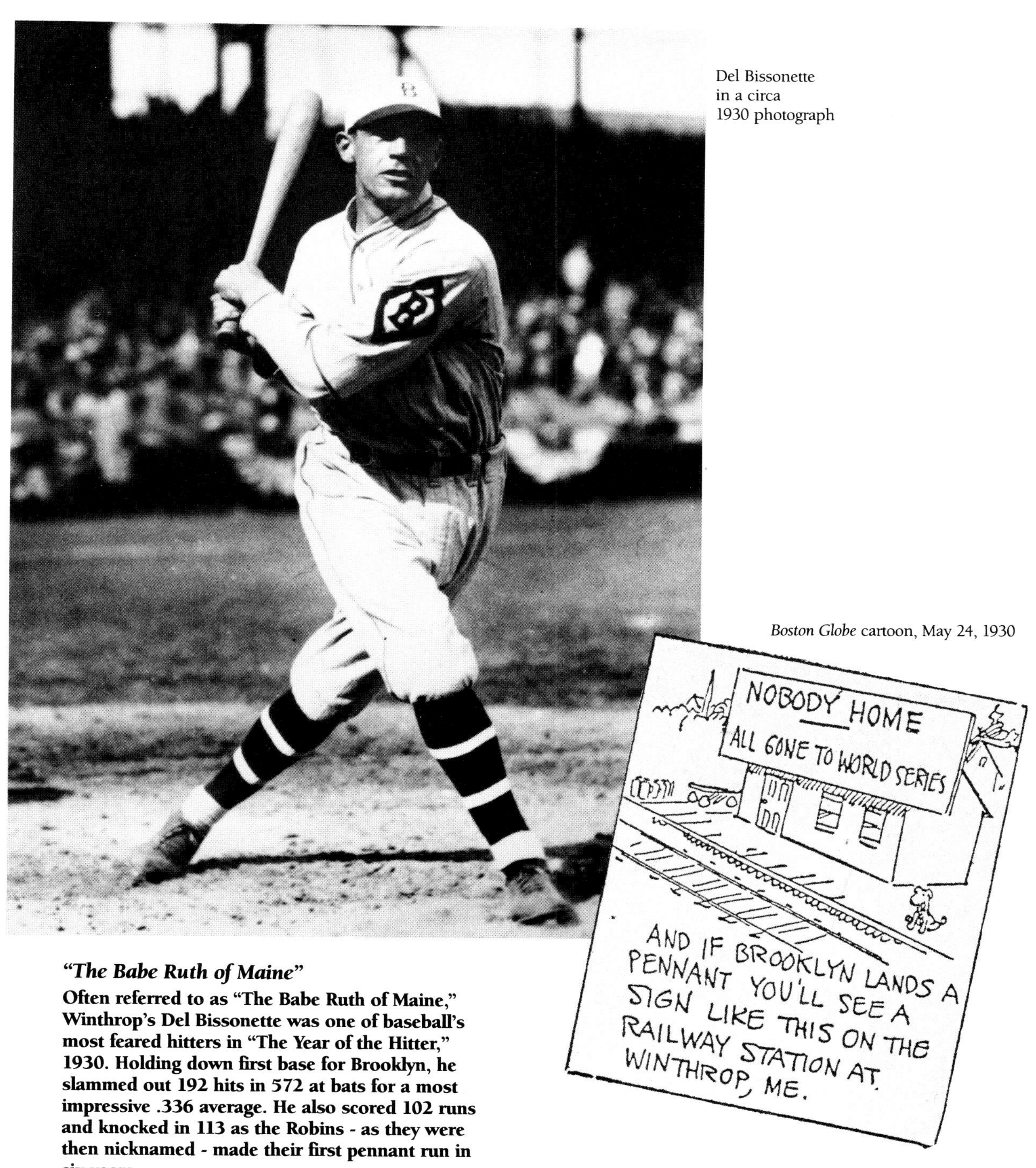

Del Bissonette in a circa 1930 photograph

Boston Globe cartoon, May 24, 1930

"The Babe Ruth of Maine"

Often referred to as "The Babe Ruth of Maine," Winthrop's Del Bissonette was one of baseball's most feared hitters in "The Year of the Hitter," 1930. Holding down first base for Brooklyn, he slammed out 192 hits in 572 at bats for a most impressive .336 average. He also scored 102 runs and knocked in 113 as the Robins - as they were then nicknamed - made their first pennant run in six years.

The Icicle Strikes Out The Iron Man

The third Mainer to appear in a World Series - following in the footsteps of Freddy Parent, shortstop for the Red Sox in the 1903 tilt, and Bill Carrigan, catcher, also for the Red Sox, in 1912 and catcher-manager for them in both 1915 and 1916 - was Augusta's Don Brennan. He was the first to see the Series from the vantage point of the mound. A power pitcher to begin with - it is said he could poke holes in the sides of barns around Augusta with his fastball - Brennan's career was side-tracked via a string of sore arms. But the big guy - he stood six feet tall and weighed anywhere from 200 to 240 pounds (the 1938 edition of *Who's Who In The Big Leagues* described him as "portly") - hung in there. He saw service with the Yankees (a 5-1 record in 18 games in 1933), the Reds (15-11 in 117 games, mostly in relief, from 1934 to 1937), as well as minor league teams from Newark (26-8 in 1932) to Jersey City to Toronto. Obtained by New York Giants' manager Bill Terry for his team's pennant drive in 1937, Brennan - nicknamed "The Icicle" because of his composure on the mound - responded with a 1-0 mark in six games.

It was his Series work, though, that was his career highlight. The 1937 Fall Classic was a "Subway Series" (or, more aptly, a just-walk-across-the-bridge Series . . . for the Giants and the Yankees then played across the Harlem River from one another. Now they're a little further apart.). The Yankees vs. the Jints. The Yankees were heavily favored: not surprising when you consider that their lineup included Lou Gehrig, Red Rolfe, Poosh 'Em Up Tony Lazzeri, Bill Dickey, Tommy "Old Reliable" Henrich, George "Twinkletoes" Selkirk, and 23-year-old Joe DiMaggio, who had belied the "sophomore slump" with 46 home runs, 167 RBIs, and a batting average of .346 during the course of the season, his second in the majors.

True to expectation, the Bombers took the first game handily, winning 8-1 as Joe D's single with the bases loaded capped a 7-run sixth inning. The second game was more of the first. Again the Yankees prevailed easily, winning by an identical 8-1 count. Game three saw the Series move to the Polo Grounds, but even in their home lair the Giant bats remained dormant. The score was 5-1, Yankees.

Don Brennan, however, made his first appearance and did the old home state proud. Pitching the ninth inning, he got future Hall of Famer Bill Dickey to fly to rightfield, got Twinkletoes Selkirk on a pop foul to Mel Ott (playing third for the Series), and got Myril Hoag to line out to short. Three up, three down. In game four the Polo Grounders finally unlimbered their attack, scoring six big runs in the second as their ace, Carl Hubbell, held the Yanks to just 6 hits.

In the fifth game the Giants were again plagued by a lackluster offense. They could do little against the savvy of Yankee mainstay Vernon "Lefty" Gomez. (Lefty, known almost as much for his zaniness as for his considerable pitching skill, was so much in control that he found time to gape at a plane as it flew overhead in the seventh inning. "He has an overpowering weakness for planes," *The New York Times* explained. And it is a fact that the Yankee ace once stood gaping at a passing plane while a runner on third stole home!). In the eighth inning, with the score 4-2 in favor of the Yankees, manager Bill Terry once more turned to Don Brennan. "The Icicle" responded by retiring Myril Hoag on a long fly to left, and then, after George Selkirk had singled to right, getting always tough Tony Lazzeri to pop to short, and Gomez to line to left. In the ninth, with the score still 4-2, Brennan walked Frankie Crosetti, got Red Rolfe on a sacrifice bunt, and induced Jolting Joe to hit a soft popup to shortstop Dick Bartell.

Continued on page 47

He Came to Pitch

Don Brennan, left, in an Augusta Loggers' uniform, summer, 1942. With him, in the center, are two unidentified BIW batsmen. Far right is manager Val Picinich, who caught eighteen years in the bigs (1916-1933), moved to Nobleboro to raise chickens in 1937, managed BIW in 1942, died in Nobleboro that December.

"A Hit at the Home Plate"

I enjoy advertisements with a baseball motif. This one dates from October of 1937 and was obviously meant to capitalize on the excitement of the World Series. I like the graphics. You'll like the prices.

ad, *Portland Press Herald,* October 12, 1937

The Iron Horse
You can bet Lou wasn't smiling after Don Brennan struck him out in the fifth game of the 1937 World Series.

ad, *Portland Press Herald,* May 6, 1937

His last challenge: none other than the Iron Horse himself, Lou Gehrig (who'd whacked 37 homers, driven in 159 runs, and had a .351 batting average during the regular season). With the count one and one, our hero threw a called strike past Lou. On the next delivery Larruping Lou swung . . . and missed. The Pride of Augusta had struck Lou Gehrig out.

Alas, the Jints could do nothing in their half of the ninth. The Series was over. Don Brennan, however, could be justly proud. He'd faced the mightiest team in the land . . . and subdued them with but a solo hit and no runs over a full third of a game. Not bad for a guy who'd grown up throwing strikes against the sides of barns in Kennebec County.

World War II

The Second World War played havoc with most every aspect of life in America. Baseball was no exception. Team after team was depleted of most of its regulars. The result was that players who might ordinarily have been considered too old, too young, or too infirm were given an opportunity. Pete Gray, with one arm, patrolled the outfield for the St. Louis Browns in 1945, batting .218 in 234 at bats; Joe Nuxhall, all of 15 years old, found himself on the mound for the Reds one afternoon in June of 1944 (although not for long: he gave up 2 hits and 5 walks against the Cards in two-thirds of an inning. Nuxhall, though, did return to the majors and won 135 games in a "grown-up career" that spanned fifteen seasons, 1952-1966.); Tommy Brown, aged 16, played 46 games at shortstop for the Dodgers in 1944; etc.

No youngsters from Maine benefited from the war's opportunities, but a pair of "oldsters" did. Our friend Clyde Sukeforth found himself re-activated by the Dodgers in 1945 after an eleven-year absence as a major league player. Catchers were especially scarce and, as Sukey explains it: "I was always managing farm clubs. And I was always throwing batting practice so my arm was as good in '45 as it ever was because I never let up." It seemed his batting eye hadn't let up either: in 51 at bats for the Dodgers that year - at age 45 - Clyde batted a solid .294.

Another Mainer who got a second chance during the war was 35-year-old Raymond "Bobby" Coombs. Born in Goodwin's Mills, Bobby had a short stint with Connie Mack's Athletics in 1933. He then wound his way through the minors for the next ten years. From Syracuse to Birmingham to St. Paul to Shreveport to Jersey City, Bobby saw a lot of minor league parks. In 1943, after winning 18 games for Jersey City, he had a chance to see the majors again. Called up by the Giants, Bobby saw action in nine games before he, too, was drafted by Uncle Sam. His warmest memory of his stay at the Polo Grounds is of Carl Hubbell: "My locker was next to his. He was a great guy. The only difference was that he had twenty pairs of shoes and I had two."

He Got a Second Chance

Born in Goodwin's Mills and a longtime resident of Ogunquit, Bobby Coombs saw limited action on the mound for Connie Mack's Philadelphia Athletics in 1933; then bounced back in a New York Giant uniform ten years later.

"When All Hell Broke Loose"

That dean of sportscasters, Red Barber, has termed 1947 the year "when all hell broke loose." The reason, of course, was Jackie Robinson. Hailed as the first Negro to play in the majors, actually he was not. Almost three-quarters of a century earlier, in 1884, Fleet and Welday Walker had played for Toledo in the American Association, then considered a major league. The Walkers were brothers who had starred at Oberlin College. Both were very definitely black. And both were intensely disliked by baseball's original Mr. Bigot, Adrian "Cap" Anson. Quite simply, Anson refused to play against them. And given his status as the game's greatest hero at the time, that's all it took. A color barrier was established that would last for the next six decades.

Enter Jackie. And, once again, enter Clyde Sukeforth. Sometimes touted as "the man who discovered Jackie Robinson," Clyde is not. No one is more adamant on that point than Sukey himself. He did, however, play a significant role in the signing of Jackie. And he was there the day that Robinson made his first field appearance in a Dodger uniform. The day was April 15, 1947. The place was Ebbets Field, Brooklyn, New York. And the manager for the Dodgers was Clyde Sukeforth.

It was an historic day if ever there were one. Here's how Clyde recalled it in an interview I had with him at his home in Waldoboro in November, 1990: "Well, I knew that there was a lot at stake. I mean he stood a chance to do not only something for himself but for his race. He had a chance to carry the flag - in fact, he would be carrying the flag - for the entire colored race. But you didn't have to tell him. He knew that. He had the determination."

Robinson went 4 for 5 in a 5-3 Dodger win over the Braves that day; went on to help Brooklyn win the 1947 National League flag; was voted Rookie of the Year; is now, of course, enshrined in the Hall of Fame.

It Was Quite a Day

A pensive Clyde Sukeforth and his opposing manager, the Boston Braves' Billy Southworth, pose for the camera before Jackie Robinson's historic first major league game, Ebbets Field, Brooklyn, New York, April 15, 1947.

Jackie as he looked in his brand-new Dodger blue uniform, April, 1947

Professional Baseball Returns to Maine

It was 1946. The war was over! And the New England League started up again. Under the aegis of super baseball fan John J. "Magnate" Haley, Portland was one of the eight teams in the circuit. Managed by ex-spitball hurler Rip "Lanky" Jordan (see page 165), the team was called the Gulls. By season's end it had earned many another sobriquet. The team was just plain dismal. In its home debut - before a sparse crowd of 550 - the Gulls were clobbered by the Manchester Giants, 12-1. The Giants banged out five home runs, a double and a triple. "For a time it looked as though they couldn't hit a single," commented the *Press Herald* the next day.

Things got worse. The only salvation was that the Fall River Indians were equally maladroit. The two waged a battle all season long to see who would garner last place honors. For better or worse, Portland "won"; their mark of 20-99 being just that much worse than Fall River's 30-94. With a won-lost percentage of .168 (which means that the team lost five games for every one victory), the 1946 Gulls make the 1962 Mets - the most futile team in recent times - look good: the Mets won 40 and lost 120 for a mark of .250.

A name change appeared in order for 1947. The team became the Pilots. It had a new manager, too. Del Bissonette - manager of the Braves in 1945, a coach for the Pirates in 1946, and probably the greatest name in Maine baseball annals - took over. The team's performance picked up, although they were still far from pacesetters. The Pilots hovered around the middle of the standings for much of the season, finally finishing in seventh, ahead of only the Lowell Stars. For a second year in a row the Lynn Red Sox won the loop . . . but Portland was gaining. In 1946 they'd finished 60½ games off the mark. In 1947 they were only 41½ games behind.

The Pilots Come Close

"The Year That Could've Been" was 1948. The Braves - they were the *Boston* Braves then: of "Spahn and Sain and pray for rain" fame - took the National League flag . . . their first since 1914. The Red Sox could have - and probably should have - taken the American League crown. Instead they lost it in a one-game playoff with Lou Boudreau and Gene Bearden and the Cleveland Indians on October 4th. And the Pilots, again managed by Del Bissonette, could have won New England League honors.

For the first time in history, in that year of 1948, a Maine team was affiliated with a major league outfit. The Pilots were part of the 15-team minor league system of the Philadelphia Phillies (who had finished seventh in 1947 but who were rebuilding toward their "Whiz Kids" success of 1950). It helped. The Phillies took ads in both the *Press Herald* and the *Evening Express* extolling Philly - "Fightin' Phillies" - pride. More importantly, Del was given better players. The Pilots lost their opener but then reeled off seven wins in a row. They found themselves in first place, and in a dogfight with the ever-powerful Lynn Red Sox for most of the summer. The Nashua Dodgers made it a three-way affair in August. When all was said and done in September, Lynn was once more atop the league, Nashua was second, and the Pilots a close third . . . with the remainder of the loop far, far behind. Led by the hitting of outfielder Jim Pokel (nicknamed "The Big Poke," and whose 30 homers set an all-time New England League mark), shortstop Mike Romello (nicknamed "Midget Mike" and/or "Mike the Tyke" because of his diminutive 5′4″ frame), and thirdbaseman Jackie Cusick (who would later play 114 games at shortstop for the Cubs and Braves in 1951-52), and the pitching of Carl Kolosna and Will Koszarek (nicknamed "King Carl" and "Silent Will"), the 1948 Pilots earned a shot at the Governor's Cup: a playoff between the top four teams in the league. Here's where the Bissonettemen really had their chance. Down two games to one to Lynn in a best-of-five series, they rallied to take the fourth game, 2-0, and had the rubber game won by a 2-1 margin going into the bottom of the eighth. But Lynn scored one that inning, and then came through with another - on a very hotly-disputed play at the plate - in the ninth. That was it. The Governor's Cup was not to reside in Portland. (Note: Nashua won it. After knocking off fourth-place Pawtucket, the Dodgers trimmed Lynn in what was getting to be a habit. They'd done precisely the same in 1946 and 1947.).

The Governor's Cup Comes to Portland

In what was to be its swan-song year, 1949, the New England League obliged with another of its quirky seasons . . . a season that worked out exceedingly well for the Pilots. With Del Bissonette having moved on to manage Toronto, then in the International League, the club had a new skipper. He was 38-year-old Lamar "Skeeter" Newsome, a former (1935-1947) major league infielder with the Athletics, Red Sox, and Phillies. Fan support was strong. Hugh Duffy, back in 1915, had labeled Portland "the best day in and day out minor league city in New

Continued on page 55

Looking Good

Here's how Del Bissonette and his Portland Pilots looked in 1947. That's Del in the middle of the front row. Other notables include outfielder Cliff Blake, a Cornish, Maine native who led the New England League in batting that year with a .340 average (back row, far left); pitcher Bob Tanner, later baseball coach at Portland High School (back row, third from left); and pitcher Ed Hadlock, also later baseball coach at Portland High and the man for whom Portland's Hadlock Field is named (middle row, fourth from left). Herb Swift (not shown in photo), father of the Seattle Mariners' Billy Swift, hurled a few games for the Pilots that year, too. What he recalls most: "It was a thrill just being there."

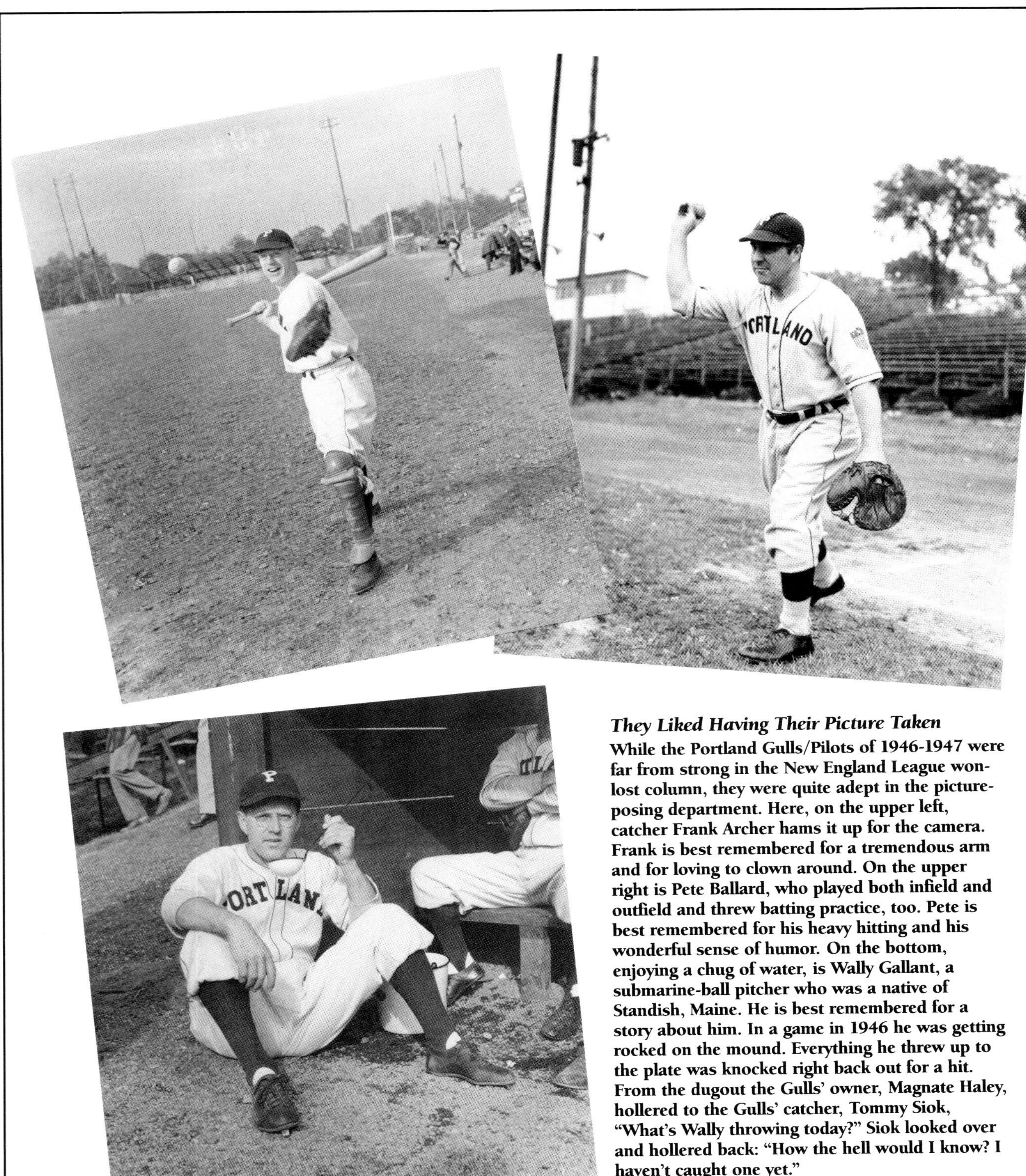

They Liked Having Their Picture Taken

While the Portland Gulls/Pilots of 1946-1947 were far from strong in the New England League won-lost column, they were quite adept in the picture-posing department. Here, on the upper left, catcher Frank Archer hams it up for the camera. Frank is best remembered for a tremendous arm and for loving to clown around. On the upper right is Pete Ballard, who played both infield and outfield and threw batting practice, too. Pete is best remembered for his heavy hitting and his wonderful sense of humor. On the bottom, enjoying a chug of water, is Wally Gallant, a submarine-ball pitcher who was a native of Standish, Maine. He is best remembered for a story about him. In a game in 1946 he was getting rocked on the mound. Everything he threw up to the plate was knocked right back out for a hit. From the dugout the Gulls' owner, Magnate Haley, hollered to the Gulls' catcher, Tommy Siok, "What's Wally throwing today?" Siok looked over and hollered back: "How the hell would I know? I haven't caught one yet."

Here's How

Pilot pitcher Charlie Dyke shows an unidentified Portland Stadium fan how to throw a curve ball. Charlie, alas, is best remembered for not being able to get anybody out.

Official program and score card from 1949, the year the Pilots won the New England League Governor's Cup

England." It showed in the late '40s. The Pilots had led the league in attendance by a wide margin in 1948, when 117,606 spectators passed through the turnstiles at Portland Stadium. For their home opener in 1949 a hefty crowd of 5,122 turned out as the Pilots took on - and beat - the Springfield Cubs.

The team won nine of its first twelve, was in first place for a brief burst in mid-May. The club's natural level, however, was more like third or fourth place. Playing slightly better than .500 ball, the Pilots jockeyed with the Cubs for third all through June and July, with the Nashua Dodgers and Pawtucket Slaters well ahead in the battle for the top spot. Then the league began to crumble. Providence, which had drawn an abysmal 7,327 paying customers for its first nineteen home games, dropped out on June 21st. There was much talk of adding Auburn (Maine), which had just completed a new stadium, to the league. Augusta was also mentioned as a possibility. But nothing came of it, and when Lynn, Fall River, and Manchester all folded on July 20th, league management decided to see the season out with just the remaining four teams. Everything was started anew. All four had a fresh chance. Skeeter and his boys responded by winding up, at season's end in September, a strong second to Pawtucket. It was in the Governor's Cup match, however, that the Portlanders really shone.

In an odd arrangement, number one Pawtucket - led by Bob Montag, who was tops in the league with a resounding .423 batting average, and who'd zoomed along at an even more resounding .500 for the first fifty games of the season - was paired against number three Springfield in a best two-out-of-three, with the Pilots to meet the winner in a best-of-seven match. The Cubs (Springfield) surprised, beating the Slaters two out of two. That set the stage: Springfield vs. Portland for the Cup. The opening game was nothing short of a rout. The Pilots pounded out twenty hits en route to a 20-4 victory. Hero of the day was definitely leftfielder Charlie Hood, who hit for the cycle and then added another homer for good measure. The Pilots also took game two, 7-3, in a game highlighted by Pilot thirdsacker Walt Derucki's three-run 400-foot shot over the centerfield wall. The Cubs, however, charged back in game three, winning 10-2. Dusty Rhodes, later to gain considerable fame with the Giants for his bat (if not his glove!), was the Cubs' big gun with three hits in five trips to the plate. The Pilots took a commanding lead in the fourth game, winning 7-2, as the old pro, player-manager Skeeter Newsome himself, logged four hits including a home run. Again, though, the Cubs fought back: they won game number five, 9-0, as Dusty hit an inside-the-park grand slam, and they took game number six as Dusty scored the winning run in an 11th-inning 4-3 cliffhanger.

That brought it all down to the seventh and deciding game. After the very first inning, however, little suspense remained: the Pilots romped for eight runs right off the bat. Final score: 11-0, with skipper and shortstop Skeeter leading the attack with a double, two singles, and four RBIs. The Governor's Cup was Portland's!

All This for 60¢ General Admission

Far more important than the 1949 Governor's Cup success, however, was the opportunity the fans of Maine had to watch some pretty darned good ballplayers. Passing through Portland Stadium - the home of the Gulls/Pilots from 1946 through 1949 - were the likes of Roy Campanella (Campy batted .290 with 95 RBIs for Nashua in 1946; later went on to win three MVP awards with the Dodgers; is now in the Hall of Fame), Don

Newcombe (who won 33 games while losing only ten during his two years, 1946-47, with Nashua; went on to three twenty-game seasons with Brooklyn), George Crowe (who walloped .354 and led the league with 102 RBIs while playing first base for Pawtucket in 1949; later had some very satisfying seasons with the Braves and the Reds), Walter Alston (who was player/manager for Nashua in 1946; went on to manage the Dodgers for almost a quarter of a century), Dale Long (first-sacker for Lynn in 1948 when he hit .302 and knocked in a league-leading 119 runs; later starred for the Pirates, Cubs, and Senators; is best remembered for his eight home runs in eight games for the Bucs in 1956), Billy Klaus (who hit .327 for Springfield in 1949; went on to play over 2,500 games at short, second, and third for a host of major league teams), and James Lamar Rhodes (better known as "Dusty," who batted .290 in 119 games for Springfield in 1949; later had several noteworthy seasons with the Giants; almost singlehandedly pulverized the Indians in the 1954 World Series). Other future major leaguers who saw action in the New England League in 1946-1949 included Dan Bankhead, Matt Batts (I've always loved that name!), bonus babies Wayne Belardi ($17,000) and Billy Loes ($23,000), Alex Campanis, Billy Hunter, Gino Cimoli, Marion Fricano, Don Hoak, Clint (old "Scrap Iron") Courtney, Fred Hatfield, Don Liddle, and Bob Cain (the man who, in 1951, had the distinction of pitching - or *trying* to pitch - to the Browns' 3'7" midget, Eddie Gaedel). All that for 60¢ general admission!

Two Who Made It Big

Big Don Newcombe, top, and Roy Campanella, bottom (being congratulated by Gil Hodges, number 14, and Carl Furillo, number 6, after clouting a first-inning three-run blast on May 7, 1957), were just two of the parade of greats who played at Portland Stadium during their postwar 1940s' New England League days.

The Shot Heard 'Round the World

In early autumn, 1951, my family followed the legions of others in our ranch house tract development in Ardsley, New York: we acquired our first television set. It was just in the nick of time! I, a baseball-eyed ten-year-old, had the chance to witness what most baseball historians rank as the single most dramatic event in the game's history: Bobby Thomson's "Shot heard 'round the world." I can yet recall it vividly. The stage was being set - Clint Hartung was going in to pinch run for the injured Don Mueller; Thomson was getting set to advance to the plate - just as my mother walked in the room and joined me to watch. A native of Brooklyn, she had a strong fondness for the Dodgers. As Thomson stepped in I kiddingly remarked "Watch him hit one." Her response was "Oh, Will, don't say that." Then, boom!!! (I often wonder if the course of history would have been different if my mother hadn't walked in when she did!).

But let's back up. Let's review just what made Bobby Thomson's homer so dramatic. By August there was no doubt who was going to win the National League pennant. The Dodgers - led by the hitting of Gil Hodges, Duke Snider, Roy Campanella, Pee Wee Reese, and Jackie Robinson, and the pitching of Don Newcombe and Preacher Roe - built a lead that could only be called commanding. As of August 12th they stood 13½ games ahead of the second-place team, their longtime arch rivals, the Giants. Then strange things began to happen. The Giants began to win and win and win. And the Dodgers began to lose and lose and lose. It was virtually impossible . . . but at season's end the Giants - led by Monte Irvin, Alvin Dark, Don Mueller, a rookie named Willie Mays, Larry Jansen, and Sal "The Barber" Maglie - had caught up with Brooklyn. The two teams finished in a dead heat. An exact tie.

That set up a best two-out-of-three Playoff Series. Game number one, played at Ebbets Field on October 1st, saw the Giants win, 3-1. The Dodgers returned the favor the next day, when the action shifted to the Polo Grounds, romping to a 10-0 shutout. That left it all to October 3rd. Game number three, at the Polo Grounds, for all the marbles. The contest was a 1-1 cliffhanger until the eighth inning, when the Dodgers came up with three big runs. Nothing happened in the bottom of the eighth or the top of the ninth . . . so that's the way it stood, 4-1 Dodgers, going into the bottom of the ninth.

With just three outs to go, however, it was obvious that the Dodgers' starting pitcher and ace, Don Newcombe, was worn out. Alvin Dark squeezed a single up the middle. Don Mueller, nicknamed "Mandrake" because of his proficiency with the bat, hit a bouncer into right. Dark motored to third. Monte Irvin, however, popped up to firstbaseman Gil Hodges. Dodger fans breathed a sigh of relief. But Whitey Lockman, the Giants' firstsacker, poked Newk's second pitch - high and outside and a good six inches out of the strike zone - down the leftfield line, good for a double. Dark scored. Don Mueller, sliding into third, pulled the ligaments on both sides of his ankle. Giant manager Leo Durocher sent Clint Hartung in to pinch run. The score was now 4-2, with two on and only one out. Dodger skipper Charlie Dressen finally made a move. It was time to take Big Newk out. Dressen conferred - for the umpteenth time - with his bullpen catcher and coach who was - you can guess, of course! - Clyde Sukeforth. Once more, let's pick up the happenings in Sukey's own words, relayed to me in my November 8, 1990 interview with him:

> "My claim to fame: I sent in the wrong pitcher in the Polo Grounds in the playoff game in 1951. I'm in the bullpen. We have two pitchers. We have Carl Erskine and Ralph Branca. Dressen tells you who to take to the bullpen. Dressen's the manager. I was the bullpen coach and catcher. And I'm catching next to the wall where the telephone is and I'm catching Branca. We're synchronized: I'll catch Branca's pitch and throw it back and then catch Erskine's pitch

and throw it back. Well, Erskine had more or less chronic arm trouble. He would have won 20 (games) every year had he been sound all the time, because he had one of the finest overhand curveballs you ever looked at. And his fastball was highly adequate. And he had good control. And he was a good competitor. Well, Charlie's calling. This is the third and deciding game. Newcombe is breezing along with a 4-1 lead. He'd gotten in a little trouble in the seventh and eighth innings and both our pitchers (in the bullpen) have been throwing for two innings. I mean they were ready all the time in case he (Dressen) wants one or the other of 'em. Charlie keeps calling me - and I knew Charlie: I played with Charlie in Cincinnati - and he keeps calling. 'Who's ready?' I said that Branca was 'loose and good.' I didn't say anything about Erskine. I didn't see his good curveball. I didn't see his better fastball. And knowing the boy is a good competitor and the importance of the game I just assumed he doesn't feel like pitching. And Branca's throwing good.

"(So Branca goes in.). He only made two pitches. He threw one strike. (It was) the Polo Grounds (known for its short distance down the lines). He (Bobby Thomson) hit a 250-260 foot home run (off the second pitch). But it made me famous. Oh yeah, Charlie passed the buck. The only time all year he ever called me. That was the first time in the whole year that he ever asked my opinion."

Bobby Thomson: he liked Ralph Branca's second pitch.

Structural Change Comes to the Game

In 1952-54 a shot of a different nature was heard throughout baseball-land. The same sixteen-team structure that had been in place for over five decades, since 1903, ceased to exist. Teams began - with league consent, of course - to switch cities. After the 1953 season the hapless St. Louis Browns moved to Baltimore, becoming the Orioles. The following year, the Athletics (on the way to their eventual berth in Oakland) moved to Kansas City. Later, at the conclusion of the 1957 season, the Dodgers and Giants would desert their familiar stomping grounds for the more fertile fields of California. But the team that started it all, and benefited the most quickly in terms of on-the-field success, was the Braves. One of the National League's founding clubs in 1876, the Braves had fallen upon hard times in Boston. Pennants (1914 and 1948) since the turn of the century were scarce, fan support meager. In 1948, when they won what was to be their last title in Boston, the Braves drew 1,455,431. In 1949 that figure dropped to 1,081,795. In 1950 it was 844,391. Only 487,475 showed up in 1951. And 1952 saw an unbelievably low 281,278 fans go through the turnstiles. Something clearly had to be done. Owner Lou Perini also owned the Milwaukee franchise in the American Association. In March of 1953 the league's permission was given: bye-bye Boston, hello Milwaukee.

The Suds City loved its new team. By the thirteenth home game more fans had already payed to see them play than had in the entire 1952 season at Boston! The team's performance zoomed at about the same rate: from seventh in 1952 they jumped to second in 1953. It was the first of four successive second or third-place finishes. Finally, in both 1957 and 1958, the Braves took the crown. The team's offense was its hallmark. Hank Aaron, Eddie Mathews, Joe Adcock, Frank Torre,

Continued on page 61

The Rookie from Cherryfield

In his rookie year with the Braves, in 1958, Cherryfield's Carlton Willey posted a 2.70 ERA and led the National League in shutouts.

A Happy Pair

This was the Braves' one-two punch on May 10, 1959. Milwaukee had just trimmed the Reds, 2-1, behind the hitting of Hank Aaron, left, and the hurling of Carlton. Aaron's single in the ninth drove in the winning run. Carlton pitched all the way for the victory.

Wes Covington, Red Schoendienst, "Hurricane" Bob Hazle (who clouted .403 in 134 key at bats in 1957): all were calculated to bring fear to the rest of the league. But the pitching was no slouch, either. Warren Spahn seemed to get better as he got older. At age 36 in 1957 he was 21-11. The following year he added one notch to both his age and his wins. He went 22-11. Lou Burdette (17-9 in 1957; 20-10 in 1958) made for a strong one-two punch. But there were others. Bob Buhl was 18-7 in 1957. Ex-Cub Bob Rush won 10 games in 1958. A Mainer was there to help out, too. Carlton Willey, of Cherryfield, posted a most impressive 21-6 mark for the Wichita Braves, Milwaukee's top farm club, in 1957. That earned him a shot with the parent club in 1958. After a month or so, however, he was sent back down to Wichita. A no hitter, though, convinced the Braves' brass he was ready. He was. During the course of the rest of the season Carlton tossed a league-leading four shutouts, had a fine 2.70 ERA, and picked up nine big wins. Here's how Carlton - who still lives in Cherryfield: I interviewed him there in April, 1991 - recalls the thrill of that first season in the bigs:

> "The first one (game) I pitched I remember the most. It was against the Giants. In San Francisco. I beat 'em 8-0. It was a five-hitter, I think. They had Willie Mays, Orlando Cepeda, Ray Jablonski, Jim Davenport. They had a good ballclub." (Ed. note: the score of the game, played June 23rd, was 7-0, and it was a six-hitter . . . but all six were singles, one of which was Willie Mays' 1,000th big league base hit!). "The fellows that we had on our club - Aaron, Mathews, and Spahn and Burdette - they were the best. You'd never know that Warren Spahn was the kind of pitcher that he was. And won as many games as he did. Because you never heard him say anything, bragging or anything. And the same with Aaron. (He was) just as quiet. You had to pump him to get words out of him. Burdette, though, was a real card. I'll tell you a story. We were playing against the Cubs. It was the ninth inning. There were two outs. Burdette was pitching; (Del) Crandell was catching; and Ernie Banks was hitting. Well, he (Burdette) got the ball back from Crandell. He had two strikes on Banks. He had a big chew of gum in his mouth. He spit that gum into his glove, turned his back around and just pushed that ball into the glove. He threw the damned ball and Banks missed it by at least two feet. We went in the clubhouse and Burdette and Crandell were laughing like heck . . . that gum was still stuck on the ball. It didn't come off when it hit Crandell's mitt!"

45 rpm record, late 1957

Move Over, Elvis

After notching three wins over the Yankees in the 1957 World Series, Lew Burdette had his share of limelight . . . including a shot at show biz. Elvis and Fats and Chuck Berry needed have no fear, however: Lew was far better on the mound than behind the mike.

> (Note: Carlton also pitched an inning in the fifth game of the World Series against the Yankees. He went into the game in the ninth, and did about as well as was possible: he struck Moose Skowron and Gil McDougal out, induced Tony Kubek to hit an easy-out popup. Three up, and three down. Still, though, it's obvious Carlton's best memories of that championship season were his first victory, and just the joy of playing with the likes of Hank Aaron, Eddie Mathews, Warren Spahn, and, of course, Lou Burdette. And who can blame him?!).

After four more not-overly-wondrous seasons (he was 19-33 over the four), Carlton found himself amidst the helpless - and just about always winless - New York Mets. He was sold to New York after the 1962 season. Just how bad were the Mets? Well, the inaugural 1962 squad lost 120 games (out of 160) . . . the most by any team this century. That was the season of firstbaseman "Marvelous Marv" Throneberry (who had a real weakness for ground balls hit right at him, and who, in a game in June, managed to miss both first and second in running out what would otherwise have been a triple), catcher Choo Choo Coleman (who was okay on low pitches, but suspect on everything else), and, of course, manager Casey Stengel, beloved for statements like "Now we haven't been doin' so great but let me tell ya why that is . . . ."

Carlton missed out on that "glorious" first year, however. He arrived in 1963, when the team - with the inimitable Casey still at the helm - was starting to make its slow move toward respectability. But it was slow. The Mets still dropped 112 games. The team's mainstay on the mound, Roger Craig, lost 18 consecutive decisions. Carlton, nevertheless, tasted a heady measure of success. He equalled his high-watermark with the Braves - nine wins (remember, this is a team that won but 51 games all season long!) - while leading the staff with a very respectable 3.10 ERA. As in 1958, he kicked in with four shutouts. Again - this time on how it felt to be a part of one of the very worst clubs in baseball history - Carlton's own reflections:

> "Oh, God, I loved 'em. I loved the Mets. It was a great club to play for. I didn't want to be traded to New York. But now I'm glad I did, because it's the best place to play in the world. The fans are great. The fans know baseball.
>
> "We were all a great big family. We'd just go up to the ballpark and see how we were going to lose. Somebody'd make an error or somebody (on the other team) would hit a home run. We were kind of loose about it. We had to be: there's not much we could do about it."

On the Mound for the Mets
In his inaugural with the Mets, 1963, Carlton Willey had a most respectable 3.10 ERA; accounted for almost 20% of the team's total wins.

Does Carlton have a Casey Stengel story? Of course. It would be difficult not to! He recounts the time the Mets were losing badly to the Pirates at Forbes Field. It was the fourth inning or so and it was raining quite hard. Casey killed about as much time as possible out on the mound talking to his pitcher, figuring the umpires would call the game. But they didn't. So old Case got a hold of one of the groundskeeper's raincoats - "a real sou'wester with a hat and everything" . . . to prove his point about how hard the rain was coming down - called time, and went out to the mound again. As Carlton beams: "I thought those people in Pittsburgh would go crazy from laughing so hard."

Talking it Over with Casey

Here Carlton, just obtained from the Braves, lines up with manager Casey Stengel, left, and fellow Met pitchers Roger Craig, second from right, and Jay Hook, far right, during spring training of 1963.

The Decade of the Pitcher

Since 1945, when Clyde Sukeforth came out of "retirement" to hit .294 in 51 at bats for the war-weakened Brooklyn Dodgers, there have been but two non-pitcher Mainers to appear in the major leagues. Dick Scott of Ellsworth played three games at shortstop for the 1989 Athletics, and catcher Ron Tingley of Presque Isle has been with the Padres and Angels off and on since 1982. That's it.

In this same four-and-a-half decade span Maine has, however, fared rather well with respect to pitchers. In no decade was that more apparent than the 1970s. Nine Mainers took to the mound at one time or another in search of fame and fortune . . . and strikeouts and miserly earned run averages. In alphabetical order there was:

Ralph Botting, of Houlton, who was 2-0 for the Angels in 1979 (and 2-3 lifetime over two seasons, both with California, 1979-1980).

Danny Coombs, of Lincoln and Brewer, who was 10-14 with a 3.30 ERA for the Padres in 1970 (and 19-27 lifetime over nine seasons with the Astros and Padres, 1963-1971).

John Cumberland, of Westbrook, who was 9-6 with a 2.92 ERA for San Francisco in 1971 (and 15-16 lifetime over six seasons with the Yankees, Giants, Cardinals, and Angels, 1968-1974).

Larry Gowell, of Lewiston, who was 0-1 with a 1.29 ERA with the Yankees in 1972 (his only season in the majors).

Fred Howard, of Portland, who was 1-5 with a 3.57 ERA for the White Sox in 1979 (his only season in the majors).

Pete Ladd, of Portland, who was 1-1 with a 3.00 ERA for the Astros in 1979 (and 9-17 lifetime over four seasons with the Astros and the Brewers, 1979 and 1982-1984).

Bert Roberge, of Lewiston, who was 3-0 with a 1.69 ERA for the Astros in 1979 (and 12-12 lifetime over six seasons with the Astros, White Sox, and Expos, 1979-1985).

Bob Stanley, of Portland, who was 15-2 with a 2.60 ERA for the Red Sox in 1978 (and 115-97 lifetime over thirteen seasons, all with the Bosox, 1977-1989).

Stan Thomas, of Mexico, who was 4-4 with a 2.29 ERA for the Indians in 1976 (and 11-14 lifetime over four seasons with the Rangers, Indians, Mariners, and Yankees, 1974-1977).

Some of these Maine moundsmen hurled, of course, with more success than others. Danny Coombs started 27 games for the Padres in his most shining year, 1970. The 6′4″ southpaw also struck out 105 batters in 188 innings that year. John Cumberland became the first Mainer to appear in a League Championship Series when he started game number two for the Giants against the Padres in 1971. Pete Ladd earned a very real taste of glory when he repeatedly shut down the Angels in relief in the 1982 Angels-Brewers League Championship Series. "Bigfoot" (he wore size 14EEE shoes!) appeared in three of the five games, struck out five in 3.1 innings pitched, and chalked up two saves. As both a starter and a reliever in his long career with the Red Sox, Bob Stanley won in double figures five times and holds several club records.

The most intriguing of the nine, however, may have been Larry Gowell. A Seventh Day Adventist, Gowell's religion prohibited work from sundown Friday to sundown Saturday. When you're a professional ballplayer, pitching is work. A perennial strikeout leader, Gowell's religious beliefs posed no real problems in his impressive minor league career . . . but management at the parent club, the Yankees, were less than thrilled that one of their staff would be out of commission two days a week every week. So Larry's pinstripe days were short. But they were rather sweet: over two games the fastballer fanned seven in seven innings as well as rapping out a double in his only time at bat. (Note: ironically, Larry Gowell is now a Baptist; has been for a number of years. Had he been a Baptist then - in 1972 - there's no telling what honors he might have garnered.).

They All Came From Maine

A complete team - nine players in all - of major league pitchers. And they all pitched in the 1970s. And they all hailed from Maine.

Ralph Botting

Danny Coombs

John Cumberland

Larry Gowell

Fred Howard

Pete Ladd

Bert Roberge

Bob Stanley

Stan Thomas

Maine's Flirtation with Triple A Baseball

This is the part of WAS BASEBALL REALLY INVENTED IN MAINE? that I find very difficult to write. I love minor league baseball. One of the reasons I moved to Portland in 1987 was that there was minor league ball close by. What a great way to spend a summer evening: sitting at The Ballpark, enjoying the game. And since I rarely cared which team won, I think I enjoyed it all that much more . . . for the sheer relaxation and rhythm of the sport. I know I cried after the last game.

The gyrations and legal maneuverings of the Maine Guides/Phillies could fill twenty pages. Probably more. But it would be boring. The story starts with Jordan I. Kobritz, a Bangor attorney who wanted to bring minor league baseball back to Maine. Portland, "The Metropolis of Maine," was the logical choice. But, in the fall of 1982, the city's City Council rejected the idea. Undaunted, Kobritz went ahead and purchased the Triple A Charleston (West Virginia) Charlies of the International League for $650,000 in December. It took two months, but Kobritz found a home for his team: in February of 1983 it was announced that the team would play in Old Orchard Beach. First, though, a stadium had to be constructed. Eventually christened simply The Ballpark, it opened for play on April 18, 1984. The Charlies (who'd continued to play in Charleston during the 1983 season) needed a name, too. Kobritz, in time-honored tradition, opened up the selection to the fans. A statewide contest drew over 10,000 responses, representing over 1,000 different names. The 1,000 were pared down to 100, then 10, and then, finally, one. That one was the Guides (other top ten finalists included the Schooners, Beacons, Sails, Vacationers, Coasters, and Deer).

Play Ball

With a new name, a new ballpark, and an affiliation with the Cleveland Indians (named in honor of a Mainer, it will be recalled!), professional baseball returned to Maine in grand style in April of 1984. This was Triple A. We were on a par with the likes of Denver, Buffalo, Louisville, Omaha, Des Moines, Portland ("the other Portland," the one in Oregon), Albuquerque, Phoenix, San Antonio, etc. We were big time!

After a six-game road trip, during which they were 5-1, the Guides made their Old Orchard debut on the afternoon of April 18th . . . and came through with a 13-9 bombardment of the Rochester Red Wings. Although it was but 38 degrees at game time, 6,104 hardy souls donned football-weather gear and came on out to watch and cheer. It was the start of a good year. The Guides jumped into first place; held it until mid-June; were in contention all the way; finished second to the Columbus Clippers at the finish. The top four teams - Columbus, the Guides, the Toledo Mud Hens, and the Pawtucket Red Sox - in the eight-team loop then vied for the honor of winning the International League's Governor's Cup. The Guides made short work of their first opponent, the Mud Hens. They swept all three games, 8-2, 7-4, and 3-2. They continued to roll against their next and final foes, the Pawtucket Red Sox (who had been victorious against Columbus). Behind future major leaguer Jerry Reed, they coasted 8-1 in the opener of the best-of-five series. Game two saw the Guides again triumph, 8-6. With the Pawtucket part of the set over, and the Guides back at The Ballpark, taking the Cup apeared almost certain. It was not to be. The Pawsox won game number three, 5-2. Then they won number four as well, 9-2. That left it all up to the

Five Years

Five years of Maine Guides'/Maine Phillies' memorabilia . . . and memories. Pictured on the cover of the 1984 program is manager Doc Edwards; on the 1987 program, manager Bill Dancy.

The Stars Came Out at Old Orchard Beach
In alphabetical order, from upper left to bottom right, are six of today's stars who made their way through The Ballpark on the road to the big time: Cecil Fielder, Mike Greenwell, Kelly Gruber, Fred McGriff, Kevin Mitchell, and Kirby Puckett.

evening of September 13th. Jerry Reed again pitched well . . . but not well enough. Future Red Sox and White Sox journeyman Steve Lyons whacked a Reed fastball over the right-centerfield wall in the third. That was enough. The Guides were held scoreless. Final score: Pawsox 3, Guides 0. Still, it was a heck of a season. Close to 200,000 fans came out to The Ballpark. Playing at Old Orchard at one time or another during that first year of professional baseball's return to Maine were, among others: Larry Sheets (who batted .302 for Rochester), Kelly Gruber (Syracuse), Kevin Romine (Pawtucket), Milt Thompson (Richmond), Sid Fernandez (Tidewater), Otis Nixon (the Guides), and, ironically, both of the players who five years up the road, in 1989, would lead their respective leagues in home runs: Fred McGriff (Syracuse) and Kevin Mitchell (Tidewater) . . . as well as the player who would top the American League in batting that same year, Kirby Puckett. Called up to the parent Minnesota Twins from Toledo before a game at The Ballpark, Kirby was asked, "Where will they play you?" "Anywhere they want," was Kirby's answer. He's been playing - and superstarring - ever since.

In their second season, 1985, the Guides again finished in second place, this time behind the Syracuse Chiefs. Guides' first-baseman Jim Wilson led the league in both home runs (with 26) and RBIs (with 101). Leftfielder Dwight Taylor topped the circuit with 52 stolen bases. This year the team was even more determined to win the Governor's Cup for manager Doc Edwards. Again, however, they were to be foiled. Their opponent in the first best-of-five match-up was the Tidewater Tides, the Mets' top farm club. The Tides took game number one handily, 7-1. The Guides tied it at one apiece as they limited the Tides to just one run (a Kevin Mitchell homer) and took the second game, 3-1. Game number three, played at The Ballpark, was the heartbreaker: the Guides had two runners cut down at the plate, lost 3-2. After the fourth encounter, though, the Guides and the Tides (how nicely that rhymes!) were tied once more, as DH Rick Lisi drove in both runs in a 2-0 victory with his first home run in two years. The end came in the deciding game: the Guides' bats were less than hot and the Tides, behind another Kevin Mitchell circuit clout, took it, 3-1. (Note: the Tides, in what was billed as the mini-Subway Series, went on to beat the Yankees' top minor league team, the Columbus Clippers - managed by Mainer Stump Merrill - three games to one.). Future major leaguers that fans had a chance to see at Old Orchard in the Guides' second year included Mike Greenwell, Kevin Romine, and Todd Benzinger (all Pawtucket), Kelly Gruber (Syracuse), Henry Cotto, Dennis Rasmussen, and Dan Pasqua (all Columbus), Rick Aguilera, Lenny Dykstra, and Kevin Mitchell (all Tidewater), and the Guides' own Jerry Reed.

The Beginning of the End

In 1986, unfortunately, financial woes began to overshadow the team's performance on the field. Actually, the two went hand in hand. With firstbaseman Jim Wilson, who'd led the International League in both homers and RBIs in 1985, back, and Cory Synder, up from Double A Waterbury where he'd led the Eastern League in homers and RBIs in 1985, playing third, the Guides were expected to be a powerhouse. They weren't. Frustrated by rainouts galore, the team slowly sank toward the bottom of the standings in mid-May. Only the Toledo Mud Hens saved them from the basement. Comments the likes of "Last night's attendance was only 429" (*Evening Express*, May 22nd) and "The announced attendance last night was 249" (*Evening Express*, June 13th) began to appear all too frequently. After dropping 18 out of 25 during an especially dismal stretch in late May and well into June, the Guides fell below the Mud Hens into the bottom slot in the standings.

To offset declining attendance, Jordan Kobritz began scheduling concerts for weekends the Guides were on the road. One of these, by Canadian rock group Loverboy on August 6th, earned him a court summons for violation of Old Orchard Beach's noise ordinance. Less than three weeks later, on August 26th, Kobritz announced an agreement with Northeast Baseball, Inc., of Scranton, Pennsylvania, where Scranton would get the Triple A Guides and Kobritz and his partners would get $2 million and ownership of the Double A Waterbury franchise. The Guides, meanwhile, finished last in the league in both the standings (with a 58-82 mark, 4½ games behind seventh-place Toledo and 22 games behind front-running Richmond) and in attendance (with just over 100,000 admissions, down over 25% from 1985).

From here on it gets complicated. On the first of October, Kobritz failed to make a mortgage payment to FAME (the Finance Authority of Maine, which had loaned Kobritz $2.2 million to pay for the construction of The Ballpark). On October 21st Kobritz announced that the sale to Northeast Baseball was terminated. The people in Scranton disagreed. (The case would eventually go to court twice: the first time the decision would be in Kobritz's favor; the second, in Northeast Baseball's favor.).

Meanwhile, back to baseball. While the fans at The Ballpark were decidedly fewer in 1986, those that did turn out were rewarded with the opportunity to see a number of future major league standouts: Cecil Fielder hit 18 homers for Syracuse; Mike Greenwell also had 18 homers while batting .300 for Pawtucket; Jody Reed batted .282 for the Pawsox; Fred McGriff had 19 circuit clouts and 74 RBIs for Syracuse; while Doug Jones, Dave Gallagher, and Cory Snyder (called up to the Indians after hitting .302 with 9 homers in 49 games for the Guides) all did their thing for the home team.

The home opener for the 1987 Guides came against the Columbus Clippers on April 19th after two successive rainout days. Clippers' manager Bucky Dent, in his first-ever trip to Maine, described the weather as "duck soup." (Although I suspect what Bucky meant to say was "pea soup."). The team - now an affiliate of the Philadelphia Phillies - played a doubleheader. They lost both games, then lost one more the next day to give the Clippers a clean sweep. By the end of the month, before the season was really even off the ground, the Guides were mired very near the bottom of the standings. They remained there, in sixth or seventh, until August, when they found themselves in the unfortunate position of possibly falling into last. By the end of the month (and the season), however, the Guides were back solidly entrenched in seventh place. Their final record was 60-80, good enough to put them 3½ games ahead of Richmond . . . but 21 games behind the champion Tidewater Tides. The worst was yet to come, though. On October 13th the U.S. 1st Circuit Court of Appeals ruled that Northeast Baseball, Inc. could buy the Guides for $2 million. That, effectively, sealed the doom for Triple A baseball in Maine. The team's fans, however, did get a reprieve: with their new stadium not scheduled to be completed until 1989, Northeast Baseball announced, on December 18th, that the team - rechristened the Maine Phillies - would play one more season at Old Orchard Beach.

The Ballpark

The Ballpark was intimate. Translation = small. It seated 5,300, the lowest number in the International League. It was not beautiful. But it had real grass, advertising signs in the outfield, an excellent view from any seat in the house. And it had charm.

August 17, 1988

August 27, 1988

A good game . . . and a beach towel, too. Who could ask for anything more?

The "crowd" lining up to get in.

August 27, 1988

Phillies' secondbaseman Tommy Barrett on deck with shortstop Greg Legg (love that name!) at bat.

August 27, 1988

My favorite Maine Phillie - Tommy Barrett: brother of Marty, good player, great guy - smiles for the camera.

People

What really made The Ballpark such a special place, of course, was the people who filled it: the players, the fans, the employees.

August 27, 1988

Syracuse Chiefs' David Walsh enjoying conversation between games of a doubleheader.

August 17, 1988

Phillies' catcher-firstbaseman Al Pardo signs autographs.

Soda vendor Matt Sherm. When I asked Matt if I could take his picture he asked me what he should do. I said all he had to do was look reasonably intelligent. He laughed and said, "That's gonna be tough."

August 30, 1988

Left to right, fans Angela Crozier, Standish, Wendy Donovan, Gorham, Heidi Donovan, Gorham, and Jack Donovan, Portland. Jack: "It's kinda sad. I've enjoyed bringing my daughters to see Triple A baseball. It's part of what makes Portland such a nice place to live."

September 1, 1988

Standing for our National Anthem on The Ballpark's next-to-last day as a ballpark.

August 31, 1988

Before the start of the lame-duck club's last season in Maine the International League and the American Association got together to form what they termed the Triple A Alliance. With the American Association strong in the Midwest and as far west as Denver and Oklahoma City, it brought some teams from distant places to The Ballpark. Both leagues - although there was cross league play - were divided into an eastern and a western division. The Maine Phillies shared the IL east with the Tidewater Tides, Pawtucket Red Sox, and Richmond Braves.

Over 1,600 fans greeted the start of the last year at Old Orchard on a sunny afternoon on April 10th. They saw the Phillies lose a 10-inning heartbreaker to the Braves, 7-5. It was prophetic. The Braves and the Phillies were to wage battle almost all season. But, alas, the battle was to see which team would finish last. The Phillies actually had a good team - with future big leaguers Ricky Jordan, Ron Jones, Marvin Freeman, Kevin Ward, and Todd Frohwirth, plus sparkplug secondbaseman Tommy (brother of Marty) Barrett all contributing - but they never seemed to get untracked. Fan support was not great (understandable given the team's lame-duck status) but there were some healthy crowds at times. The biggest turnout of the year came on August 18th when 4,321 showed up for Helmet Night. It was telling, however, in that it was Red Sox Helmet Night. (Joked Phillies' manager George Culver: "When we go into Pawtucket, I think they should offer Maine Phillies' batting helmets. It would draw quite a crowd."). There's no doubt that the franchise would have done a whole heck of a lot better if it had been associated with the Sox rather than the Indians/Phillies. The last games were played on September 1st. The Rochester Red Wings took the first game of a twin bill, 4-3, but the Phillies won the last game of professional baseball likely to be played at Old Orchard, 3-2. That left the Phillies with a 62-80 mark, and last place. Bye-bye Maine . . . hello Scranton/Wilkes-Barre.

While bidding adieu to the Phillies and The Ballpark (since renamed SEAPAC - the Seashore Performing Arts Center) in 1988, fans were treated to visiting future major leaguers the likes of David Justice (Richmond), Steve Finley, Mickey Tettleton, and Craig Worthington (Rochester), Rob Dibble and Luis Quinones (Nashville), Gregg Jeffries (Tidewater), Alvaro Espinoza, Bob Geren, Roberto Kelly, and Randy Velarde (Columbus), and Brady Anderson, Sam Horn, Carlos Quintana, and Kevin Romine (Pawtucket).

Will minor league baseball ever return to Maine? I very much hope so. But I wouldn't rush out and buy a season's ticket.

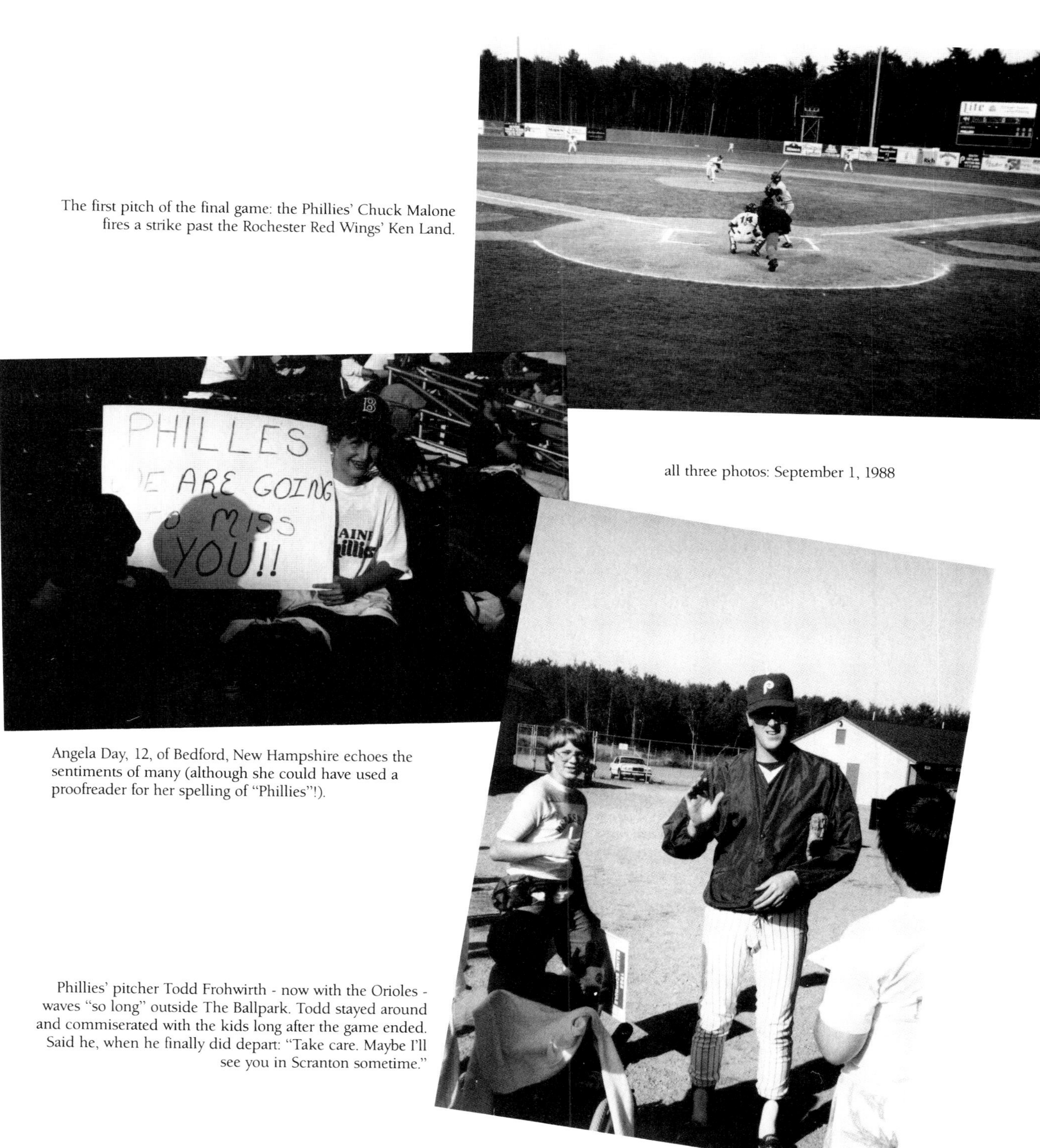

The first pitch of the final game: the Phillies' Chuck Malone fires a strike past the Rochester Red Wings' Ken Land.

all three photos: September 1, 1988

Angela Day, 12, of Bedford, New Hampshire echoes the sentiments of many (although she could have used a proofreader for her spelling of "Phillies"!).

Phillies' pitcher Todd Frohwirth - now with the Orioles - waves "so long" outside The Ballpark. Todd stayed around and commiserated with the kids long after the game ended. Said he, when he finally did depart: "Take care. Maybe I'll see you in Scranton sometime."

Into the 1990s

The first two years of the 1990s have had a definite Maine presence. We've contributed a native-born pitcher, a native-born catcher, and a native-born manager to "The Grand Old Game." And, if we cheat a little, we can also add a shortstop to our list of Mainers in the majors at the start of this century's last decade.

Our pitcher, South Portland native Billy Swift, has notched two wonderful seasons with respect to his ERA . . . 2.39 in 1990 and 1.99 in 1991. In addition, his career-high 17 saves were a major factor in the Seattle Mariners' first-ever season, 1991, with a record of more wins than losses.

Presque Isle-born Ron Tingley, in and out of the majors since his debut with the San Diego Padres in 1982, appears to have found a home with the California Angels. Ron, who also played for the Maine Guides when he was with the Cleveland Indians' organization, was brought up to the Angels in July of 1990, and was with them the whole of 1991, appearing in a career-high 45 games behind the plate.

Carl "Stump" Merrill became the fifth Mainer in the game's history to become a major league manager when he ascended to the helm of the New York Yankees in June of 1990. Born and raised in Brunswick, a key member of the University of Maine's stellar Black Bear team of 1964, and a longtime (and still) resident of Topsham, Stump spent over 20 seasons as a pro player, coach, and minor league manager before getting his major league managerial shot with the Bronx Bombers in 1990-1991. Unfortunately, frustration with the team's second-half performance in 1991 led to a "Dump Stump" movement. Despite a two-notch upward climb - the Yankees finished fifth in 1991 vs. seventh in 1990 - Stump was fired the day after the season ended. Will he get another opportunity to head up a team in the bigs? Let us hope so.

If we cheat - and let's, in this one instance only! - we can add Mike Bordick to our 1990s' list. Although not born in Maine - Mike was born in Marquette, Michigan - he's lived in Maine since his grade school days. A graduate of Winterport's Hampden Academy and an alumnus of the University of Maine's powerhouse nine, Mike was called up to the Oakland Athletics in late 1990, appeared in two games in the 1990 World Series, and became the A's regular shortstop in 1991 when veteran Walt Weiss became a fixture on the disabled list. He responded with a .238 batting average and, more importantly, a steady glove in 90 games for the defending American League champs.

Who knows what the rest of the decade will witness . . . but bring it on. We're ready for it!

After sporting a 2.39 ERA in 55 games for the Mariners in 1990, Billy Swift, photographed here at Fenway Park in September of 1991, topped both in 1991: he appeared in 71 games, all in relief, and posted a dandy 1.99 ERA.

Presque Isle native Ron Tingley enjoyed his most active major league season to date in 1991. Appearing in 45 games for the Angels, the good-with-the-glove catcher knocked out 23 hits in 115 at bats for an even .200 mark.

Brunswick/Topsham's Stump Merrill as he appeared batting one out while serving as a coach with the Yankees in 1985, and as he signed autographs at a baseball card show at the Augusta Civic Center in late January, 1991.

THE MAINE DREAM TEAM

Here it is! The Maine Dream Team!! The best firstbaseman, the best secondbaseman, etc. to have ever come out of the Pine Tree State.

To be eligible for The Dream Team - and for the "They Also Played" section that follows - a player has to have been born in the State of Maine. He has to, in other words, be a true native. As a result, a number of fine players who are closely associated with Maine - but who were actually born "away" - are not included. These include Jim Beattie (born in Hampton, Virginia), Mike Bordick (born in Marquette, Michigan), Tommy Catterson (born in Warwick, Rhode Island), Jack Coombs (born in LeGrand, Iowa), Pat French (born in Dover, New Hampshire), Ben Houser (born in Shenandoah, Pennsylvania), and Eddie Phillips (born in Ardmore, Oklahoma), among others. Sorry, guys.

Each player must also have played in the major leagues. And it is their major league record by which they have been judged. As important as minor league ball is, it's what a player has done in the majors that really matters.

While few, indeed, would credit Maine with producing an overabundance of ballplayers, we have produced some darned good ones. The Dream Team reflects that. It's a heck of a team!

Note: all statistics and the vast majority of information included both in this section and They Also Played are from that indispensable reference guide, THE BASEBALL ENCYCLOPEDIA. As authoritative as the ENCYCLOPEDIA is, however, it is not without its gaps. If, accordingly, there is a blank for a certain piece of information it is not a typographical error: it is because that information is simply not known. The number of times a hitter struck out was, for example, often not recorded until 1910 or so. Similarly, if no information is given for height or weight or righthanded/lefthanded, it is because that information, too, is not known.

Firstbaseman — Adelphia Louis "Del" Bissonette

The man who would have been the Babe Ruth of Maine: that's the label generally bestowed upon Del Bissonette. It's flattering. Yet it's sad, too. Therein lies the tale of the ballplayer from Winthrop.

Del loved baseball almost from the time he was able to walk. Large for his age, he was on an athletic par with much older kids in Winthrop from grammar school on. At Winthrop High he did some pitching, played some first base, even caught some (the fact that he was left-handed didn't deter him in the least) . . . and excelled at it all. A Yankee scout wanted to sign him as a pitcher while Del was still in high school, but Del turned the offer down, deciding he wanted to finish his education first.

After two years at Winthrop High, Del went on to do a little prepping at Kents Hill and then at Westbrook Seminary (now Westbrook College) in Portland. While at Westbrook, in 1919, he hit a resounding .600 - going 24 for 40 - to set a state record that still stands. In spite of his hitting prowess, however, Del's goal was still to be a pitcher. He attended New Hampshire State College (now the University of New Hampshire) for one year, during which time he was given a tryout by the Cleveland Indians. Steve O'Neil, the venerable Indians' catcher, had warmed up Del and seen what he had. O'Neil reputedly stated that he'd never witnessed a player who could throw as hard as Del. The Tribe, however, was in the midst of a pennant race and manager Tris Speaker really didn't give the Mainer a worthwhile look-see.

After New Hampshire, Del went on to Georgetown University in Washington, D.C. While there, playing in a basketball scrimmage, he was accidentally rammed into a cement wall, badly banging his left shoulder. As he later was to say of the injury that cost him his pitching career: "I had to carry it (his throwing arm) in a sling or in my pocket for a year and a half."

Following his shoulder injury, Del took up the outfield and then first base. He played semi-pro around Maine and eastern Canada. In 1924 and 1925 he firstbased for both Binghamton and York in the Eastern League. His performance at York in 1925 - he finished second in the league in batting with a .381 mark - earned him a shot with the Brooklyn Robins (later the Dodgers) in 1926. The first day of spring training he lined eleven consecutive balls over the rightfield fence. "Bissonette's Punch Makes Robins Chirp" headlined an article in the March 2nd *Portland Evening Express*, referring to Del as the "Winthrop Walloper." Although he was a sensation for much of the spring, a bad bout of the flu finally did him in. Del ended up back in the minors for 1926, first with Jersey City and then with Rochester. While with the Red Wings, Del adopted a new batting stance, and then brought it with him to Buffalo in 1927. In that year - while Babe Ruth was tearing up the American League - Del tore up the International League. He led the loop in hits (229), doubles (46), triples (20), home runs (31), runs (168), and runs batted in (167), all while walloping a .365 batting average. Buffalo won the IL pennant, the mayor presented Del with a gold key to the city, and, of far greater importance, with numbers such as he'd posted, there was no holding Del back any longer.

Del Bissonette in a circa 1930 photograph

DEL BISSONETTE

Born September 6, 1899, Winthrop, Maine   Died June 9, 1972, Augusta, Maine

Batted and threw left-handed   5′11″; 180 lbs.

MAJOR LEAGUE RECORD

Year	Team	G	AB	H	2B	3B	HR	HR %	R	RBI	BB	SO	SB	BA	SA	Pinch Hit AB	Pinch Hit H	G by POS
1928	BKN N	155	587	188	30	13	25	4.3	90	106	70	75	5	.320	.543	0	0	1B-155
1929		116	431	121	28	10	12	2.8	68	75	46	58	2	.281	.476	3	0	1B-113
1930		146	572	192	33	13	16	2.8	102	113	56	66	4	.336	.523	0	0	1B-146
1931		152	587	170	19	14	12	2.0	90	87	59	53	4	.290	.431	0	0	1B-152
1933		35	114	28	7	0	0	0.0	9	10	2	17	2	.246	.307	3	1	1B-32
5 years		604	2291	699	117	50	65	2.8	359	391	233	269	17	.305	.485	6	1	1B-598

Bye-Bye, Buffalo - Hello, Brooklyn

Del played four complete seasons (plus a part of a fifth) for Brooklyn. All four were good. Two were outstanding. In his rookie year, 1928, Del weighed in with a rather remarkable 25 home runs (fourth in the league, well ahead of fifth-place finisher Rogers Hornsby's 21), 106 RBIs (sixth best in the league), 13 triples (sixth best), 319 total bases (fourth best), and a .320 batting average. The 25 homers by a rookie is still a Dodger club mark. In their 102 years of existence, no one - not Babe Herman, not Duke Snider, not Roy Campanella, not Jackie Robinson, not Gil Hodges, not Frank Howard, not Steve Garvey - has surpassed it. Del is also but one of four National Leaguers to ever top the 100 RBIs' mark in his freshman season. An especial highlight that season was the Robins' victory over Carl Hubbell, also a rookie, the first time they ever faced the man who would become the ace of the arch-rival Giants' staff. It happened on August 26th. The score was 4-3 . . . and the Robins won it on a tremendous ("It cleared everything in sight": *The New York Times*) tenth inning solo shot over the Ebbets Field rightfield wall by Del.

In 1929 Del's output slipped. It's understandable. He was hit in the head (later requiring a mastoid operation) by a pitch from Lester Sweetland of the Phillies the first week of the season. He was also hampered by sinus problems for much of the season. Still he produced a .281 average, banging out an even dozen homers and knocking in 75 runs.

In the year the hitters went wild, 1930, Del did, too. He reeled off a .336 batting average, socked 16 circuit clouts, scored 102 runs, and drove in 113.

His last complete season, 1931, gave no hint that Del's playing days were winding down. In 597 at bats he banged out 172 hits for a .290 average, scoring 90 times

"No Meal Has He Ever Missed Yet"

"The Dodgers have Del Bissonette
No meal has he ever missed yet.
The question that rises
Is one that surprises:
Who paid for all Del Bissonette?"
circa 1930 verse by L.H. Addington

In an interview I had with Del's second wife, Laura, in Winthrop in June of 1991, she confirmed that Del was a hearty eater. "It was fun to cook for him," she reminisced. His favorite dish was what he called a Monday . . . vanilla ice cream swimming in chocolate syrup. "He'd have one every night at 7:00 just like clockwork," she reminisced once more.

Del reaching for a throw, circa 1930. Glenn Wright, Brooklyn shortstop from 1930 to 1933, said of our firstsacker: "I never saw anyone who can reach for them like Del. He grabs many a ball for a putout that would ordinarily be put down as an error for a shortstop or a secondbaseman."

and knocking in 87. At age 32 the next season, 1932, Del should have been at his peak. He most likely would have been, too, had it not been for a crippling - indeed, almost fatal - accident that occurred during spring training in Clearwater, Florida. He was playing a game of volleyball when teammate Dazzy Vance - all 200 pounds of him - landed on Del's left ankle. At first Del thought nothing of it. Three weeks of pain later, however, he learned that he'd severed his Achilles tendon. He was operated on and expected to be out of action for two months. A week after the operation, however, he developed blood poisoning. He hovered on the brink of death for days; did not gain strength back for months. It was 1933 before Del recovered sufficiently to try to resume his career. Brooklyn management was doubtful he'd ever be the same. In spite of Del's assurance that he was ready and raring to go, they obtained veteran Joe Judge from the Senators. When Judge got hurt early in the season Del worked his way back into the lineup . . . but not to stay. With a disappointing .246 average, no home runs and 10 RBIs after 35 games, the Dodgers packed him off to Baltimore - then in the International League - in exchange for outfielder Ralph Boyle and $12,500 cash.

Bye-Bye, Brooklyn - Hello, Baltimore

It would be wonderful to report that Del bounced back after being shipped to Baltimore. But he didn't. From Baltimore he went to Albany. Then it was on to the Montreal Royals, in the International League. At age 37, Del hung up his playing shoes, trading them in for a managerial role. He managed Des Moines in the Western League in 1937, and then the Glace Bay team in the Cape Breton (Nova Scotia) Colliery Baseball League in 1938. In 1939 Del led Quebec to the championship of the Provincial League. In 1941 he joined the Boston Braves' organization, debuting with their Bradford, Pennsylvania entry in the Pony (Pennsylvania-Ontario-New York) League. From 1942 through 1944, Del was at the helm of Hartford in the Eastern League, leading his club to a pennant in 1944. For 1945, the Braves brought him up to Boston as their third base coach. The war was still on and the Braves, a perpetually weak club, were even weaker than usual. It was more than Braves' skipper Bob Coleman - who'd succeeded Casey Stengel after the 1943 season - could take. On July 30th, with the team mired in seventh place with a 42-49 mark, he tossed in the towel. The Braves' management picked Del to take over. The new manager's goals - as expressed in an interview shortly after taking over the reins - were to get the team hustling, have it take more chances on the basepaths, and, as much as anything, get the players to have some fun. Sounded good. Actually, though, there really wasn't much that Del could accomplish with a squad that was fundamentally lacking. Under his tenure the Braves won 25, lost 36, and ended up in sixth place. On November 7th it was announced that Del would not be rehired; that the Braves' field boss for 1946 would be Billy Southworth, an old Boston favorite who'd starred for the Braves in the early 1920s. Disappointed, Del signed on with the Pirates as a coach for 1946. For 1947 and 1948, he returned to Maine as manager of the Portland Pilots (also often referred to, during Del's time at the helm, as the "Bissonettemen") of the New England League. Then it was up to Canada, where he skippered the Phillies' top farm team, the Toronto Maple Leafs, in 1949, and Trois Rivieres in the Canadian Provincial League in 1951. After Trois Rivieres, Del returned to Winthrop, unpacking his suitcase for good. He took up poultry farming, and it appears that the only association he had with the game from there on in was when he came out of

Continued on page 88

ad for Dazzy Vance Glove, July, 1929

"STOP MAKING ERRORS"

says Dazzy Vance

"Use my patented Glove with the ball-gripping Interlaced Fingers"

"FORGET about those errors you've made so far this season," fast-pitching, star-fielding Dazzy Vance says to you. "No matter what glove you are muffing them with now, from today on make up your mind to put a stop to unnecessary errors." (Remember, last year Dazzy played 38 games without a fielding error. He made this outstanding record with the glove he designed himself and if you ask him how he did it, here's the big dope he gives you):

"The Interlaced Fingers in my Dazzy Vance Glove hold the hot ones. These interlacings running from finger to finger keep the ball from slipping through. When a ball hits the glove, the interlaced fingers snap onto the pill and hold it like a vise. This remarkable feature means one thing: Stop making errors. And I say to all infielders and outfielders who want to be star players, 'Use my Dazzy Vance glove and catch 'em all, high, wide and handsome.'"

When you buy a Dazzy Vance glove at $8.50 you get materially more than what the price suggests. You also play a better brand of ball that may put your name in the baseball hall of fame. Don't chance errors for the mere difference of a few cents in price. You can play a Vance glove fresh from the box. Every one is oil-treated and "broke in" in big league style before it leaves the factory. See this famous Vance glove at your sporting goods store. Try it on. Try it out. And you will be sold for keeps. A Junior Vance model for boys can be had for $5.00.

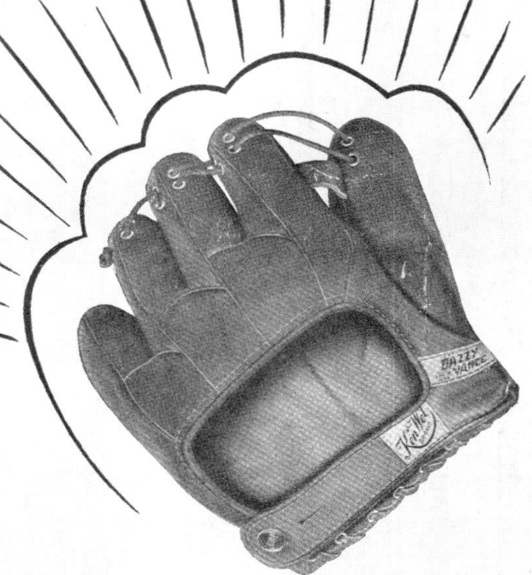

Amaze the Crowd with Spectacular Catches

Learn all about Dazzy Vance and his secrets of sensational fielding. Get wise to the inside tricks. Get the dope on this great Dazzy Vance Glove. Dazzle the crowd with some of the same swift plays that make Dazzy's fans go wild. There are some hot tips for you and they're free.

FREE! Send the coupon now and Dazzy Vance will write you a letter and send you the complete Ken-Wel Baseball Book-and-Catalog. See actual detail photographs of the gloves and equipment the great stars use. Mail the coupon now! If you play on a team, kindly write the name of your team below. Ken-Wel Sporting Goods Co., Inc., Dept. B-7, Utica, N. Y.

MAIL COUPON

DAZZY VANCE, care of
KEN-WEL SPORTING GOODS Co., Dept. B-7,
Utica, N. Y.

Please send me your Ken-Wel Baseball Book and data, fully illustrated and with pictures of big ball stars.

Name ....
(PRINT NAME)
Address ....
City .... *State* ....
Age ...... *Name of Team* ....

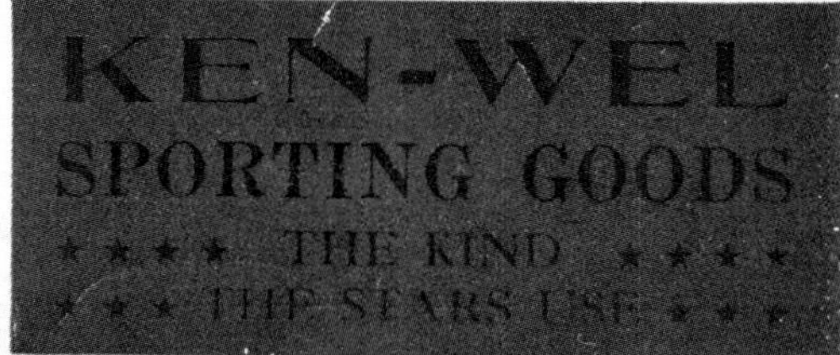

Lefty and Babe and Dazzy, Too

In his four-plus seasons with Brooklyn, Del played with some of the game's best. Among his teammates were Max Carey, Al Lopez, Lefty O'Doul, Babe Herman, Ernie Lombardi, and Dazzy Vance. Vance, whose real first name was Clarence, was a fireballer of the first order. Big - he stood 6′ and weighed in at a good 200 pounds - he topped the National League in strikeouts for an amazing seven years in a row, 1922-1928.

A youthful Del as he appeared in his Portland Taxi League uniform, circa 1923.

This marvelous photo of the York White Roses of the Eastern League was taken in 1925. What I especially like about it is that there are eighteen guys in York uniforms . . . and one in a Portland uniform. That one, of course, is Del, who presumably had just joined the team.

A Special Tribute

After WAS BASEBALL REALLY INVENTED IN MAINE? was pretty much all designed and laid out, I received a call from Laura Bissonette, Del's second wife, saying she'd found a suitcase full of old photos plus Del's personal scrapbook. Was I interested in looking at them? You bet I was!

The photos and cartoon art on these four pages are the result . . . and serve as a *special* tribute to Del Bissonette. And, of course, to Laura as well.

Here's the tall and the small of it: Del, all 5′11″ of him, towering over 5′5″ Rabbit Maranville, circa 1930.

When he arrived in Montreal to play for the Royals in 1936, Del was well received. A local men's store even came up with "The Sporty New Del Bissonette Ensemble" . . . a set of clothes named in the slugger's honor!

Cartoon Art

Cartoon art, which goes back well into the 1800s, reached perhaps its sports' pinnacle in the 1930s and 1940s. Here are some fine examples from that golden period . . . all featuring Del, of course.

. . . when Del was one of the "Flatbush Fusiliers," 1930

. . . when Del was being courted as manager of the Montreal Royals, 1940

. . . when Del became the Boston Braves' new skipper, July 1945

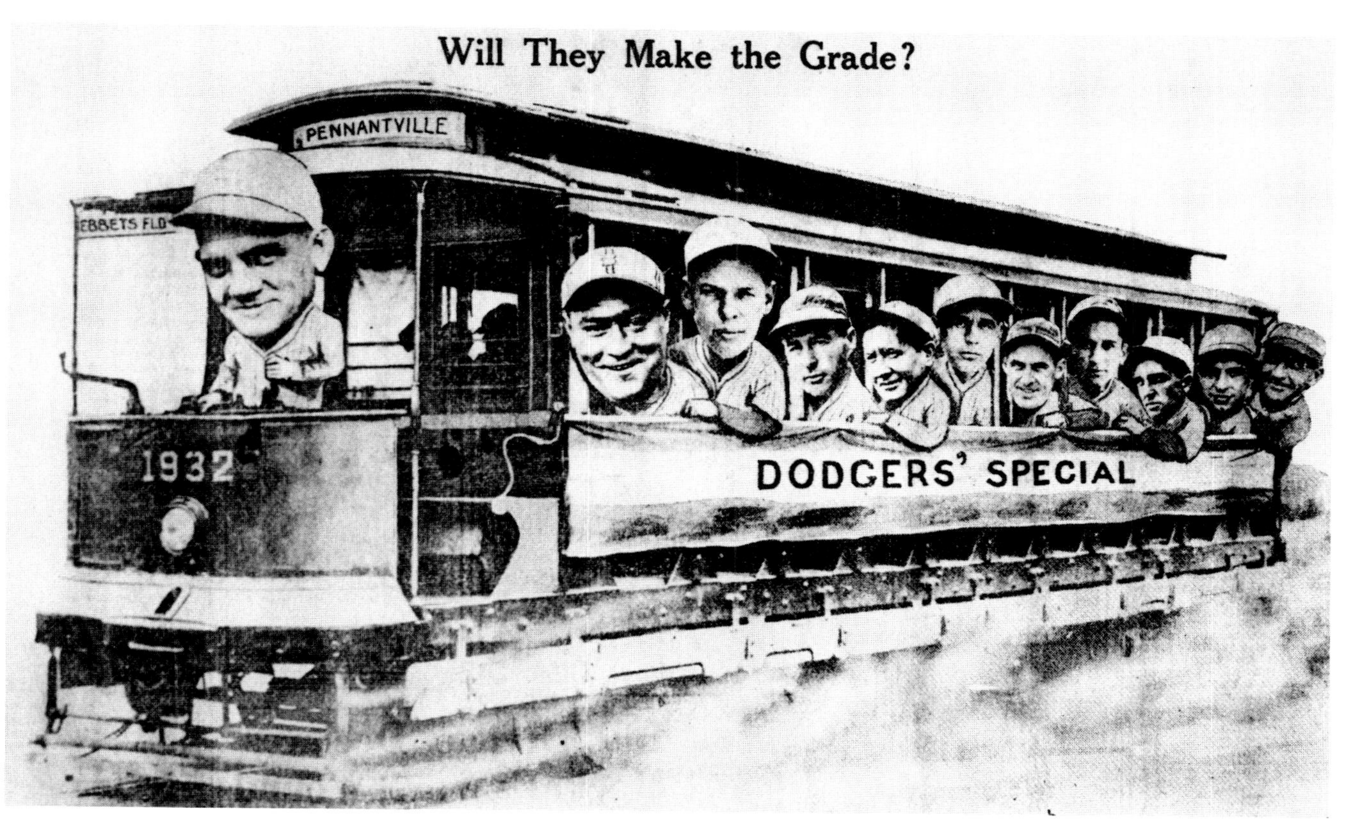

. . . when Del was aboard the "Dodgers' Special," February, 1932. With him - bound for Pennantville? - are, left to right, manager Max Carey, Hack Wilson, Babe Herman, Lefty O'Doul, Dazzy Vance, Del, Mickey Finn, Al Lopez, Wally Gilbert, Glenn Wright, and Casey Stengel.

P.S. The Cubs won the flag in 1932. The Dodgers, in spite of all the legendary names, wound up in third-placeville.

circa 1940 postcard view

It Was Small

Ebbets Field: the home of the Brooklyn National League club from 1913 through 1957, and where Del starred from 1928 through 1931, was a bit of a bandbox. It was, in fact, so intimate that Red Barber could write in 1954: "When you have a box seat at Brooklyn, you are practically playing the infield."

"retirement" to coach a Winthrop Little League team in the late 1950s. He quit even that, however, when his team won all the games. As Laura put it: "The other coaches got a little upset."

On June 3, 1972, Del Bissonette was found in a Winthrop apple orchard with a gunshot wound in his abdomen. Police concluded that it was self-inflicted. He died a week later in an Augusta hospital. Brooklyn teammate Lefty O'Doul once called Del "the gamest guy I've ever met. Most other people would have quit with all his problems." During his baseball career, Del had undergone arm surgery, a mastoid operation, a dozen sinus operations, and, finally, the severed Achilles tendon that hastened the end of his playing days and almost killed him, too. It appears that, at age 72, troubled by worsening emphysema and bouts of depression, "The Winthrop Walloper" finally did quit. Yet, even though Del Bissonette was often referred to as "the unluckiest man who ever played baseball," Del didn't see himself that way. He once remarked, "In the overall picture, I've been pretty lucky just to play in the majors."

"He Wanted to Stay Home in Winthrop"

Here's Del in his 1945 Boston Braves' manager's garb. In 1954 he was offered the job of once more managing the Braves, this time in Milwaukee. He turned it down. As Laura recalls: "He had retired and he wasn't going back for anything. He wanted to stay home in Winthrop."

Secondbaseman — George Henry "Topsy" Magoon

Our Dream Team secondbaseman was first and foremost a shortstop . . . but he also played more games at second than any other Mainer ever has. Plus we need him at second . . . so that's where you'll find George "Topsy" Magoon in our defensive alignment.

Topsy - presumably so-called because of his spinning top-like movements around the infield - was born in St. Albans, Maine on March 27, 1875. His family moved to South Lebanon, Maine while George was an infant, and it was there that he did his growing up.

As with so many of our Dream Teamers, a key ingredient in that growing up was baseball. From grammar school on, young George was a whiz on the diamond. His only problem appeared to be which position to play. He loved to gobble up ground balls as an infielder; but he loved to pitch, too. It was as a pitcher, as a matter of fact, that he began his career, twirling for a Milford, Massachusetts semi-pro outfit in 1891 at the tender age of sixteen.

Topsy's fielding abilities, however, were to be his ticket to the big leagues. He honed those skills in the ballfields around South Lebanon and neighboring East Rochester, New Hampshire in 1892 and 1893. In 1894 he set out for the more challenging pastures of Camden, Maine, where he held down second base for a strong semi-pro nine. Somewhere along the line he was spotted by Doc Keay, a former top-flight centerfielder for Portland in the New England League. Doc arranged a tryout with the Portlands. Result: Topsy was signed to play in the Forest City in 1895.

For Portland, Topsy played third. And he played it exceedingly well. "Brilliant" is how *The Sunday Telegram* characterized his fielding. Topsy's hitting was timely, too. "A batsman of far more than average ability," was how the paper put it. He hit in the middle part of the order all season; occasionally even batted cleanup. On one such occasion, on May 18th, he responded by, as *The Sunday Telegram* so wonderfully phrased it, "lifting the spheroid over the left field fence." Translation: he socked a homer over the leftfield wall. In that same game, incidentally, *The Telegram* couldn't resist chiding Bangor, losers of the game by a rather lopsided score of 15-3. "The Bangor league team has at last reached bottom, and the bubbles where the team went down have about quit coming up. Poor Bangor!" crowed one of *The Telegram's* scribes, adding that the "Penobscot farmers" were the poorest excuse for a team that the Portlands had seen in quite a spell. (Ed. note: the "Penobscot farmers" ended up third in the league at season's end. The Portlands? Well, they finished a little further on down the road . . . seventh in an eight-team loop.).

The year of 1896 saw Topsy again playing a mean third base for the Portlands. He also played some second base in July. By mid-August, though, he wasn't playing anywhere for Portland. He was playing for Brockton.

But let's back up. On August 9th, *The Sunday Telegram* was especially generous in praise of Topsy. Commenting on a 3-1 loss to Bangor, the paper noted that: "The feature of the game was the magnificent playing of Magoon at third. He made three stops and one running catch that were little short of marvelous." The paper further reflected that Walter Woods (a Portland pitcher who would later spend three seasons in the majors) and Topsy "should be in a faster club than the Portlands." In those days, "faster" meant "better." Lo and behold, within a week Topsy did sever his connection with the Portlands - who were on the verge of dropping out of the league, anyway - and sign up with Brockton, one of the powerhouses of the New England League. For the Massachusetts team he resumed his clever fielding and more-than-satisfactory batting. For the season he ended with 106 hits in 396 at bats, an average of .268. In the field he led all NEL thirdbasemen with a .922 fielding percentage.

After another year at Brockton, in 1897, Topsy was ready for the majors. But it didn't appear as if the majors were ready for Topsy. Our future Dream Teamer saw the season of 1898 open with him still holding down the hot corner for Brockton. Down in Brooklyn, however, the Bridegrooms (the nickname - honest - of the Brooklyn National League club from 1890 through 1898) were in a pickle. Manager Charlie Ebbets had tried a handful of players at that most pivotal of positions, shortstop. None of them had done the job. The Bridegrooms, as *The New York Times* put it rather ungently, were "lamentably weak at short stop." Charlie - the man for whom Ebbets Field would later be named - decided Topsy was the man for the job. He was right. Topsy came aboard the last week in June; played his first game on June 29th. *The Times* was not long in acknowledging his presence. Said the paper's baseball writer on July 10th: "The addition of Magoon at short stop has greatly strengthened the team."

In that first year in the bigs, Topsy played in 93 games. He batted a disappointing .224 . . . but was rock solid in the field. He undoubtedly would have continued to call Brooklyn home were it not for a heavy dose of what could only be termed intra-club collusion. Before the start of the 1899 season, Ebbets and Harry B. Von der Horst, owner of the original Baltimore Orioles (then in the National League), worked out an arrangement whereby Baltimore shipped most of its best players to Brooklyn. Von der Horst, while still in charge of the Orioles, was allowed to purchase a controlling interest in the Brooklyns. Virtually half the Orioles - excluding John McGraw and Wilbert Robinson, both of whom refused to be part of the charade - suddenly found themselves wearing Brooklyn uniforms. Conversely, of course, a like number of Ebbets' charges suddenly found themselves in the Star Spangled City. Topsy, who went to Baltimore, was - in effect - swapped for veteran Bill Dahlen, who made the move north.

While such shenanigans would never be countenanced today, Von der Horst's and Ebbets' moves had their desired effect in 1899. Brooklyn, on the strength of a 20-game winning streak, moved into first place on May 22nd and never lost the top rung thereafter.

In Baltimore, meanwhile, the switcheroo worked out well for John McGraw. He was given his first taste of managing . . . and liked it. Even with a weakened club he turned in a fine 86-62 record, good enough for a strong fourth place finish (in what was a twelve-club circuit, it should be noted). Topsy was there, playing right beside Muggsie - who held down third as well as managing - for the first half of the season. During that first half Baltimore led all twelve clubs in turning double plays . . . undoubtedly one of the major factors in the Orioles' positive performance. In the heat of the Baltimore summer Topsy was released to Chicago. All told, for both clubs combined, he batted .242, up eighteen points from his 1898 mark.

The year 1900 found Topsy with Indianapolis of the brand new American League.

George "Topsy" Magoon in a 1903 *Sporting Life* magazine photo

GEORGE "TOPSY" MAGOON

Born March 27, 1875, St. Albans, Maine   Died December 6, 1943, Rochester, New Hampshire

Batted and threw right-handed   5′9″; 165 lbs.

MAJOR LEAGUE RECORD

Year	Team	G	AB	H	2B	3B	HR	HR %	R	RBI	BB	SO	SB	BA	SA	Pinch Hit AB	Pinch Hit H	G by POS
1898	BKN N	93	343	77	7	0	1	0.3	35	39	30		7	.224	.254	0	0	SS-93
1899	2 teams	**BAL N** (62G — .256)			**CHI N** (59G — .228)													
1899	total	121	396	96	13	4	0	0.0	50	52	50		12	.242	.295	0	0	SS-121
1901	CIN N	127	460	116	16	7	1	0.2	47	53	52		15	.252	.324	0	0	SS-112, 2B-15
1902		45	162	44	9	2	0	0.0	29	23	13		7	.272	.352	1	0	2B-41, SS-3
1903	2 teams	**CIN N** (42G — .216)			**CHI A** (94G — .228)													
1903	total	136	473	106	17	3	0	0.0	38	34	49		6	.224	.273	1	0	2B-126, 3B-9
5 years		522	1834	439	62	16	2	0.1	199	201	194		47	.239	.294	2	0	SS-329, 2B-182, 3B-9

It was so brand new, in fact, that it was not considered a major league. Under the guidance of Ban Johnson, however, it soon would be. Ban had taken the old Western League and was steadfastly shaping it into a league to rival the National. In 1900 he was close to that goal, close enough for him to unveil the "American League" name. Topsy was part of the excitement of it all. In addition, he turned in a whale of a season for Indianapolis. Portland's *Daily Eastern Argus* was filled with glowing reports of his work, both in the field and at the plate. In one column he was referred to as "electrical." That's powerful stuff!

Topsy Magoon's second tour of the bigs began with the Cincinnati Reds in 1901. His average increased again . . . up to .252. He played 127 games, knocking out 116 hits in 460 at bats, and stole 15 bases. It was his most successful season. "A wonderful one-handed catch by Magoon of Leach's liner, on which he made a double play, was easily the (game's) feature," applauded *The New York Times* on May 12th. It typified the appreciation shown Topsy's work with the glove. But the weak-hitting Reds also appreciated his steady work with the bat, too. He batted fifth for most of the summer, was even the cleanup hitter on at least one occasion (July 14th - on which he responded with 3 hits in a 7-0 win over Brooklyn).

A highlight of a different sort in Topsy's 1901 season took place on May 4th. The Reds were playing the Cardinals in St. Louis. The score was tied, 4-4, in the 10th inning . . . when the grandstand caught fire and burned down. In the earliest days of the century, with grandstands almost universally constructed of wood, such conflagrations were not all that unusual. Still, it must have made quite an impression on Topsy. The players of both teams, incidentally, were credited with saving the day when the fire broke out. They

circa 1899 photo, John McGraw

Two of the Great Ones

In 1899, the year that Topsy shared the infield with John McGraw for the original Baltimore Orioles, Mugsie hit a resounding .391 and pilfered 73 bases! He was, in short, a great ballplayer as well as an outstanding manager.

Two years later, in 1901, Topsy found himself on the Cincinnati Reds and playing with another all-time great, Wahoo Sam Crawford. Best recalled for his prodigious triple output - he's hit more of them than any other player in the game's history! - Sam could belt out home runs, too. In 1901 he led both leagues with 16 roundtrippers.

1911 Turkey Red card, Sam Crawford

remained calm and collected, and the *Cincinnati Times-Star* lauded the manner in which they lined up and assisted the fans out of the stands. "The encouragement of the players had not a little to do to avoid a panic, and to their coolness and advice is largely due the quick and effective emptying of the stands," wrote the reporter who covered the game.

Topsy's average rose once again for 1902. He hit a career-high .272. Unfortunately, though, his hits were spread across but 162 at bats in 45 games, mostly all at second base. On July 15th Topsy rapped out a pair of doubles - off the great Christy Mathewson, no less! - in a 10-2 rout of the Giants by the Reds. The next day, July 16th, he supplied a single in a 7-2 Reds' win. Then he disappears from box scores for the remainder of the season. A thorough reading of the three Portland newspapers of the time, *The Rochester* (N.H.) *Courier,* the Cincinnati papers, and *The New York Times* provides no reason for the disappearance. Our secondsacker was most likely injured, but no mention was made of it. Nor do the Cincinnati Reds, themselves, have a clue as to what happened to Topsy all those summers ago.

Topsy did come back to the Reds for the season of 1903. He got off to a slow start, though, and on June 9th he was traded to the White Sox for outfielder Cozy Dolan and secondbaseman Tom Daly. He failed to ignite with the White Sox either, batting .228 in 94 games, virtually all at second.

That was to be it for Topsy's major league career. But he yet had many seasons of meritorious minor league ball left in him. In 1904 he was with Indianapolis in the American Association. In 1905 it was Toronto in the International League. Then it was off to Des Moines (or "DeMoines," as *The Rochester Courier* spelled it) of the Western League. Next came Trenton, New Jersey in the Tri-State League for two

State Champs
Topsy coached the University of Maine's varsity nine in 1912 and 1913. This photo shows the 1912 squad, winner of the State Championship. Looking appropriately proud is Topsy, second from the left in the back row.

seasons, 1907 and 1908. He last played some - and managed, too - for Savannah in the South Atlantic League in 1910 and 1911.

Topsy's involvement with baseball continued on after his professional playing days ended. He coached the game at the University of Maine in 1912 and 1913. He was coach at the University of New Hampshire in 1915. And he umpired many a game in the semi-pro leagues that abounded in eastern New Hampshire and southwestern Maine in the years prior to World War II.

From 1917 through 1920 Topsy served the City of Rochester as City Marshal, the equivalent of Chief of Police. He later was employed as a special officer at the Rochester Fair and at Rockingham Park Race Track.

On December 6th, 1943, George "Topsy" Magoon died of a heart attack in his sleep at his home in Rochester. He was 68 years old. In his 16-plus seasons in the majors and the minors he most likely scooped up more ground balls than any other native-born Mainer ever has, before or since. It's quite a feat.

Thirdbaseman — Harry Donald Lord

Another couples of miles west and the Maine Dream Team would've lost Harry Lord to New Hampshire. Porter, where our guardian of the hot corner was born in 1882, is that close to the state line.

But Harry was born in Maine and we're glad of it, for Harry Lord was a ballplayer's ballplayer. Growing up in Kezar Falls, he learned an early love of the game, and went on to star in it - and football, as well - at Bridgton Academy. From there it was on to Bates, where he again excelled in both sports. It was at Bates that he first came to consider baseball as a possible career. As Harry explained years later: "As a little chap I played the game, but never with any thought or desire to use baseball as a means of gaining a livelihood. In fact, I had ambitions in other fields. During my high school baseball days I gave the team the best that was in me, yet I never regarded the game with serious thought until I entered Bates College. There I settled down to study baseball. The further I advanced in baseball the more I saw in the line of making plays. The game interested me beyond the mere physical enjoyment derived."

The "other fields" that interested Harry were along legal lines. He had planned to be a lawyer. But he also wanted to get married and start a family . . . and he realized that he would most likely do better financially on the diamond than in the law office. After further sharpening his skills - and switching from second base to third - playing summer ball in and around South Portland in 1904 and 1905, he accepted an offer from Jesse Burkett to join Worcester in the New England League. Burkett, one of the golden players of the 19th century, was a demanding drillmaster. Harry learned well. He batted .280 and helped Worcester win the league flag. He advanced to Providence in 1907, again playing a rock-solid third base and hitting a very respectable .278. Up the road, meanwhile, the Red Sox were re-building. The players who had spear-headed them to championships in 1903 and 1904 were either gone or in the process of going. The club's owner, John I. Taylor, was intent upon finding a re-placement at third for the great Jimmy Collins, whom he had traded to the Athletics during the 1907 season. The man he wanted - and got - was Harry Lord.

Harry played the better part of three seasons with the Sox. With them he developed into one of the game's premier thirdbasemen. He was of the old school: if he couldn't stop the ball with his glove he'd stop it with his chest. He gave way to no man on the basepaths either. That included Ty Cobb. In fact, Cobb so respected the fiercely competitive play of Harry - and vice versa, it should be noted - that they became fast friends off the field. And Harry was no slouch with the bat. In his first full season in the majors, 1908, he contributed a .260 average, 23 steals, and 61 runs scored. *The Boston Post* wrote: "The crowd always looks to Lord or McConnell to start something. They gen-erally succeed, too." In 1909 Harry really came into his own, leading all Sox regu-lars - one of whom was Tris Speaker! - with a .311 mark. His stolen base and runs scored counts also increased measurably, to 36 and 85, respectively. *The Boston Globe*, in September, honored him by writing: "Harry Lord is by all odds the best run getter among the thirdbasemen of the American League." Highlights that season, as the Bosox surged to third place, their

Harry Lord as depicted on a 1909 Sweet Caporal Cigarettes' card

HARRY LORD

Born March 8, 1882, Porter, Maine   Died August 9, 1948, Westbrook, Maine

Batted left-handed; threw right-handed   5′10½″; 165 lbs.

MAJOR LEAGUE RECORD

Year	Team	G	AB	H	2B	3B	HR	HR %	R	RBI	BB	SO	SB	BA	SA	Pinch Hit AB	Pinch Hit H	G by POS
1907	BOS A	10	38	6	1	0	0	0.0	4	3	1		1	.158	.184	0	0	3B-10
1908		145	558	145	15	6	2	0.4	61	37	22		23	.260	.319	1	0	3B-143
1909		136	534	166	12	7	0	0.0	85	31	20		36	.311	.360	1	0	3B-134
1910	2 teams	**BOS A** (77G — .250)			**CHI A** (44G — .297)													
1910	total	121	453	121	11	8	1	0.2	51	42	28		34	.267	.333	3	1	3B-114, SS-1
1911	CHI A	141	561	180	18	18	3	0.5	103	61	32		43	.321	.433	2	0	3B-138
1912		151	570	152	19	12	5	0.9	81	54	52		28	.267	.368	0	0	3B-106, OF-45
1913		150	547	144	18	12	1	0.2	62	42	45	39	24	.263	.346	0	0	3B-150
1914		21	69	13	1	1	1	1.4	8	3	5	3	2	.188	.275	0	0	3B-19, OF-1
1915	BUF F	97	359	97	12	6	1	0.3	50	21	21		15	.270	.345	3	1	3B-92, OF-1
9 years		972	3689	1024	107	70	14	0.4	505	294	226	42	206	.278	.356	10	2	3B-906, OF-47, SS-1

best showing since the championship year of 1904, included a two-hit performance in the Grand Opening of Shibe Park (later Connie Mack Stadium) before 32,000 fans on April 12th; three hits, three stolen bases, and two runs scored in a 6-1 win over the Senators, April 17th; being the lead runner (i.e., the one who steals home!) in that rarity of rarities, a triple steal, in a 6-2 win over the Athletics on April 21st; fielding in "sensational style" (*New York Times*) as the Red Sox take their third game in a row from the Browns, 3-2, on June 9th; going four for four in a 9-6 win over the Yankees, June 22nd; a two hit/two steals/two runs scored game against the Yankees, July 28th; knocking out two hits in both ends of a doubleheader sweep of the Tigers, August 3rd (before a crowd of 29,781 at the Huntington Avenue Grounds, the most people ever to witness a Boston American League contest up to that point); going three for four with two runs scored in a 5-4 win over the Indians, August 12th; again going three for four as the Sox take Washington, 3-1, September 9th; going three for four in a 9-7 win over the soon-to-be-champion Tigers, September 30th; and, to top it all off, being selected team captain in September.

The Buffalo Buffeds

This was Harry's Federal League team as it appeared in August of 1915. Harry is in the front row, far left. Other notables on the team included Hal Chase (back row, far left), who would lead the National League in batting in 1916 and had a .291 lifetime average over fifteen major league seasons; pitcher Hugh Bedient (back row, third from the left), who'd been 20-9 with the 1912 Red Sox; and pitcher Howard Ehmke (back row, fourth from right), who would go on to win 166 games for the Tigers, Red Sox, and Athletics.

Harry, incidentally, took a fair share of abuse for his somewhat craggy looks. During his banner season with the Bosox, 1909, the *Boston American* went so far as to write, tongue in cheek of course, that "Harry was handsome as a child, according to family history, but the nurse dropped him one day and from that time on he took few prizes at beauty shows."

But could he ever play third!

Harry's .311 average for the season placed him fifth in the league. He was in fast company. Ahead of him were Ty Cobb (.377), Eddie Collins (.346), Napoleon Lajoie (.324), and Wahoo Sam Crawford (.314). *Behind* him were the likes of teammate Tris Speaker (.309), Home Run Baker (.305), Hal Chase (.283), and an aging Wee Willie Keeler (.264).

After his superlative 1909 season the sky seemed the limit for Porter, Maine's contribution to baseball. An injury to his hand, though, changed all that. On July 1st, batting in his customary number two slot in the Red Sox attack in a game against the Senators, Harry was whacked on the hand by a Walter Johnson fastball. Ouch! Actually, double ouch: The Big Train's fastball was so fast it was once said "He can throw a lamb chop past a wolf." Harry's finger was broken. It took him but two weeks to mend well enough to get back into the lineup, but it was still long enough for management to seemingly become enamored of Clyde Engle, the man who'd filled in for the two weeks. Harry was inserted back into his old position for a week, then benched in favor of Engle. On August 9th he was traded to the White Sox - along with secondbaseman Amby McConnell - for pitcher Frank Smith and thirdbaseman Billy Purtell. Delighted to be playing again, Harry batted a healthy .297 in 44 games for the White Sox over the rest of the season.

With the White Sox

Harry had a somewhat controversial career with the White Sox. An acknowledged team leader (he was once more selected to be captain), excellent fielder and batsman, he resented owner Charlie Comiskey's parsimonious ways. (Comiskey's tightfisted policies, history now accords, were the primary cause of the Black Sox scandal of 1919.). Harry, however, hung in there . . . and strung together three strong seasons for the Pale Hose. His numbers for 1911 were especially impressive: 180 hits in 561 at bats for a .321 average; 43 stolen bases; and 103 runs scored. By 1914, though, Harry had had it with Comiskey. His salary requests were seldom met. His manager, Nixey Callahan, was a conservative sort whose goal was to downplay the fiery brand of ball so espoused by Harry. What really did it, however, was when he was told that hit or take signals would be flashed to him from the sideline when he was at bat. After but 21 games into the season, he asked for his release and left the team.

After sitting out the remainder of the summer of 1914, Harry went aboard the Federal League, the "outlaw" third major league that existed in 1914-1915. Two months into the season (actually, Harry joined the team as a player on May 24th; was made manager two weeks later, on June 5th), he was signed as player-

Big Ed

Big Ed Walsh won 82 games, including back-to-back 27-win seasons in 1911 and 1912, in the five years that he and Harry Lord were White Sox teammates. He was elected to the Hall of Fame in 1946.

manager by Buffalo. When he joined them the team, known alternately as the Buffeds (ugh!) or the Blues, were mired in last place - with a 15-30 record - and seemed destined to remain there. Harry, though, stirred them up, got their juices flowing, and got them to begin winning.

front cover of souvenir program, Harry Lord Day

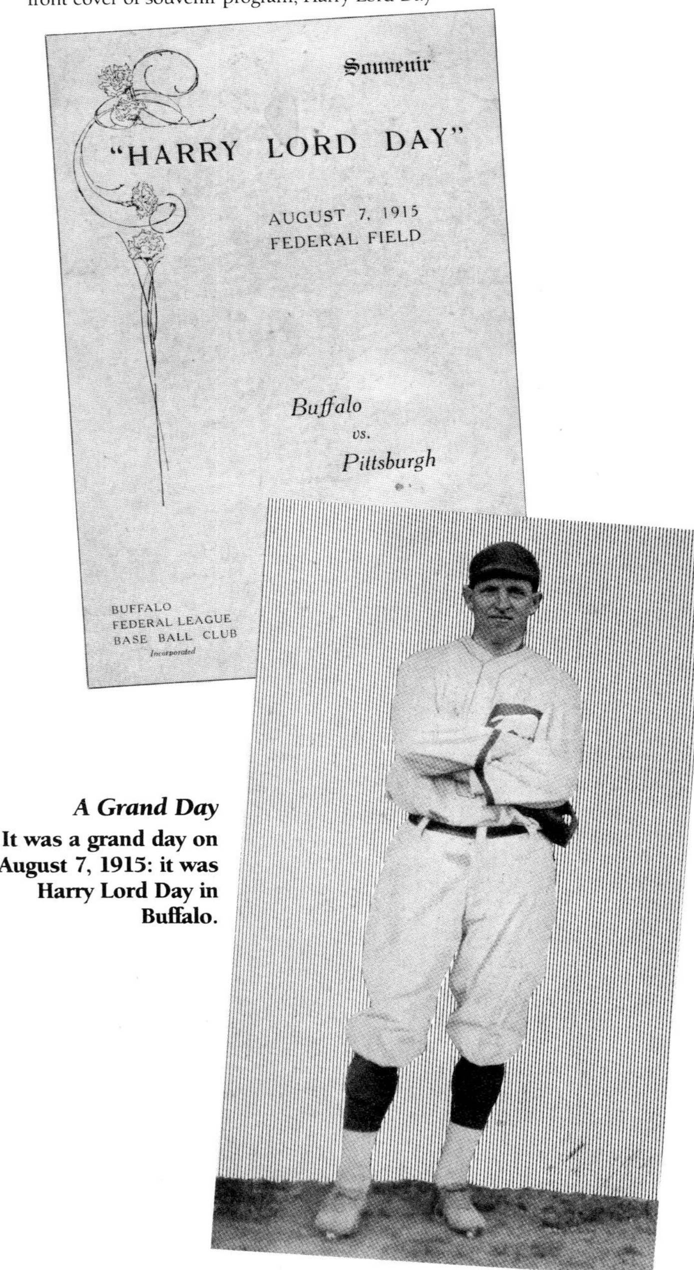

A Grand Day
It was a grand day on August 7, 1915: it was Harry Lord Day in Buffalo.

photo of Harry Lord, Harry Lord Day souvenir program

Under his reign the club - referred to as "Harry Lord's fighting Federal League team" - took 59, lost 48, and moved up to a relatively strong sixth-place finish. That the fans of the Niagara Frontier appreciated his work was shown on August 7th: it was Harry Lord Day at the ballpark, a fitting tribute to Harry's tenacity and leadership.

After the demise of the Federal League, Harry came home to New England. He managed and held down third for Lowell in the New England League in 1916. The following year he was with Portland in the Eastern League, batting .266 in 102 games. Harry then tried his hand in the grocery business: he purchased a store in South Portland, close to his home in Cape Elizabeth. It afforded him plenty of time to do one of the things he enjoyed most: share life with his wife and his son and daughter. He loved to hunt and fish, too. He also kept close to the game. He coached at South Portland High, was player-manager of a semi-pro team, later managed a spirited Dixfield nine. In 1925 Harry went into the coal business as co-proprietor of the Portland Lehigh Coal Company. He would remain in it the rest of his life.

After several years of a lingering illness, the great old thirdbaseman passed away in Westbrook on August 9, 1948. His one regret: that he had exited the White Sox before the Black Sox infamy of 1919. He was a leader among the Sox players, was trusted by them. "I'm sure," he voiced in his later years, "that if I could have been there, Joe Jackson and Buck Weaver, whom I still don't believe were in it, and the others would have listened to me. I could have stopped it if I'd had to punch the ringleader in the nose." And that's probably exactly what Harry Lord, if that's what it would have taken, would have done.

Shortstop — Frederick Alfred Parent

Our starting shortstop was one of the heroes of the first modern (i.e., played between the winners of the American and National Leagues) World Series, in 1903, a scrappy little guy who was born in Biddeford and who became synonymous with Sanford.

After his schooling ended, Freddy Parent went to work in a Sanford mill. There he toiled at a loom from 7:00 AM to 6:00 PM, Monday through Friday. Come Saturday, though, he was out playing baseball every day the weather would permit. Finally, in 1898, he decided to follow his heart and give ballplaying a full-time shot: he signed on with New Haven in the Connecticut League. He did well enough to get a brief (two games at second) shot with the St. Louis Cardinals in mid-July of 1899, before being returned to New Haven. In 1900 he moved up to Providence in the International League, where he batted leadoff and was a mainstay both offensively and defensively. He came up to the major leagues to stay, with the Boston entry in the brand-new American League, in 1901.

In his first season in Boston, Freddy showed that, though he stood but 5′5½″ tall and weighed but 148 pounds, he could play with the best of them. In 138 games he poked a solid .306, scoring 87 runs and driving in 59 more, as Boston finished second only to Chicago. The following year, 1902, Freddy led the league both in times at bat (567) and number of assists (496) while batting a credible .275.

It is the year 1903, however, for which Freddy Parent is best remembered. There's good reason. For one thing, it was the year that the National League deigned to recognize the American League as an equal, and agreed to play an inter-league playoff at season's end. For a second thing, the Red Sox (then generally called the Pilgrims, sometimes the Somersets or Puritans) captured the AL flag. For a third, the Pilgrims/Somersets/Puritans then went on to win the inter-league playoff at season's end, taking the Pirates, five games to three. And most of all, because the shortstop from Sanford played like a whiz kid . . . both during the regular season and against the Bucs. Some statistics: batting in the fifth slot in the Boston attack, Freddy led all American League shortstops with a .304 batting average, stole 24 bases, scored 83 runs, and knocked in 80 (second best on the club).

But Freddy was more than statistics. In his book, THE BOSTON RED SOX (New York City: G.P. Putnam's Sons, 1947), Frederick G. Lieb wrote of him: "Parent was built close to the ground . . . but he had surprising dexterity in getting over the ground, took the spikes of the toughest base runners, was a fast runner himself and a dangerous hitter in the clutch." Garry Herrmann, president of the Cincinnati Reds, went considerably further in lavishing praise: in 1904 he called Freddy Parent the best shortstop in the major leagues.

But, back to 1903. Barney Dreyfuss, owner of the National League champs, the Pirates, was so confident that he could put the upstart "Junior Circuit" in its place that he challenged the Bostons to a best-of-nine series. Henry J. Killilea, the Pilgrims' prexy, accepted. The match was on!

At the outset of the contest it certainly appeared as if Dreyfuss' prediction would prove correct. Game number one, played in Boston on October 1st, saw Pittsburgh score four times in the first inning and go on to win handily, 7-3. Freddy accounted for two - one of which was a triple - of the Pilgrims' total of six hits, and scored one of the team's three runs. In game two the Bostons bounced back, with Big Bill Dinneen shutting down the Bucs, 3-0. The third game was pretty much a repeat of the first: Pirate hurler Deacon Phillippe (who would pitch five of the eight games!) bested Boston's ace, Cy Young, with Pittsburgh winning, 4-2. In game four, with two days of rain giving his arm some rest, the Deacon came back . . . and won again, this time by a score of 5-4. The Pirates now had a rather commanding 3-1 lead in games. Game five, however, saw a turnaround. The Bostons belted the Bucs, amassing 14 hits in an 11-2 romp. Freddy contributed two of the 14 hits and scored a run. Game number six was more of the same. Freddy managed to get hit by a pitch in one at bat and he socked a triple in another and scored two runs (plus his fielding was noted as a feature of the game in the media accounts of the day) as the Pilgrims again came out on top, 6-3. The seventh game saw an overflow crowd of 17,308 jam its way into the Pirates' Exposition Park. With fans taking over much of the outfield it was agreed that any ball hit into the crowd would be a ground-rule triple. The result was that there was an almost unheard of total of seven triples in the game, with Freddy's bat accounting for one of them. He also chipped in with a single, two runs scored, and fielding that the press again applauded. That gave the Bostons the advantage . . . plus play shifted back to their home park, the Huntington Avenue Grounds. Two days of rain postponed the excitement . . . and again allowed Deacon Phillippe enough rest to take the mound one more time. He pitched well, too. But not well enough. Big Bill Dinneen did better, holding the Bucs to four hits (it would have been five but Freddy made a great grab of a liner off the bat of Fred Clarke). To the "almost frenzied delight" (*The New York Times)* of 17,000 rooters, the home team won, 3-0. It was October 13, 1903. And the Bostons were the world's first world champions!

What's especially noteworthy - at least from a Maine Dream Team point of view - is how one shortstop outplayed the other all during the Series. And the one that did the outplaying was the one from Maine. It may well, in fact, have been the difference in the Series' outcome. At the bat Freddy clearly outshone his counterpart, the one and only Honus Wagner. Wagner, considered by most to be the greatest shortstop in baseball history, had batted .355 during the regular season, winning the second of his record eight batting championships. In the Series, however, he slumped to .222, with but one extra base hit (a double), two runs scored, and three runs batted in. He struck out four times. Freddy, meanwhile, chimed in with a .281 average, had three extra base hits (all triples), scored eight runs, and knocked in three. He struck out but once. In the field, too, Freddy shone. Accounts of the day make mention of his fielding in several instances. Little is said about the play of "The Flying Dutchman." In terms of cold, hard statistics, the box scores show that Freddy made 17 putouts to Honus' ten; had slightly more assists, 29 vs. 27; and, most telling, that Honus made five errors to Freddy's two. Eight games, of course, do not a career make, and no one is about to suggest that Honus Wagner's plaque in Cooperstown be replaced with Freddy's. Still, for half a month in an autumn classic of long ago, one Frederick Alfred Parent was clearly king of the shortstop hill.

In 1904, the boys from Boston took the league again. Surprisingly, they did it

circa 1903 photograph

FREDDY PARENT

Born November 25, 1875, Biddeford, Maine   Died November 2, 1972, Sanford, Maine

Batted and threw right-handed   5′5½″; 148 lbs.

MAJOR LEAGUE RECORD

Year	Team	G	AB	H	2B	3B	HR	HR %	R	RBI	BB	SO	SB	BA	SA	Pinch Hit AB	Pinch Hit H	G by POS
1899	STL N	2	8	1	0	0	0	0.0	0	1	0		0	.125	.125	0	0	2B-2
1901	BOS A	138	517	158	23	9	4	0.8	87	59	41		16	.306	.408	0	0	SS-138
1902		138	567	156	31	8	3	0.5	91	62	24		16	.275	.374	0	0	SS-138
1903		139	560	170	31	17	4	0.7	83	80	13		24	.304	.441	0	0	SS-139
1904		155	591	172	22	9	6	1.0	85	77	28		20	.291	.389	0	0	SS-155
1905		153	602	141	16	5	0	0.0	55	33	47		25	.234	.277	0	0	SS-153
1906		149	600	141	14	10	1	0.2	67	49	31		16	.235	.297	0	0	SS-143, 2B-6
1907		114	409	113	19	5	1	0.2	51	26	22		12	.276	.355	12	2	OF-47, SS-43,
																		3B-7, 2B-5
1908	CHI A	119	391	81	7	5	0	0.0	28	35	50		9	.207	.251	0	0	SS-118
1909		136	472	123	10	5	0	0.0	61	30	46		32	.261	.303	0	0	SS-98, OF-37,
																		2B-1
1910		81	258	46	6	1	1	0.4	23	16	29		14	.178	.221	0	0	OF-62, 2B-11,
																		SS-4, 3B-1
1911		3	9	4	1	0	0	0.0	2	3	2		0	.444	.556	0	0	2B-3
12 years		1327	4984	1306	180	74	20	0.4	633	471	333		184	.262	.340	12	2	SS-1129, OF-146, 2B-28, 3B-8

WORLD SERIES RECORD

Year	Team	G	AB	H	2B	3B	HR	HR %	R	RBI	BB	SO	SB	BA	SA	Pinch Hit AB	Pinch Hit H	G by POS
1903	BOS A	8	32	9	0	3	0	0.0	8	3	1	1	0	.281	.469	0	0	SS-8

1905 photograph

The Winningest Pitcher of Them All

The years, 1901-1908, that Cy Young spent in Boston were almost identical to the years, 1901-1907, that Freddy spent. And it was while he was in a Boston uniform that the winningest pitcher in baseball history hurled the game that he always considered his best. It happened against the Philadelphia Athletics on May 5, 1904. Cy pitched a perfect game: 27 batters up, 27 batters down. Freddy, of course, was there: he handled five plays at short, went two for four at bat.

without a single .300 hitter in the lineup. Freddy's .291 was second highest on the team, exceeded only by centerfielder Chick Stahl's .295. With moundsmen the likes of Cy Young (26-16, with an ERA of 1.97), Big Bill Dinneen (23-14, with a 2.20 ERA), and Jesse Tannehill (23-11, with an ERA of 2.04), though, who needed much hitting? Actually the race for the pennant was a seesaw battle with the New York Highlanders (better known as the Yankees today) right down to the very wire. The title, in fact, was not decided until a doubleheader played in New York on October 10th. If they won either game, the Pilgrims were the champions. If they lost both, however, the New Yorkers would have it. In little Highland Park, with a seating capacity of 12,000, over 28,000 enthusiasts wedged their way in. They saw a humdinger. With the score deadlocked at 2-2 in the top of the ninth, Highlander pitcher Jack Chesbro (who was going for his 42nd win of the season!) allowed leadoff batter Lou Criger to reach first via an infield hit. Pitcher Bill Dinneen sacrificed Criger to second. He then went to third on an out by Kip Selbach. That brought Freddy to the plate. Chesbro reared back with his best pitch - the spitter, then still legal - but it sailed out of his hand and over Freddy's head for a wild pitch. In trotted Lou Criger with the run that won the pennant.

There would be no World Series that year, however. John T. Brush, owner of the National League-winning Giants (and a man with a zealous hatred of the American League: he referred to the Highlanders as the "Invaders"), simply refused to allow his team to play. His club was, as he phrased it, "content to rest on its laurels."

Those pennant-winning years of 1903 and 1904 were Freddy's banner seasons. He played three additional years for Boston, but his bat had lost some of its sting. He dropped to .234 in 1905, rose a notch to .235 in 1906 (the infamous year when both Boston teams finished dead last), improved to .276 in 1907. It was in this latter year that Freddy began to do some outfielding as well as playing shortstop.

In April of 1908, Freddy was peddled to the White Sox for an undisclosed amount of cash. There were those who thought that he'd slowed down to the point where, at age 32, his playing days were numbered; that playing just shy of 1,000 games in his seven years with Boston had taken its toll. Freddy did his best to prove the critics wrong. His time with the White Sox, however, was a disappointment to him. In 1908 he batted but .207 in 119 games, all at shortstop. By splitting duties between the infield and the outfield in 1909 he had his last good season: a .261 mark - with a career high total of 32 stolen bases - in 136 games. In 1910 he plummeted to .178, mostly as a part-time outfielder. He was released by the Sox after three games in 1911.

After a very full dozen years in the bigs, Freddy drifted on back to the minors. There was no way he was ready to quit yet. He played short or second - and coached some, too - for Jack Dunn's International League Baltimore Orioles from 1911 through 1914. That the old pro could still play was evidenced by his .306 batting average in 149 games in 1912. From 1915 to 1917 Freddy played and managed semi-pro ball in Maine, returning to organized ball as player-manager for Springfield of the Eastern League in 1918 and, closer to home, manager of the Lewiston Red Sox in the New England League in 1919. From 1922 through 1925 Freddy was head baseball coach at Colby. He was then junior varsity coach at Harvard from 1926 until 1928. After that it was back to Maine for good . . . where he played some and coached a lot right up through the 1940s. He also owned and

When the Red Sox Became the Red Sox

Although he played for the White Sox from 1908 until 1911, Freddy is best known for his work with the Red Sox. In fact it was while he was with them, in 1907, that the Red Sox became the Red Sox. Up until then the team had been known, variously, as the Somersets, the Puritans, and the Pilgrims. When club owner John I. Taylor got wind, in the spring of 1907, that the Boston entry in the National League was going to abandon their red stockings, he immediately ordered red hose for his team . . . and christened them the "Red Sox."

Hassan Cigarettes' baseball card, 1911

operated a filling station. But most of all Freddy Parent was a rabid supporter of Little League and American Legion ball. He once, in fact, gave his old playing days' mitt to the most valuable player for one of the local Little League squads. Talk about a treasure!

Right up until the last of his days Freddy was always ready to discuss the game. Not surprisingly, he had more respect for the way it was played in "the good old days." He opined to an interviewer in the late 1960s that "most of the clubs today are stocked with Class A players. There are about three or four major leaguers on each team." As for great running catches, he was totally unimpressed. "If the outfielder was playing the hitter right, he wouldn't have to run so far," he remarked on more than one occasion. The best player he ever saw: Napoleon Lajoie. The best of the modern (at that time, in the late 1960s): Carl Yastrzemski ("that Boston fellow," as Freddy, who had trouble pronouncing the Red Sox outfielder's last name, referred to Yaz).

Mr. World Series Shortstop of 1903 died in a Sanford nursing home on November 2, 1972, just three weeks short of his 97th birthday. On the day of his funeral hundreds of fans and friends turned out to say goodbye. Freddy was that kind of guy.

"Babe Ruth! Babe Ruth! (We Know What He Can Do)" sheet music, 1928

Freddy Knew What the Babe Could Do

Freddy was always proud of his role in the discovery of Babe Ruth. Our man from Maine was playing for Baltimore when the Babe joined the Orioles, then a minor league team, as a left-handed pitcher in the spring of 1914. Later that same season Red Sox manager Bill Carrigan wanted to know about Ruth and teammate Ernie Shore. Freddy's advice: "If you can get those two you'll win the pennant." The rest is history.

Leftfielder — Walter Miller Thornton

In a number of ways Walter Thornton's story is the most bewitching of our Maine Dream Team cast of players. His was a tale of rags to riches . . . and then back to rags again. Or was it? It's a tale shrouded in mystery.

Born on what the very few articles written about him describe as "a bounder-bound farm" on the outskirts of Lewiston in 1875, Walter Thornton became an orphan early-on in his life. At age 12 he became a wanderer, taking to the road with his brother George. The brothers became separated, however. George drifted west into the Indian Territory, became a U.S. Marshal, was eventually killed in a skirmish. Walter drifted further . . . to about as far as you can go, to Snohomish, in the state of Washington. There he involved himself in various occupations. He was a hosteler; he was a farm laborer; he was the driver of a bakery wagon. The latter was undoubtedly his favorite: it afforded him the chance to play ball. If he happened upon a game he would often just park the wagon, hop out, and join in. He loved it!

Somewhere along the way in Snohomish, Walter became close friends with a local newspaper editor. The editor, who had connections at Cornell College (in Mount Vernon, Iowa; not to be confused with Cornell University, in Ithaca, New York), whetted Walter's quest for knowledge. Through the editor's influence, Walter was admitted to Cornell Academy (the college's secondary school division), and later to Cornell College itself, trading his skills as a pitcher for tuition, room and board. At Mount Vernon he became more or less the all-American boy. He pitched the school's baseball team to local prominence; he played halfback on the football team; he fell in love with his elocution teacher, eventually marrying her. But it was his baseball prowess that made him a real standout. Word traveled the 200 or so miles to Chicago . . . and soon Cap Anson signed Walter Thornton to play for the Colts (as the Cubs were then nicknamed).

What's especially intriguing about Thornton is that he, without too much stretch of the imagination, could be likened to Babe Ruth. He could pitch (he was a southpaw, as was the Babe). But he could hit, too.

In his first year with the Colts, 1895, he didn't do much of either, however. He started two games as a pitcher and, in spite of a 6.08 ERA, he finished both and he won both. He also played first base, did a little relief pitching, and managed 22 at bats. In those at bats he knocked out seven hits, including a double and a home run. Amazingly enough, in his next season, 1896, he also had 22 at bats. This time he connected for eight hits. That works out to a .364 average. On the mound, he also won two games again. He was 2-1, with an ERA of 5.70. (His ERA dropped each of his four years in the majors.). His batting average was going up. His ERA was going down. Who could ask for anything more? What Walter needed though, was more playing time. He got it in 1897. And, as a hitter, it was his most productive season.

For the first half or so of 1897, Walter played the outfield - generally left field - and batted in either the fourth or fifth slot. He was one of the team's acknowledged hitters. Available box scores indicate that he lived up to that acknowledgement. He usually had at least one hit; very often two.

By August, however, Walter's pitching

What's In A Name?

The Cubs, the only team in continuous existence since the National League's birth in 1876, have gone through a flock of names in their 116 years on the diamond. They began as the White Stockings, a tribute to the white hose that they wore. As the White Stockings they became baseball's first dynasty, capturing five flags between 1880 and 1886. In 1888 the team took to wearing black hose . . . and the name Black Stockings came into brief use. In 1890 most of the team jumped to the newly formed Players League. That left manager Cap Anson with a collection of unseasoned "colts," the nickname the local press soon bestowed upon the team.* Other names - the Orphans, the Rainmakers, the Cowboys, and the Desert Rangers among them - were in vogue briefly. In 1901 numerous raids by the fledgling American League left the team, once more, with an abundance of young and unseasoned players. Reporters took to calling them, accordingly, the Cubs. The name stuck and - except for very limited experiments with the likes of the Panamas, the Zephyrs, the Trojans, and, surprisingly for a team far, far from "The County," the Spuds - it's been the Cubs ever since.

***Another version of the origin of "Colts" has it that it resulted from Cap Anson's appearance in a moving picture entitled _A Runaway Colt_.**

arm was pressed into service on the pitching-weak team. Although far from pacesetting efforts, he did win his first three outings in August . . . by scores of 16-8, 10-9, and, in a game in which he set down ten Washington Senators via strikeouts, 6-4. Ironically, when he did pitch a superb game - a six-hitter against the champion Baltimores on August 25th - he ended up losing, 3-1.

Who's That Guy in Left Field in the Bathrobe?

Three days after his loss to Baltimore, Walter was involved in what could certainly be termed one of the season's most colorful contests. On the 28th the Giants and the Colts played to an eight-inning 6-6 tie at the Polo Grounds in New York. Walter went the route for the Colts. The game was punctuated by a near total brawl between the two teams as a result of a vicious spiking of Colt shortstop Tim Donahue by Giant catcher Jack Warner. An estimated 1,000 fans swarmed onto the field to better view - and, unfortunately, to encourage - the hostilities. The police then charged into the crowd, dispersing them only with difficulty. The real excitement, however, occurred two days later when the game was replayed. With considerable tension still in the air, there was almost constant beefing from both sides, but especially the Chicago side. Umpire Emslie finally had enough and, after fining him $25.00, booted Colt manager and firstbaseman Cap Anson out of the game in the eighth inning. That startled the Colts because they had no other available players in uniform. Leftfielder George Decker was shifted to first and, to replace him, reserve pitcher Danny Friend was rounded up and sent to left . . . dressed in a bathrobe. Giant skipper Bill Joyce protested that Friend should not be allowed to play, that he was in violation of the rule that specified that only uniformed players could take part in the game. Umpire Emslie's response: since Friend was wearing a long robe he could well have a uniform on underneath it . . . and that, with darkness setting in, he didn't care to go out to left field to investigate. Score one for the bathrobe (and one for the Colts, too: they won 7-5).

Walter struggled through most of September, but then finished strong. On the 25th he three-hit Pittsburgh for an 8-1 victory. On October 2nd he did one hit better: he two-hit the St. Louis Browns

From Lewiston to Chicago to Cornell College to Snohomish, Washington...there is nowhere a likeness of Walter Thornton to be found. The mystery man continues to mystify: no image of him - be it a photo or sketch - is known to exist. What *is* pictured here is a piece of *Chicago Tribune* cartoon art from 1895, the year Walter joined the Colts. It was meant to be representative of the entire team...and that, although he may not have fully applauded it, included Walter Thornton.

WALTER THORNTON

Born February 18, 1875, Lewiston, Maine Died July 14, 1960, Los Angeles, California

Threw left-handed 6′1″; 180 lbs.

MAJOR LEAGUE RECORD

Year	Team	G	AB	H	2B	3B	HR	HR %	R	RBI	BB	SO	SB	BA	SA	Pinch Hit AB	Pinch Hit H	G by POS
1895	CHI N	8	22	7	1	0	1	4.5	4	7	3	1	0	.318	.500	0	0	P-7, 1B-1
1896		9	22	8	0	1	0	0.0	6	1	5	2	2	.364	.455	1	0	P-5, OF-3
1897		75	265	85	9	6	0	0.0	39	55	30		13	.321	.400	1	0	OF-59, P-16
1898		62	210	62	5	2	0	0.0	34	14	22		8	.295	.338	2	0	OF-34, P-28
4 years		154	519	162	15	9	1	0.2	83	77	60	3	23	.312	.382	4	0	OF-96, P-56, 1B-1

("Thornton, the Chicago's pitcher, had the Browns at his mercy to-day," scribed *The New York Times*) in a 3-2 Chicago win. And he triumphed again in the very last game of the year, knocking back the Brownies once more, 8-1, the very next day.

Tosses a No-Hitter

Walter Thornton played well for Chicago in 1898. Mindful of his strong finish the previous September/October and his ever-decreasing ERA (it had dropped to 4.70 in 1897), management concentrated more on his pitching than his hitting. He started 25 games, finished 21 of them, had a 13-10 won-lost record, and again lowered his earned run average . . . to a very credible 3.34. Two games especially stand out. Walter shut out the Philadelphia Athletics on a sparkling 11-inning seven-hitter, 1-0, before 5,900 delighted fans at Chicago on August 6th. He then twirled a no-hit masterpiece against Brooklyn, defeating them 2-0 before 10,000 even more delighted Chicago fans on August 21st. Lauded *The New York Times*: "Thornton pitched the game of his life, shutting his opponents out without the semblance of a hit." *The Chicago Tribune* praised the hurler's "magnificent speed." One of those he no-hit, incidentally, was Topsy Magoon. The St. Albans, Maine native was batting fifth and playing shortstop for the Bridegrooms that day.

Clark Griffith, later to be longtime Washington Senator owner, was one of Walter's more noted teammates. Here's how "The Old Fox" appeared in 1898 when he was 26-10 and led the National League with a miniscule 1.88 ERA.

For the year, Walter's hitting was again strong. (He even cracked out two hits the day of his no-hitter!). In 1897 he'd slugged .321 in 265 plate appearances. While he dropped somewhat in 1898 - to .295 in 210 at bats - it was nevertheless a most satisfying season.

But then Walter Thornton was gone. At age 24 he disappeared from the majors, becoming what could only be termed a mystery man. Stating that he was desirous of quiet and a home life, he had threatened to quit baseball after the 1897 season if a requested advance in salary wasn't forthcoming. It appears that he followed through with this desire - to leave the rigors of baseball behind him - a year later. One report had him marrying well-known-at-the-time actress Sara Andrews in 1900. Another report had him near death in a Washington State insane asylum in 1916, his mind affected from a beaning he'd suffered while playing for the Colts. In 1948, still very much alive, Walter Thornton wrote to Cornell College, requesting that his education records be deleted from their files. And, on July 14th, 1960, he was found dead at age 88 in a skid row neighborhood in Los Angeles. Even in death, however, accounts of what really happened to Walter Thornton varied. One version was that the lifetime .312 hitter was indeed destitute, that he died down and out. The other version - clearly the one that I like better - was that he lived in cheap hotels only to be close to the derelicts that he was unselfishly and unstintingly aiding, and that he'd preached to at a nearby midnight mission. The mystery of Walter Thornton . . . from rags to riches to ?

Rightfielder — Louis Francis "Soc"/"Sock" Sockalexis

From Old Town to legend. That was *almost* the story of Louis Sockalexis.

Born on Indian Island in Old Town on October 24, 1871, Louis could have stepped out of a book of mythology. He was a grandson of a chief of the Penobscots. He could throw with the velocity and impact of a lightning bolt. He could run like the wind.

As a teenager, Louis attended St. Anne's Convent School (later Old Town High School). There he starred in track, football, and, especially, baseball. Even in the heavyweight uniforms of the day he could run the 100-yard dash in ten seconds flat. And could he throw! Louis would give exhibitions during fair time in Bangor, hurling a ball over the length of the grandstand to a recipient at the other end. At Poland Spring he reputedly won a bet by tossing a ball over the top of the tower of the Hiram Ricker Hotel. Later, while at Holy Cross, one of his throws measured in at 414 feet (or 404 or 408 feet, depending on which account one chooses to believe: whatever, all were far greater than your ordinary outfield toss!).

Batting left-handed - he threw with his right - Louis could hit a ball astonishing distances. No matter how far away or high a wall was it seemed as if Louis could hit the ball over it.

After St. Anne's, Louis attended Ricker Classical Institute in Houlton. So good was he in baseball that Ricker easily won game after game. When the team played an away game, the school's administrators often closed down the institution so that the whole of the student body could go down to the train station to see Soc - as he was nicknamed - and his teammates off to another triumph.

During the summers, Louis played in various semi-pro leagues in and around Maine. One such league was the Knox County League, a strong circuit with teams in Rockland, Warren, Thomaston, and Camden. The manager of the Camdens was one Gilbert Patten (please see pages 34-35), who, under the pen name Burt L. Standish, would soon create that archtypical American hero, Frank Merriwell. It is said that it was Louis Sockalexis who inspired Patten to create his mythical superboy.

Word of Soc's prowess in the field and at the plate spread throughout the northeast. He had offers to play in the New England League. Instead, however, he chose to go to St. Mary's School in Van Buren, and then to the College of Holy Cross, located in Worcester, Massachusetts. At the time, 1894, Holy Cross was one of the major powers in American college baseball. Louis fit right in. Lewis Hatch, later to be headmaster at Phillips Exeter, recalled that when his Williams College team played Holy Cross, Soc hit a shot over the centerfielder's head and had crossed home plate before the unfortunate fielder had even chased down the ball. Hatch also recalled that few were daring - foolhardy might be a more apt word - enough to try to score from second on any hit in the vicinity of Sockalexis: if they did they'd find the catcher, ball in hand, ready and waiting to greet them at the plate. Soc would have gunned the ball - on a straight line in the air; no bounces for him - with plenty of time to spare. In his first year at Holy Cross, Louis socked - if you'll pardon the pun - opponent pitching for a .436 batting average. With an average such as that there's generally nowhere to go but down. Not so with Soc, though: he rapped out an even more

circa 1897 photograph

LOUIS SOCKALEXIS

Born October 24, 1871, Old Town, Maine Died December 24, 1913, Burlington, Maine

Threw right-handed; batted left-handed 5′11½″; 190 lbs.

MAJOR LEAGUE RECORD

Year	Team	G	AB	H	2B	3B	HR	HR %	R	RBI	BB	SO	SB	BA	SA	Pinch Hit AB	Pinch Hit H	G by POS
1897	CLE N	66	278	94	9	8	3	1.1	43	42	18		16	.338	.460	0	0	OF-66
1898		21	67	15	2	0	0	0.0	11	10	1		0	.224	.254	4	1	OF-16
1899		7	22	6	1	0	0	0.0	0	3	1		0	.273	.318	2	0	OF-5
3 years		94	367	115	12	8	3	0.8	54	55	20		16	.313	.414	6	1	OF-87

impressive .444 the next season. One of his hits was a grand slam homer against Brown that traveled so far it smashed through a fourth-story window well beyond the outfield's normal reaches.

From Holy Cross, Louis moved out to South Bend, Indiana, to play for Notre Dame. In mid-March, however, he was visited on campus by Patsy Tebeau, manager of the Cleveland team, then called the Spiders and then in the National League. Tebeau, who'd first taken notice of Soc during the Mainer's wonder years at Holy Cross, signed the outfielder extraordinare to contract on the spot.

A trio of Holy Cross future major leaguers as they posed for the camera in the spring of 1895. Left to right: Soc, Mike Powers (who caught eleven years in the bigs, mostly for the Athletics), and Walter "Doc" Curley (who played briefly for the Cubs in 1899).

"The Deerfoot of the Diamond"

Legend has it that Louis was a full-blooded Indian. He was not. The last full-blooded Penobscot had died in 1853. Nor was Soc the first Native American to play in the major leagues. To Jim Toy, who had played 153 games in the American Association - then considered a major league - in 1887 and 1890, goes that honor. But Louis was the first to be recognized as an Indian. And to be ballyhooed as such. The press and the fans showered him with nicknames: "The Deerfoot of the Diamond," "Chief Sock-em," just plain "Chief," and, of course, "Soc" or "Sock," were all favorites. Louis didn't let the nicknames down. Not at first, anyway.

Playing right field and batting either third or clean-up, Louis was a smash. "Sockalexis Does Some Great Work: He Makes a Decided Hit With the Fans and Three of Them for the Team" rang out the *Cleveland Plain Dealer* of April 27th, referring to Soc as "Warrior Louis Sockalexis." The article continued on to say that, playing in Cincinnati, the fans initially greeted the Native American with derisive war whoops and Indian yells, but as the game progressed and Soc began to show his stuff, he was given an ovation. Such it was throughout the league: throngs came to deride, then stayed to cheer. Many, in fact, began to refer to the team as the Indians (the name it would eventually adopt; please see pages 28-29). So did the press, which loved Soc. On May 1st, "The Chief" led a ninth-inning rally to beat the St. Louis Browns. The *Plain Dealer*'s writer had fun with that one: "Sockalexis socked it to 'em. Tonight he is the real medicine. In that fatal ninth he stepped into the batter's box with the score a tie and the bases full and his bat in hand. And Donahue (Ed. note: Red Donahue, the Brownies' pitcher) was sending them in like pills. Sock-it-on-the-nose, or whatever his name is, bruised the ball on the forehead and it went sailing into the ozone, heading for the next county." Soc ended up with a triple and the Spiders went on to win, 8-3.

Day after day the praises rang out. On May 5th Soc went "shooting in the air like a skyrocket to pull down an awful line drive far out in right field" and then "threw the ball like a shot to the plate and cut off a runner trying to score from third." As superb as Soc's fielding was, his work with the "war club," as the press liked to refer to Louis' bat, was as good. He batted very near .400 for much of the early part of the season. Legend says that in Soc's first appearance in New York - an event built into majestic proportions by the New York press - he blasted a home run that traveled some 600 feet in his first at bat against the New Yorkers' ace, future Hall of Famer Amos Rusie. While there's no way Soc's smash could have flown that unwieldy distance, he did hit a homer and *The New York Times*, citing Soc's "phenomenal stick work," characterized the shot as a "beautiful line drive over the right field ropes." And, on May 31st, all attendance records were broken at Brooklyn's Eastern Park when the Spiders came to play. Noted *The Times:* "It can safely be said that Sockalexis, the full-blooded Indian, was what brought many of the people."

Such good times were not to be everlasting, however. There are various stories regarding Soc's downfall. All involve alcohol. While there is some evidence that Soc drank before he arrived in Cleveland, most accounts of his life represent that he did not. The most generally accepted view is that the beginning of the end came after Soc made an especially spectacular catch to save a game for the Spiders. He'd raced back (and back and back) to make a virtually impossible one-handed snare of the ball. So overcome with glee was a contingent of fans that they swarmed onto the field, carried their star off the diamond, and, unfortunately, trooped to a local saloon. There, in the spirit of victory and camaraderie, Soc was induced to take his first drink. Alas, he discovered that he liked alcohol's taste and, especially, its effects. Drinking long and hard became a way of Soc's life. Naturally enough, his play fell off. But his drinking did not. He became, as Trina Wellman wrote in an excellent 1975 paper entitled *Louis Francis Sockalexis: The Life-Story of a Penobscot Indian,* what could be termed an "instant alcoholic." Cleveland management offered all kinds of monetary rewards if he'd quit drinking. As Spider manager Patsy Tebeau would later recount: "No other player to my knowledge ever sacrificed so much on the altar of his appetite than did this red man." Continued Tebeau, "When he began to drink and stay out all night, I promised him $6,000 for the next season and $10,000 for 1899 (Ed. note: both were almighty sums in those days!) if he would stay sober and play ball. He promised all right but he couldn't let the strong stuff alone."

During an especially wild night of celebrating on the 4th of July, Soc hurt his right foot. Combine this with his heavy

Louis Sockalexis in his Lowell uniform in 1902. Hughie Jennings, who played and/or managed in the major leagues from 1891-1920, would later write that Soc "had the most ability of any man who ever played the game."

The Cleveland Ball Club Company
This is the letterhead design of the Cleveland Baseball Club as it appeared in 1913. Two years later the club would adopt the nickname Indians . . . in honor, of course, of Soc.

drinking and you had one sorry ballplayer. Although he would sometimes show flashes of his old brilliance, Louis Sockalexis was basically washed up before the end of his first season in the majors. He ended the season with 94 hits - including nine doubles, eight triples, and three home runs - in 278 at bats for a .338 average. Now .338 is far from bad - in fact it's very good - but it was a far cry from what it could have been. In 1898, Soc played in but 21 games, batting .224 in 67 at bats. The excessive drinking was ever more evident. Soc made a token run at an outfield berth in 1899, but the magic was gone. After seven games the Spiders gave their former hero his release.

After his fall from grace, Soc drifted on back east. He tried to catch on in both the Eastern League (with Hartford) and then the Connecticut League (with Waterbury) that same year, 1899. Another comeback attempt was made with Lowell in the New England League in 1902. Again, he showed moments of his former greatness, but alcohol had too much of a hold to allow for any real consistency. Soc pretty much summed up his own heartbreaking career when, arrested on a vagrancy charge in Holyoke, Massachusetts in August of 1900, he told the judge: "They liked me on the baseball field, and I like firewater."

Louis finally returned home. To Old Town. There he got himself together. He married and settled down, working as a woodcutter during the winter months and helping to run the Indian Island ferry during the summer. He also did more than a fair share of coaching and umpiring in various local baseball leagues. And did he still play, too? You bet he did. Though much of his speed was gone, Soc could still hit the ball just about where he wanted to.

Louis Sockalexis' life appeared to be quite stable and quite satisfactory when, on Christmas Eve of 1913, he was found dead in the woods outside the lumber camp in which he worked in Burlington, Maine. All reports indicated that he'd had a heart attack. He was 42 years of age. In the pocket of his blue flannel shirt there was found a wad of aged newspaper clippings . . . accounts of his wondrous heroics all those years earlier. Reading and re-reading them had been Soc's way of remembering how good he was. And, perhaps, of forgetting how brief his moment of glory had been.

Centerfielder — George F. "Piano Legs" Gore

Read me some names from a faded box score
Culled from the distant ago;
Anson, Dalrymple, Williamson, Gore,
Flint, Delahanty and Lowe.
Verse, author unknown

Maine's only batting champ - to date! - was most definitely one of the outstanding performers of his day. That his day was a long, long time ago should not detract from his achievements. A batting champ of one era is not likely to hit .214 in another!

George F. "Piano Legs" Gore was born in Hartland, Maine in 1855. It was in Hartland that he learned a love of the game, playing as often as he could in fields and pastures in and around town. He eventually moved to Saccareppa (Westbrook), where he found ample opportunity to play - and play well - for the S.D. Warren paper mill team. In one game he blasted a ball 450 feet. Word spread, and soon George was persuaded to leave Maine and give pro ball a try. Playing briefly in 1877, George hit .319 in 33 games for Fall River in the New England League. The next season, 1878, he really began to show his stuff: he socked a solid .324 for the New Bedford Whalers, also in the New England League. "They paid me $55 a month and expenses. That was good money for a youngster in 1878," George would later reminisce. A.G. Spalding, owner of the Chicago White Stockings, was impressed: he offered George Gore $1,200 to play in Chicago in 1879. George said "No." He wanted $2,500. Many credit him, accordingly, with being baseball's first holdout. The two eventually compromised on $1,900 . . . and George started his 14-year major league career.

George Gore's first year was a disappointment. The rookie batted .263 in 266 at bats; the White Stockings finished fourth. His second year, however, was in no way disappointing. The Mainer led all National League batsmen with a .360 average; the White Stockings took the flag by a wide margin. George knocked out 116 hits in 322 plate appearances, well ahead of teammate Cap Anson, who had 120 safeties in 356 at bats (good for a .337 mark). George also led the league in slugging percentage (with .463) and was third in hits. That there was a heartwarming degree of local pride in George's accomplishments was reflected in the *Daily Eastern Argus*, Portland's most prominent newspaper at the time. Baseball coverage was thin, but included in a now-and-again column entitled "Sporting Matters" were bits and pieces of information. George Gore was mentioned more times than any other player. This was especially true early in the season, before the intense coverage of the forthcoming Hancock-Garfield presidential election dominated the press. Thus - wedged in between rather fascinating tidbits the likes of "Cincinnati pays its base ball club $11,750 in salaries" and "The Baltimores appear to lack good judgment. In the arrangement of their dates they have several times agreed to play with two clubs on the same date, thus causing

The Evolution of the Distance Between Home and the Pitcher's Mound

It is well worthy of note that 1880 - the year George Gore led the National League with a healthy .360 batting average - was considered a Year of the Pitcher. Not one, but two, perfect games were hurled. Scores were low, lower, and lowest. Pitchers so dominated the game that, at season's end, the club owners got together and voted to increase the distance from the pitcher's mound to home plate by five feet: from 45 feet to 50 feet. It was moved to its present-day 60′6″ in 1893. (The extra 6″ came about by accident. The intention was that the distance be an even 60 feet, but somebody goofed in reading the diagram the rulemakers had provided . . . and it's been 60′6″ ever since.).

much trouble and disappointment." - we have the following mentions of the man who a scant four years earlier was playing for S.D. Warren:

> "The management of the Chicago club appears to have come to the conclusion that Gore is too good a man to keep as a substitute. He is filling the position of center field every game the club plays, and right nobly is he keeping up his reputation as a first-class base ball player. The good plays credited to him have been numerous, and we have not yet seen an error charged against his name." (May 13th)
>
> "In Saturday's run at Chicago Gore made the first home run that has been made on the home grounds this season." (May 24th)
>
> "Gore of the Chicagos still continues to make heavy hits, brilliant plays and no errors." (May 29th)

Averaged More Than a Run Scored Per Game

Although George would not again lead the league in hitting, he would top it in a pair of other categories; bases on balls, three times (with 29 in 1882; 61 in 1884; and 102 in 1886) and runs scored, two times (with 86 in 1881; 99 in 1882). It is his run production, in fact, that most distinguished the man from Hartland's career statistics. He averaged 1.02 runs scored, lifetime, per game. Contrast that with Hank Aaron (.66) or Lou Gehrig (.87) or Ted Williams (.78) or any other player you can think of and you will be very impressed with the 1.02 mark. At various times George had six hits in six at bats, five consecutive extra base hits, and seven - yes seven! - stolen bases . . . all in a single game. His speed coupled with his high walk/low strikeout ratio made him the ideal leadoff man. George was, truly, one of the few players of his time who fully earned the accolade of "star." More than one baseball historian has likened George to Ty Cobb or Tris Speaker.

Nor were George Gore's achievements limited to the bat. In the days of gloveless heroics, he was right up there with the best. William McMahon, in the book NINETEENTH CENTURY STARS, credited George with being a "fine thrower and fielder." The White Stocking outfield of Abner Dalrymple, the legendary King Kelly, and George was the equal of any in the 19th century.

Played on Seven Pennant Winners

In the seven-year span between 1881 and 1886, the White Stockings rang up five first-place finishes. George was a key ingredient in every one of them: over the seven years he racked up batting averages of .360 (his batting crown year), .298, .319, .334 (third in the league), .318, .313 (fifth in the league), and .304. From 1887 through 1889 George played for the New

photograph, 1891

GEORGE GORE

Born 1855, Hartland, Maine Died September 16, 1933, Utica, New York

Batted left-handed; threw right-handed 5′11″; 195 lbs.

MAJOR LEAGUE RECORD

Year	Team	G	AB	H	2B	3B	HR	HR %	R	RBI	BB	SO	SB	BA	SA	Pinch Hit AB	Pinch Hit H	G by POS
1879	CHI N	63	266	70	17	4	0	0.0	43	32	8	30		.263	.357	0	0	OF-54, 1B-9
1880		77	322	116	23	2	2	0.6	70	47	21	10		.360	.463	0	0	OF-74, 1B-7
1881		73	309	92	18	9	1	0.3	86	44	27	23		.298	.424	0	0	OF-72, 3B-1, 1B-1
1882		84	367	117	15	7	3	0.8	99	51	29	19		.319	.422	0	0	OF-84
1883		92	392	131	30	9	2	0.5	105		27	13		.334	.472	0	0	OF-92
1884		103	422	134	18	4	5	1.2	104		61	26		.318	.415	0	0	OF-103
1885		109	441	138	21	13	5	1.1	115	51	68	25		.313	.454	0	0	OF-109
1886		118	444	135	20	12	6	1.4	150	63	102	30		.304	.444	0	0	OF-118
1887	NY N	111	459	133	16	5	1	0.2	95	49	42	18	39	.290	.353	0	0	OF-111
1888		64	254	56	4	4	2	0.8	37	17	30	31	11	.220	.291	0	0	OF-64
1889		120	488	149	21	7	7	1.4	132	54	84	28	28	.305	.420	0	0	OF-120
1890	NY P	93	399	127	26	8	10	2.5	132	55	77	23	28	318	.499	0	0	OF-93
1891	NY N	130	528	150	22	7	2	0.4	103	48	74	34	19	.284	.364	0	0	OF-130
1892	2 teams	**NY N** (53G — .254)				**STL N** (20G — .205)												
1892	total	73	266	64	11	3	0	0.0	56	15	67	22	22	.241	.305	0	0	OF-73
14 years		1310	5357	1612	262	94	46	0.9	1327	526	717	332	147	.301	.411	0	0	OF-1297, 1B-17, 3B-1

York Giants, helping them to flags in 1888 and 1889. A highlight came on August 25th of his first season with the Jints. Playing against his old teammates, he had four hits as the New Yorkers took the White Stockings, 9-1. In its account of the game *The New York Times* described the ex-Chicago player as "the happiest man in the metropolis."

For the Giants, George performed well, but "old age" - and, some would say, wine and women - was beginning to slow him down. George's average fell to .290 in 1887, and tumbled all the way to .220 (in but 64 games played) in 1888. In 1889, however, he again topped the magic .300 plateau, turning in a .305 mark in 120 games. After a season with the New York team in the Players League in 1890 (the league's sole season) in which he batted .318 and walloped ten home runs, it was back to the Giants. For them he played his last noteworthy season in 1891, hitting

The Champs

Looking properly victorious, here are the National League champion Chicago White Stockings of 1885. George, who batted .313 and was among the league leaders in walks (68), triples (13), and runs scored (115), is in the back row, far left. Other notables include Hall of Famers Cap Anson (back row, third from the left), Mike "King" Kelly (back row, second from right), and John Clarkson (front row, second from right). Next to Clarkson, in the front row far right, is rightfielder W.A. Sunday . . . later to gain a considerable measure of fame as evangelist Billy Sunday.

New York, New York

Appearing majestic indeed is this artist's rendition of the original Polo Grounds in 1887, George's first year with the Giants. That's George himself as depicted on an Old Judge Cigarettes' card from that same year. When George was traded to New York after the 1886 season he vowed that the White Stockings would not win another National League flag as long as he was playing. They did not.

.284 in 528 plate appearances. In George's last year in the majors, 1892, he split his time between the Giants and the Cardinals, batting an uninspiring .241 overall. George returned to pro ball briefly in 1894; nearing forty, he had a .319 mark in 48 games for Binghamton in the Eastern League.

After his retirement from baseball George Gore became, in the words of the few later-day articles written about him, a "successful businessman." He resided in Nutley, New Jersey the last 13 years of his life; would often make the short trip into New York City to take in a ballgame at the Polo Grounds or Yankee Stadium. He died at the Masonic Home in Utica, New York on September 16, 1933.

Catcher — Clyde LeRoy "Sukey" Sukeforth

If Maine were to ever select a Mr. Maine Baseball the odds are that the man so honored would be Clyde Sukeforth. Player, manager, coach, scout: for six decades Sukey was on the scene in one capacity or another.

Clyde was seemingly born into the game. When I interviewed him in the autumn of 1990 - as he was approaching his 89th birthday - he openly admitted to a lifelong love affair with baseball. And only baseball. "It was a different world back then," said Sukey about his youth in Washington, Maine. "Football was nothing. Basketball was nothing. Every kid had a ball and a glove, and threw the ball. You'd throw the ball seven days a week." The result, of course, was kids with strong arms. Sukey put his strong arm to advantage as a catcher. Sure, he pitched and played other positions, too, both in Washington and in Waterville, where he graduated from Coburn Classical Institute. But he was mostly a catcher. As he explains it: "In order to have a game somebody had to catch. That's how I got started. No one else wanted to."

In the years after World War I, Maine had an especially well-organized semi-pro program. Many of the industrial plants sponsored a club, and they'd often recruit better college players from all over New England. They also recruited Sukey. After his high school days at CCI, the future Maine Dream Team catcher played for Great Northern's team in Millinocket. He also did some "pastiming" - as the press used to call "ballplaying" - for the Augusta Millionaires. The team was so called because they had, at one point in the early 1920s, a then-lordly payroll of $750.00. Out-of-town scribes couldn't resist bestowing the "Millionaires" sobriquet upon them.

Next stop in Clyde's career was Georgetown University, where he was an undergrad for two years. His standout work behind the plate at that highly respected institution attracted the attention of the Cincinnati Reds. Almost before you could say *New England produces great catchers* - Mickey Cochrane, Gabby Hartnett, Carlton Fisk, Jim Hegan, Birdie Tebbetts, Connie Mack, Clyde Sukeforth - Sukey had signed on the dotted line with the Reds.

Clyde's professional career began, appropriately enough, in the New England League. In his first season, 1926, he played for both Nashua and Manchester. Combined, he clouted the league's hurling for a robust .367 clip, knocking in 44 runs in 64 games. Late in the season Cincinnati brought him up for a quick look-see. Very quick. Clyde had one time at bat, as a pinch hitter. He struck out.

In 1927 Sukey came up to stay. But not to play very much. The Reds' number one receiver was Eugene "Bubbles" Hargrave, whose .353 in 1926 marked the first time a catcher had ever won a major league batting title. So Sukey benchwarmed in 1927 and 1928 while either Bubbles or Val Picinich did the bulk of the backstopping.

In 1929, Clyde's waiting paid off. He finally, platooning with Johnny Gooch, got to show his stuff. And show it he did: the Mainer rapped out 84 hits in 237 plate appearances. That figured out to be .354 . . . good for eighth in the league among all hitters and tops among all major league catchers. It was also, by a margin of over 40 points, the highest average on his own

Cincinnati club. Newspaper articles of the period also praised Clyde's defensive skills, noting - as one paper so well expressed it - that he showed "fine promise as a maskman." It was, in short, one heck of a year!

Clyde's next two seasons with the Reds, 1930 and 1931, showed progress in that he appeared in more games: from 84 in 1929 he increased to 94 in 1930, and then to 112 in 1931. Not surprisingly - catching wears you down, especially in a hot and humid river town the likes of Cincinnati - Sukey's batting average fell off. Yet Sukey, who was a left-handed line-drive hitter, was still no slouch with the stick. He socked .284 in 1930; was .256 - with 15 doubles and 4 triples - in 1931.

On March 14th, 1932, Clyde was part of one of the blockbuster trades of the 1930s. He, along with Tony Cuccinello and Jersey Joe Stripp, was sent to the Dodgers in exchange for thirdbaseman Wally Gilbert, catcher and future Hall of Famer Ernie Lombardi, and Babe Herman, an outfielder who certainly deserves to be a Hall of Famer. Unfortunately, however, Sukey had injured his eye in a hunting accident in the fall of 1931. A shotgun pellet penetrated his right eye. At first doctors were doubtful that the eyesight could be saved. But prompt medical attention - plus Sukey's determination - allowed him to have partial vision out of the injured eye. As Clyde phrased it in my interview with him: "I can see some out of it but I've never been able to read out of it, and naturally it didn't help my hitting any."

With the Dodgers - and the injured eye - Sukey's playing career went the other way. He played in fewer and fewer games. In 1931 he appeared in 59 games, 22 of them as a pinch-hitter. The following two seasons saw even less action: Sukey got into but 20 games in 1933; 27 in 1934. The Dodgers, though, knew full well that Sukey had skills that transcended his playing ability. Here was a man of incredible baseball savvy.

Clyde did some catching in the Dodgers' minor league system from late 1934 right through 1939. More importantly, in 1936, with Tri-Cities (Leaksville-Spray-Draper, North Carolina) in the Bi-State League, Clyde began to manage. From Tri-Cities he moved up to Clinton, Iowa in the Three I (Illinois-Iowa-Indiana) League in 1937, Elmira in the Eastern League in 1938 and 1939, and to the Dodgers' top farm team, Montreal, in 1940, 1941, and 1942. Under his leadership the Royals finished second in the International League in both 1942 and 1943.

It was then back to Flatbush for the better part of a decade. From 1943 through 1951, Sukey was a coach for the Dodgers, playing a vital role in the team's development as the dominant club in the Senior Circuit. And in 1945 he did more than coach. With the team's catching corps woefully reduced due to wartime service, our Dream Team catcher was pressed back into duty behind the plate. Although the 43-year-old Sukey hadn't had an official time at bat since 1939 he showed that the touch was still there: in 51 plate appearances he whacked out a solid .294 average. That's not at all bad for a guy who'd had his first major league base knock almost two decades earlier!

Far more important, however, was Clyde's role in the breaking of the color barrier. No black had played major league ball since 1884 (please see page 48). Branch Rickey, the Dodgers' General Manager, set about to change that. Almost from the very day he came aboard as head man in Brooklyn in 1942, Rickey was determined to find the best candidate for the job of the 20th century's first black ballplayer. Jackie Robinson, as of 1945, was Rickey's number

Continued on page 124

March, 1934 photograph

CLYDE "SUKEY" SUKEFORTH

Born November 30, 1901, Washington, Maine Resides in Waldoboro, Maine

Batted left-handed; threw right-handed 5′10″; 155 lbs.

MAJOR LEAGUE RECORD

Year	Team	G	AB	H	2B	3B	HR	HR %	R	RBI	BB	SO	SB	BA	SA	Pinch Hit AB	Pinch Hit H	G by POS
1926	CIN N	1	1	0	0	0	0	0.0	0	0	0	1	0	.000	.000	1	0	
1927		38	58	11	2	0	0	0.0	12	2	7	2	2	.190	.224	3	1	C-24
1928		33	53	7	2	1	0	0.0	5	3	3	5	0	.132	.208	4	0	C-26
1929		84	237	84	16	2	1	0.4	31	33	17	6	8	.354	.451	3	2	C-76
1930		94	296	84	9	3	1	0.3	30	19	17	12	1	.284	.345	7	1	C-82
1931		112	351	90	15	4	0	0.0	22	25	38	13	0	.256	.322	4	1	C-106
1932	BKN N	59	111	26	4	4	0	0.0	14	12	6	10	1	.234	.342	22	3	C-36
1933		20	36	2	0	0	0	0.0	1	0	2	1	0	.056	.056	0	0	C-18
1934		27	43	7	1	0	0	0.0	5	1	1	6	0	.163	.186	5	0	C-18
1945		18	51	15	1	0	0	0.0	2	1	4	1	0	.294	.314	5	0	C-13
10 years		486	1237	326	50	14	2	0.2	122	96	95	57	12	.264	.331	54	8	C-399

A Sukey Scrapbook

. . . with Great Northern Paper Company's team, 1921 and 1923

. . . with the Reds, 1926-1931

. . . with the Dodgers, 1932-1934

. . . during spring training, March, 1933

. . . with, left to right, all-time greats Pie Traynor, Wally Gilbert, and Heinie Manush at Sloppy Joe's in Havana, Cuba, October, 1930. Sukey - certainly the most dapper of the group in his white suit! - was part of a pair of all-star teams that barnstormed Cuba during the fall of that year. Other greats on the tour included Bill Terry, Rabbit Maranville, Glenn Wright, Paul Waner, and Carl Hubbell.

. . . with his daughter Helen and Dodger manager Barney Shotton, Ebbets Field, August, 1947

. . . and, still looking dapper, Sukey outside his Waldoboro home in November, 1990

one choice. But he wanted the opinion of others. He especially wanted the opinion of Sukey. Here are the events of that long ago August of 1945 as relayed to me by Clyde himself in an interview at his home in Waldoboro in November of 1990:

> "He (Rickey) told me to go to Chicago and see the Lincoln Giants and the Kansas City Monarchs (for whom Jackie Robinson was playing). He said, 'Pay particular attention to a shortstop named Robinson, particularly his arm.' Now he said, 'Identify yourself. Tell him who sent you.' Well, up to that point we didn't identify ourselves. We bought our tickets and we made ourselves as inconspicuous as possible. Well, I contacted Robinson. He (Robinson) wondered why Rickey would be interested in him. He kept pressing me on that point. So I told him the nature of my errand. I said, 'Now, Mr. Rickey is interested in your arm.' He asked why. I said, 'That's a good question but I don't have the answer.' He said, 'Well, I'd be happy to show you what arm I have but I fell on my shoulder the night before last and I'm not going to be able to play for several days.' Well, I knew there was a great deal of interest in the guy. Rickey had told me, 'If you like his arm bring him in, if his schedule will permit. If his schedule won't permit, make an appointment and I will come out there.' That showed the interest there was . . . that he (Rickey) would drop everything.
>
> "So I asked him (Robinson) to meet me down at the hotel after the game. The Stevens Hotel. Well, I get him down to the hotel and I talk to him for a long, long time. And the more you talk to the guy the better you like him. He's intelligent. He's got determination written all over him. So I said, 'I have to see a doubleheader in Toledo on Sunday (which was two days hence). How about meeting me in Toledo? We'll check the train schedules, and I'll have made the Pullman reservations for us and we'll go into Brooklyn and Rickey can tell you what you want to know.'
>
> "So we got into New York in the morning and I introduced him (Robinson) to Mr. Rickey. 'But I haven't seen his arm,' I said. Well, evidently he didn't hear me. That was the start of that famous meeting."

Out of that meeting - which took place on August 28th and which lasted three hours - came the signing of Robinson to a Dodger contract. Out of that meeting also came a line destined for baseball immortality. At one point in the talks Robinson asked Rickey: "Are you looking for a Negro who is afraid to fight back?" Rickey replied: "I'm looking for a ballplayer with guts enough not to fight back."

Clyde was also the Brooklyn manager on the day, twenty months later, when Jackie Robinson stepped onto the diamond at Ebbets Field to make his first appearance as a Dodger. For more on that historic occasion please turn to pages 48-49.

Before the start of the 1952 season, Sukey followed Branch Rickey from Brooklyn to Pittsburgh. For the Bucs he performed as coach, scout, and all-around troubleshooter through 1958. He had the opportunity to manage the club in late 1957. Mired deep in last in August, the Pirates fired Bobby Bragan and asked Sukey to take over. He politely said, "No."

Although Sukey "retired" from the game after the season of 1958, he couldn't resist the lure of bouncing back into it from time to time thereafter. He got "the itch" - as he puts it - in 1963 and went back with the Pirates' organization for three years, doing some scouting and then managing Gastonia in the Western Carolinas League in 1965. From 1966 through 1975 he covered New England as a scout for the Atlanta Braves. Add it all up and Clyde's involvement with major league baseball totals some 45 years and spans six decades. That's a whale of a lot of ball!

Today Clyde Sukeforth is a remarkably spry gentleman of 90 . . . a man who still bird hunts every morning during the season, who still follows baseball actively, and who - with his second wife Grethel - lives the good life on the shores of lovely Medomak Bay in Waldoboro.

Braintrust Legends

Clyde with two of the game's braintrust legends, Branch Rickey, left, and Leo Durocher, right. The occasion was Leo's selection of Sukey as one of his coaches for the 1943 season. Rickey, then Dodger prexy and GM, and Leo the Lip, then Dodger field manager, were both oft-quoted. Rickey is credited with the likes of "Baseball is a game of inches" and "Trade a player a year too early rather than a year too late." Leo, less genteel, is recalled for such as "Nice guys finish last," "Show me a good loser and I'll show you an idiot," and "You don't save a pitcher for tomorrow. Tomorrow it may rain." My favorite Leo quote, though, concerns the fans of Brooklyn. (I once lived in Brooklyn for seven years. It's quite a place.):

> "It was Brooklyn against the world. They were not only complete fanatics, but they knew baseball like the fans of no other city. It was exciting to play there. It was a treat. I walked into that crummy, flyblown park as Brooklyn manager for nine years, and every time I entered, my pulse quickened and my spirits soared."

March 1, 1943 photograph

Left-Handed Pitcher — Michael Joseph "Kid" Madden

Kid Madden's career was meteoric . . . and tragically short. Born in Portland on October 22, 1866, the Kid took an early liking to pitching. Though frail and almost childlike in appearance - he weighed but 124 pounds spread thinly over a 5′7″ frame during his peak pitching years - Madden developed an assortment of breaking pitches second to none. "He throws the most puzzling drops and curves" is how one Portland sportswriter of the time summed up the Kid's stuff. Even years after his death, his curve, especially, was recalled with awe: "I think he could toss as wide a curve as ever was thrown" wrote columnist Nat Colcord in a May, 1909 *Portland Evening Express* feature story on Mainers who'd played in the major leagues.

Madden hurled successfully for a number of amateur clubs in and around Portland throughout his teenage years. Given a trial by the Portland club of the New England League in 1886, he responded favorably, pitching especially well as he developed confidence - he was, after all, but 19 years of age - during the course of the season. His crowning achievement came at the very end of the season: the Portlands, pennant winners in the NEL, hosted the National League Boston Red Stockings (later to become the Boston Beaneaters; then the Boston Braves; then the Milwaukee Braves; now the Atlanta Braves) in an exhibition game on October 12th. Madden, on the mound for the home team, spun his breaking-ball magic and held the major league contingent to but nine hits and four runs, going the entire route in a 7-4 Portland victory.

So impressed was Boston manager John Morrill that he signed Madden (as well as the Kid's batterymate, Tom O'Rourke) to a Boston contract for the following year. Again, the Kid did not disappoint. In fact, as a 20-year old rookie in 1887, Kid Madden won 22 games while losing 14. In addition, he led the team's staff in ERA: his mark of 3.79 was considerably lower than future Hall of Famer Old Hoss Radbourn's 4.55; and the other two pitchers on the four-man staff, Dick Conway and Cannon Ball Bill Stemmyer, had higher still numbers. The Kid started 37 games and, as was the custom of the day (124 pounds or not), what he started he was expected to finish. Of the 37 starts, he went the distance in all but one of them. There were no relief specialists in 1887!

A "Boy Wonder"

The press of the day was high on Kid Madden. The *Evening Express*, in their edition of May 20th, reflected that "Madden is pitching intelligently," then went on to add that "A good season's work may be expected of him." Later that same month, after the Kid had bested league-leading Detroit, the paper wrote "Young Madden acted like a veteran and fooled the heavy hitters of the league completely, doing magnificent work when the bases were occupied." A nifty seven-hit shutout of the Philadelphia Athletics on June 2nd earned more *Express* accolades: "Madden, by his fine work in the box strengthened the statement that he is a 'boy wonder.' " No less an authority than *The New York Times* was also impressed. After the Pride of Portland threw a two-hit shutout over the New York Giants on September 8th, the *Times*' sportswriter commented: "The old saying that the

circa 1888 photograph

MICHAEL "KID" MADDEN

Born October 22, 1866, Portland, Maine　　Died March 16, 1896, Portland, Maine

Threw left-handed　　5′7″; 124 lbs.

MAJOR LEAGUE PITCHING RECORD

Year	Team	W	L	PCT	ERA	G	GS	CG	IP	H	BB	SO	ShO	Relief Pitching W	L	PCT	SV	ERA
1887	BOS N	22	14	.611	3.79	37	37	36	321	317	122	81	3	0	0	—	0	—
1888		7	11	.389	2.95	20	18	17	165	142	24	53	1	0	0	—	0	4.22
1889		10	10	.500	4.40	22	19	18	178	194	71	64	1	1	0	1.000	1	2.81
1890	BOS P	4	2	.667	4.79	10	7	5	62	85	25	24	1	1	0	1.000	0	6.43
1891	2 teams	**BOS AA** (1G 0-1)			**BAL AA** (32G 13-12)													
1891	total	13	13	.500	4.19	33	28	21	232	249	94	62	1	1	0	1.000	1	4.09
5 years		56	50	.524	3.92	122	109	97	958	987	336	284	7	3	0	1.000	2	4.31

Madden John, laborer, h. 173 Washington
Madden Michael, laborer, h. 78 Anderson
Madden Michael J., base ball player, bds. 19 Winthrop
Maddox Bradley B., cooper 276 Commercial, h. 4 Tate
Maddox Joseph H., machinist, h. 21 Brackett
Maddox Melvin, cooper 276 Commercial
Maddox Oliver C., carriage maker 60 Union, h. 13 Boyd

Occupation - "Base Ball Player"

Before the days of telephone directories there were city directories . . . in which was listed each occupant's occupation as well as his/her street address. Here's Kid Madden's listing in the PORTLAND DIRECTORY for 1887, the year he was a 20-game winner. "bds." meant "boards." Winthrop Street is on Munjoy Hill, just off Fox Street and below Washington Avenue. The Kid would later move to the Bramhall Hill/Western Promenade section of town; die there in 1896.

New Yorks cannot bat left-handed pitching was verified here to-day, when they failed to gauge the curves of young Madden, and received a 'whitewash' at the hands of the Boston Club." And a scant two days later, after the Kid had shut down the New Yorkers again, 5-2, the paper's column headline read: "The Giants Played Good Ball But They Could Not Bat Madden's Curves."

Sad to say, however, the "Boy Wonder" was to be a one-year wonder. Whether from physical or mental exhaustion or disfavor with management, Madden pitched far less frequently in 1888 than he had in 1887. The *Evening Express* made note of this in their edition of August 11th. "Madden sits on the bench day after day. It doesn't seem to bother him whether he plays or not," was their poignant reflection. The Kid, though, did start 18 games . . . and again finished all but one of them. His last start of the season, against Pittsburgh on October 11th, was far and away his best outing: he blanked the Steel City nine with but three hits. For the year his record was a disappointing 7-11. His earned run average did drop, though, to a most respectable 2.95. (But, then again, most every other pitcher's dropped, too. That's because in 1887 - for one year only - the batters had a tremendous advantage: it took four strikes before a hitter was out. In 1888 things reverted back to the norm . . . and pitchers could again breathe more easily.).

In 1889 Kid Madden won in double figures again. But he also lost in double figures again, too. His record was an even 10-10. He started 19 games and, as you might expect, finished all but one of them. A severe cold hampered much of his spring, perhaps portending the physical difficulties that were to come. Boston, now nicknamed the Beaneaters, made a run for the National League pennant that year. Led by the hitting of Big Dan Brouthers and King Kelly and the pitching of John Clarkson (who won 49 games!), the Bostonians finished a scant one game behind the frontrunning Giants. Had the Kid been up to his 1887 form there's no doubt that the Beaneaters would've taken the flag.

On to New Leagues

Madden jumped to the newly-organized Players League for the season of 1890. He didn't jump far, however: he played for the Boston entry in the league. Nor did he have a very successful year. Although his club - fueled by Brouthers and Kelly and

The 1889 Bostons finished second to the Giants in the race for the National League crown. Shown here are, left to right in the back row, Tom Brown, Pop Smith, Dan Brouthers (who led the league with a .373 batting average), and Charlie Ganzel; middle row, left to right, John Clarkson (who was 49-19 with a league-leading 2.73 ERA), manager James A. Hart, and Mike "King" Kelly; bottom row, left to right, Bill Daley and Munjoy Hill's very own Michael "Kid" Madden.

Uncle Robbie

Kid Madden's batterymate with Baltimore in the American Association in 1891 was none other than Wilbert Robinson. Later to gain considerable fame as the long-time manager of Brooklyn - heck, the club was even called the Robins from 1914 to 1931 - "Uncle Robbie" was a pretty fair catcher in his playing days, and not a bad hitter, either. In one game in 1892, as a matter of fact, Robbie drove in 11 runs . . . a record that stood thirty-two seasons until bettered by the Card's Jim Bottomly in September of 1924 (in a game, incidentally, at Ebbets Field against the Robins . . . managed, of course, by Uncle Robbie.).

1898 photograph

much of the other talent who also made the move from the Beaneaters - took the pennant by a wide margin, the Kid had a mediocre season. He started but seven games, finished with a 4-2 record.

In 1891, with the Players League's one year existence now history, Kid Madden ended up in his third league in three years. He joined the American Association, again playing for the Boston team, nicknamed the Reds. It was to be his last year in the big leagues. After pitching but one game for the Reds (which he lost), Madden was rumored to be on his way to the league's Columbus, Ohio team. The Columbus team's management, however, came up $200.00 short in its offer. Madden refused. Instead he found himself, by early May, with Baltimore's American Association team (known, as seemingly has been the case with just about every team that's ever represented "The Monumental City," as the Orioles). There he pitched well enough, winning 13 while losing 12. His batterymate for many of those games, incidentally, was none other than Wilbert Robinson, later to gain everlasting fame as manager of the Brooklyn Dodgers' "Daffyness Boys."

His major league days behind him, Michael "Kid" Madden played for various minor league teams - Indianapolis and back home in Portland in 1892; Portland in 1893; Haverhill in 1894 - until ill health forced him to call it a career. He died of consumption - which WEBSTER'S defines as "a progressive wasting away of the body esp. from pulmonary tuberculosis" - on March 16, 1896 at his home at 48 Brackett Street in Portland. *The Portland Daily Advertiser* reported that he was "aged bout 28 years." He was 29.

Right-Handed Pitcher — Robert William "Stanley Steamer" Stanley

The winningest pitcher to ever come out of Maine did not, alas, reside in his native state for very long. The Steamer was two when his family packed up and moved from East Kidder Street in Portland to Kearny, New Jersey. Kearny was where Stanley's mother was from. And it's where job prospects appeared brighter for Stanley's father. Stanley, in later years, would label the move "break number one" in the series of events that landed him on the hill for the Red Sox. As he stated in a 1977 Quincy (Massachusetts) *Patriot-Ledger* interview: "You can play more baseball in New Jersey than Maine, so I got more opportunity to develop." Break number two was being left back a year in the second grade. As Bob relays it: "By the time I got to high school, we had such a fine pitching staff that I couldn't break into it." Bob had to play the infield and outfield for his first three years. In his senior year, however, things changed: "If I hadn't been held back, I would have graduated with all those fine pitchers and wouldn't have gotten the opportunity to pitch as a senior." But Bob did get the opportunity, and he responded with a masterful 10-1 record.

On the strength of his senior year's performance, Stanley was offered a contract by the Los Angeles Dodgers in the summer of 1973. But the Dodgers' offer fell short of what Bob had in mind. He turned it down. Six months later, in January of 1974, Bob was offered a contract by the Sox. This time he accepted.

Bob's first assignment was with Elmira in the New York-Penn League in the summer of 1974. His record was hardly earth-shattering. He was 6-6 with a 4.60 ERA. The next season saw Bob with Winter Haven in the Florida State League. At first glance his record there appears a disaster: he lost 17 games while winning but five. But the won-lost (mostly lost!) mark is deceiving. Winter Haven hitters couldn't hit. "I was 0-6 before that team even got a run for me," Stanley recounts. Bob's ERA was what did impress. It was 2.93 and it was obvious to anyone who actually saw him pitch that Stanley's sinking fastball was a pitch to be reckoned with. It caused batters to hit the ball on the ground, easy pickings for a team with a good defensive infield.

Next stop in Bob's professional career was Bristol, Connecticut in the class AA Eastern League in 1976. There he really strutted his stuff: he was 15-9 in 27 games - all as a starter - and had a spiffy 2.66 ERA.

Between class AA and the majors there's traditionally a year or so of seasoning at the Triple A level. With the Red Sox that means Pawtucket. Bob, however, went directly to Boston. His work during the spring training of 1977 was so outstanding that Sox skipper Don Zimmer decided to carry a ten-man pitching staff back to Fenway instead of his planned nine. Bob was number ten.

In his first year in a Red Sox uniform Stanley set the pattern that would forever make him such an asset to the team. He was, as the *Kansas City Star* would later crown him, the league's MVP - Most Versatile Pitcher. He was a starter. He was a long reliever. He was a short reliever. And he did it all well. His 1977 numbers include 13 starts, 28 relief appearances, and an 8-7 record.

It was in 1978 - the year of the ill-fated Bucky Dent playoff homer - that Bob

Stanley really came into his own. Appearing in 52 games, all but three in relief, he posted a sterling 15-2 mark. He was second in the league in won-lost percentage (his .882 was bettered only by Ron Guidry's remarkable 25-3/.893) and tops in relief appearance wins (with an even dozen). Toss in ten saves and just five home runs allowed in 141⅔ innings and you have one mighty fine season.

The next year, 1979, saw Bob go almost full tilt. His relief appearances dropped to ten, but his starts numbered a career-high 30. He also won a career-high 16 games, four of them - just one behind league leaders Nolan Ryan, Mike Flanagan, and Dennis Leonard - coming via shutouts. He was selected for the American League All-Star team and hurled two innings of scoreless ball against the star-studded Senior Circuit lineup.

Bob had an identical 10-8 record the next two seasons, 1980 and 1981. They came via very different routes, though: in 1980, he split his time between starting assignments (17) and the bullpen (33 appearances), while in 1981 he was used almost exclusively in relief, making but one start.

In 1982, Bob enjoyed another banner season. He set an American League record for most innings pitched by a relief pitcher (168⅓), notched a 12-7 record, and also recorded 14 saves.

In 1983, Bob's 33 saves ranked him behind only Dan Quisenberry of Kansas City (who had 45). It was a Sox single season record until broken by Jeff Reardon in 1991. As Sox manager Ralph Houk noted in a *USA Today* interview: "I can't recall ever managing anybody I could use either long or short as much as I use him." Bob did, though, post his first major league losing season. More would follow. In fact, he would not see a winning season again until 1988. Fenway fans started to get on Bob along the way. His spare tire made him an easy target. So did his $1 million salary. And a less-than-fully impressive performance against the Mets in the 1986 World Series didn't help either. As Bob joked to his teammates at one point: "Maybe I should change to Lou Stanley." That way, he reasoned, when the fans began to boo he could just say they were calling his name . . . Lou.

In 1987 the bottom really fell out. Bob was 4-15, with a dismal 5.01 ERA. To his credit, though, the "Stanley Steamer" hung in there. As he reflected on more than one occasion, when asked about the catcall treatment he received at Fenway: "I love the Boston fans and I understand them."

Two more seasons of "understanding," though, were enough. In September of 1989 - after a number of run-ins with Joe Morgan - the Steamer packed it in.

Today, Bob Stanley lives with his wife Joan and their three children in Wenham, Massachusetts, about 25 miles northeast of Fenway Park. He owns a landscaping company. Bob's also recently begun to play a little semi-pro ball. His fondest times, however, are very definitely family times. He's especially thankful for his son's recent victory over cancer, and a goodly share of Bob's time is spent participating in golf tournaments to benefit the Jimmy Fund.

The man who went from Portland to Boston - via Kearny, New Jersey - may be forever remembered as the pitcher who allowed the run that tied the sixth game of the 1986 Series. He might better be remembered as the man who's pitched in more Red Sox games - 637 - than any other player in the club's 91-year history. That's something really worth remembering!

circa 1980 photograph

BOB STANLEY

Born November 10, 1954, Portland, Maine   Resides in Wenham, Massachusetts

Batted and threw right-handed   6′4″; 210 lbs.

MAJOR LEAGUE RECORD

Year Team	W	L	PCT	ERA	G	GS	CG	IP	H	BB	SO	ShO	Relief Pitching W	Relief Pitching L	Relief Pitching SVT	Batting AV	Batting H	Batting HR	BA	PO	A	E	DP	TC/G	FA
1977 BOS A	8	7	.533	3.99	41	13	3	151	176	43	44	1	3	2	3	0	0	0	-	6	43	2	6	1.2	.961
1978	15	2	.882	2.60	52	3	0	141.2	142	34	38	0	13	2	10	0	0	0	-	10	34	1	2	0.9	.978
1979	16	12	.571	3.98	40	30	9	217	250	44	56	4	3	1	1	0	0	0	-	19	43	3	2	1.6	.954
1980	10	8	.556	3.39	52	17	5	175	186	52	71	1	4	2	14	0	0	0	-	9	42	2	8	1.0	.962
1981	10	8	.556	3.82	35	1	0	99	110	38	28	0	10	7	0	0	0	0	-	10	29	2	6	1.2	.951
1982	12	7	.632	3.10	48	0	0	168.1	161	50	83	0	12	7	14	0	0	0	-	13	43	2	4	1.2	.966
1983	8	10	.444	2.85	64	0	0	145.1	145	38	65	0	8	10	33	0	0	0	-	9	18	3	3	0.5	.900
1984	9	10	.474	3.54	57	0	0	106.2	113	23	52	0	9	10	22	0	0	0	-	7	28	2	0	0.6	.946
1985	6	6	.500	2.87	48	0	0	87.2	76	30	46	0	6	6	10	0	0	0	-	8	12	1	1	0.4	.952
1986	6	6	.500	4.37	66	1	0	82.1	109	22	54	0	6	5	16	0	0	0	-	6	14	2	0	0.3	.909
1987	4	15	.211	5.01	34	20	4	152.2	198	42	67	1	0	3	0	0	0	0	-	15	22	1	4	1.1	.974
1988	6	4	.600	3.19	57	0	0	101.2	90	29	57	0	6	4	5	0	0	0	-	7	12	2	2	0.4	.905
1989	5	2	.714	4.88	43	0	0	79.1	102	26	32	0	5	2	4	0	0	0	-	3	17	1	0	0.5	.952
13 yrs.	115	97	.542	3.64	637	85	21	1707.2	1858	471	693	7	85	61	132	0	0	0	-	122	357	24	38	0.8	.952

LEAGUE CHAMPIONSHIP SERIES RECORD

Year Team	W	L	PCT	ERA	G	GS	CG	IP	H	BB	SO	ShO	Relief Pitching W	Relief Pitching L	Relief Pitching SVT	Batting AV	Batting H	Batting HR	BA	PO	A	E	DP	TC/G	FA
1986 BOS A	0	0	-	4.65	3	0	0	5.2	7	3	1	0	0	0	0	0	0	0	-	0	1	0	0	0.3	1.000
1988	0	0	-	9.00	2	0	0	1	2	1	0	0	0	0	0	0	0	0	-	0	0	0	0	0.0	-
2 yrs.	0	0	-	5.40	5	0	0	6.2	9	4	1	0	0	0	0	0	0	0	-	0	1	0	0	0.2	1.000

WORLD SERIES RECORD

Year Team	W	L	PCT	ERA	G	GS	CG	IP	H	BB	SO	ShO	Relief Pitching W	Relief Pitching L	Relief Pitching SVT	Batting AV	Batting H	Batting HR	BA	PO	A	E	DP	TC/G	FA
1986 BOS A	0	0	-	0.00	5	0	0	6.1	5	1	4	0	0	0	1	1	0	0	.000	1	2	0	0	0.6	1.000

Mother Knows

A young - and thin - Bob Stanley pitches one in, circa 1978. Although the Steamer moved from Maine at the tender age of two, he did come back to his native state to visit most every summer. His dad's family all lived here and, as relayed to me by Bob: "I spent almost every summer of my growing years living with relatives and friends. My father and I would make a trip to Maine at the beginning of every summer. My mother knew to pack enough clothing because I always wanted to stay and lobster with my Uncle Jimmy."

Right-Handed Pitcher — Carlton Francis Willey

Our second Dream Team right-handed moundsman is a Down Easter all the way. Carlton Willey was born and raised in Cherryfield. He still lives there today.

"We played baseball every chance we could get - every day in the summertime - when we could get enough to play," Carlton told me when I visited him in his Cherryfield home in early April of 1991. He was talking about his youth, in the 1930s and 1940s, but I have a strong suspicion that he'd join in a game today given any sort of an opportunity. At age 59 he yet maintains the tall, lean look of a man who can play ball.

In his early playing days, in the makeshift fields ("We'd use rocks for bases.") around Cherryfield and for Cherryfield Academy, Carlton was both an outfielder and a pitcher. Heck, with only thirteen kids - seven girls and six boys - in his entire Academy graduating class he most likely could have played half the infield and done a little catching, too, if he'd been so inspired!

Upon his graduation from Cherryfield Academy his dad asked Carlton what he planned to do with his future. "You know, Carlton, you can't play baseball for a living," were his father's words of advice. Carlton still chuckles at that.

It was the Braves who gave Carlton his shot to do just that...play baseball for a living. They were the Boston Braves then and they had four teams in Maine stocked with prospects. The four represented Augusta, Bangor, Portland, and Waterville. Carlton, after a tryout at a Braves' camp in Brewer in the spring of 1950, was placed on the Bangor club. The four teams would play each other all summer long and then, at season's end, the Braves would invite three top prospects down to Boston for a full tryout. Carlton was one of the three. At Braves Field his fastball - later to be clocked at 93 mph - and his keen sense of competition so impressed the Braves' braintrust that they signed him to a contract.

First stop was with Quebec in the old Provincial League in 1951. There Carlton was 15-5 and led the circuit in both earned run average (1.95) and won-lost percentage (.750). In 1952 he moved up to Atlanta, then in the Southern Association, where he was 10-6.

Uncle Sam Calls

Stop number three, however, was the Army. Called into the service in 1953, Carlton spent two years in Germany. But those two years set his career back four years. As Carlton explained it: "After I got out (of the service), it took me two years to get back (in the groove). Honest to God, I couldn't do anything right. I'd pitched while in the military but I didn't stay in shape. I didn't run like I should have. And I didn't exercise. When I got out I weighed 198 pounds, the most I ever weighed in my life. I wasn't long losing the weight, but I was wild. I couldn't get the ball over the plate."

Carlton's record the first two seasons he returned to organized baseball certainly bespoke his problems. With Toledo in 1955 he was 8-10; with Wichita in 1956 he was worse, ending with a 5-10 mark. In 1957, however, things began to click again. Really click. Carlton's rhythm returned. So did his winning ways. Still with Wichita, he tore up the American Association, leading the loop in innings pitched (247), games won (21), and won-lost percentage (he was 21-6, which works out to .778). He also struck out 174, while walking only 94. To top it all off, he was selected the Association's Most Valuable Player.

Coming off his marvelous 1957 season with his parent club's top farm team should have guaranteed Carlton star-of-the-future treatment at the Braves' 1958 spring training site. It didn't. The problem was that the Braves - who'd moved to Milwaukee after the 1952 season and who had prospered immeasurably in the ensuing years - already possessed a fine pitching staff. With Warren Spahn, Lew Burdette, and Bob Buhl they'd swept the National League in 1957 and then went on to humble the mighty Yankees in the World Series, too.

The Braves kept Carlton on their roster as they moved north to Milwaukee that spring of '58. After letting him sit idle the first month of the season, though, they farmed him back to Wichita. Frustrated to say the least, Carlton nonetheless resolved to make it back to Milwaukee to stay. It took a no hitter - against Louisville on May 22nd - to get the Braves to recall him. But they did. And this time Carlton did stay.

Leads League in Shutouts

It took another month of inactivity before Carlton got his first start in the bigs...but when he did start he certainly made the most of it. On June 23rd he checked the hard-hitting Giants, 8-0, on a six-hitter. It was an historic game in another way as well: one of the Giants' six hits - all of which were singles - was Willie Mays' 1,000th major league hit.

Ironically, Carlton's second shutout came against Mays, Cepeda and company, too. Before a jubilant crowd of 34,770 at County Stadium on August 2nd, Carlton again blanked the Jints, this time in a 10-0 rout. He gave up but four hits. The Associated Press described Carlton's performance as "sparkling," further noting that the lanky rookie from Maine "mowed down the Giants with machine-gun regularity."

Carlton would notch two more goose-egg games before the season was out, giving him a total of four. Now four shutouts may not sound like a whole lot, but in 1958 it was more than teammates Spahn (who had 2) or Burdette (3). It was more than Robin Roberts (1). And it was more than 22-game winner Bob Friend (1). In fact, it was more than anyone else in the league. Carlton Willey - as a rookie who was with Milwaukee only part of the season - led the National League in shutouts in 1958!

After his impressive season of 1958 (for more on Carlton's first year, a year highlighted by a masterful one-inning relief stint against the Yankees in the World Series, please see pages 58-63), Carlton never really blossomed with the Braves the way it was hoped he would. The reason was basic: with a strong and experienced staff in place, a newcomer just doesn't get the chance to work on a regular basis. Timing slips. That's what happened with Carlton. After his first season, he was used infrequently for the next four. In what should have been his prime, he'd get an occasional start. Mostly he sat. Finally, after the 1962 season - in which he started but six games - the generally reserved Willey demanded to be traded.

He got his wish. On March 23, 1963 he was sold to the Mets. For Casey Stengel's crew, in their second year in the league in 1963, Carlton saw work. He started 28 games, led the staff with an ERA of 3.10, and struck out 101 batters. The last number has special significance: with the Mets as hapless as they were in 1963

circa 1964 photograph

CARLTON WILLEY

Born June 6, 1931, Cherryfield, Maine Resides in Cherryfield, Maine

Batted and threw right-handed 6′; 175 lbs.

MAJOR LEAGUE RECORD

Year	Team	W	L	PCT	ERA	G	GS	CG	IP	H	BB	SO	ShO	Relief Pitching W	Relief Pitching L	Relief Pitching SV	Batting AB	Batting H	Batting HR	BA
1958	MIL N	9	7	.563	2.70	23	19	9	140	110	53	74	4	0	1	0	48	5	0	.104
1959		5	9	.357	4.15	26	15	5	117	126	31	51	2	0	2	0	39	4	0	.103
1960		6	7	.462	4.35	28	21	2	144.2	136	65	109	1	1	0	0	48	7	1	.146
1961		6	12	.333	3.83	35	22	4	159.2	147	65	91	0	2	1	0	54	1	0	.019
1962		2	5	.286	5.40	30	6	0	73.1	95	20	40	0	2	2	1	11	3	0	.273
1963	NY N	9	14	.391	3.10	30	28	7	183	149	69	101	4	0	0	0	54	6	1	.111
1964		0	2	.000	3.60	14	3	0	30	37	8	14	0	0	0	0	4	0	0	.000
1965		1	2	.333	4.18	13	3	1	28	30	15	13	0	0	0	0	5	0	0	.000
8 yrs.		38	58	.396	3.76	199	117	28	875.2	830	326	493	11	5	6	1	263	26	2	.099

WORLD SERIES RECORD

Year	Team	W	L	PCT	ERA	G	GS	CG	IP	H	BB	SO	ShO	Relief Pitching W	Relief Pitching L	Relief Pitching SV	Batting AB	Batting H	Batting HR	BA
1958	MIL N	0	0	-	0.00	1	0	0	1	0	0	2	0	0	0	0	0	0	0	-

With the Bat, Too

Carlton, a lifetime .099 major league hitter, could occasionally swing a mean stick. Here he is - with batterymate Jesse Gonder, who went 4 for 5 - after clouting a grand-slam home run as part of the Mets' 14-5 rout of Houston, July 15, 1963.

(please see pages 62-63), if you didn't fan a hitter you were likely to be in trouble. To say that the Mets' defense was porous was to be charitable. As teammate Jim Hickman would later reflect: "Heck, Carlton threw better than half the pitchers in the league back then. But we were a bad team, too. And it's tough to throw knowing you can never make a mistake."

Many expected, in 1964, that Carlton would be the stopper that the Mets so desperately needed. The chances are excellent that he would have been, too. He hadn't allowed an earned run all during spring training when, unfortunately, tragedy struck: pitching against the Tigers in an exhibition game the afternoon of April 3rd, Carlton was walloped in the jaw by a vicious line drive off the bat of Gates Brown. Jim Hickman again: "The whole thing was a shame, because it was time for Carlton to blossom, and that finished his career. Nobody realized Carl was hurt that bad because he never showed the pain. He just stood there dazed after the ball hit him."

Carlton's jaw was broken. Oh, he recovered. But he'd lost weight: a wired jaw is not conducive to hearty eating. Next he hurt his arm a couple of times. The first time it was tendonitis. Then it was a torn muscle in his forearm. Carlton still winces when he talks about the pain he went through that season, a season in which he pitched but 30 total innings. After yet another disappointing season in 1965, Carlton decided it was time to pack it in. He scouted for the Phillies for the better part of a decade, first in the Midwest and then throughout New England. But the solitude and constant travel got to him. He came back to Cherryfield.

In recent years, Carlton has worked for the state as a probation/parole officer, been manager of a wild blueberry freezing plant for Jasper Wyman & Son, and raised Christmas trees. Now he's doing a little painting and a little light hauling. Plus he spends as much time as possible with his son Richie and his daughter Jill. When I asked him why - after the bright lights of Milwaukee and New York - he returned to Cherryfield, Carlton paused a second and then replied: "This is home, I guess. It's hard to get away from." It's a good answer.

Left-Handed Pitcher — Irving Melrose "Cy the Second"/"Young Cy" Young

There are great similarities between Michael "Kid" Madden and Maine's second stellar southpaw, Irv "Cy the Second" Young:

a - First of all, of course, both were left-handed.

b - Both were 20-game winners in their rookie year.

c - Both never won 20 again.

d - Both hurled for the Boston team in the National League.

e - Both hurled "long ago."

f - Both have ceased to be household words in Maine - or any other place - if they ever were.

Irving Melrose "Cy the Second"/"Young Cy" Young was born and raised in Columbia Falls, sixteen miles west of Machias. At age seventeen, Irv and his family moved to Concord, New Hampshire so that he could find employment as a fireman on the Boston & Maine Railroad. Although working sixty hours a week on the railroad, Irv managed to find time to pitch for the YMCA and other local amateur clubs on weekends. In 1904, at the rather advanced age of 27, he turned pro, joining Concord in the New England League. There he won 18 games and caught the eye of scout Billy Hamilton. Hamilton strongly recommended him to the Boston Beaneaters (later the Braves)... who bought his contract for $500.

So, at age 28 in 1905, Irv Young had his shot at the major leagues. He made the most of it. He led the league in three categories: most innings pitched (378*); most games started (42); most complete games (41*). He was also second in the league in shutouts with 7* (only the immortal Christy Mathewson, with 8, had more) and fifth in strikeouts. His earned run average was 2.90, respectable in any league. And he won 20 games. Yet, alas, he lost 21. But let's discount that. Irv Young, in playing for the 1905 Beaneaters, was playing for one of the more inept teams in baseball's long history. Let's concentrate - and celebrate - on the fact that he won 20 games. As a rookie.

Irv Young's banner season started well. He appeared in relief, pitching the final four innings of the Beaneaters' April 14th opening day game before a crowd of 40,000 at the Polo Grounds. And he pitched effectively, holding the World Champion McGrawmen to but 4 hits and 2 runs. He also knocked in Boston's only run in the 8th inning. Four days later he started the club's home opener, gaining his first major league win in a 4-2 performance over Brooklyn. Per *The New York Times*, the man whose nicknames would compare him to the legendary Cy Young "made an excellent impression, striking out six men and keeping the Brooklyn hits well scattered." On the 28th, Irv pitched the first of his seven shutouts of the year, holding the Phillies to 3 hits in a 2-0 Boston win. "Inability to hit Young's delivery was responsible for

*All these years later, Irv's 1905 total of 378 innings pitched and 41 complete games are still major league records for a rookie in this century. Needless to say, in this day and age of almost incessant relief pitching, they are records that will most likely last forever. And that's a long, long time. Irv's total of seven shutouts was also a long-standing rookie high: it stood for sixty-three years as the National League mark until tied by Jerry Koosman in 1968 and eventually broken by Fernando Valenzuela in 1981.

the home team's defeat today by Boston" was the rather quaint way *The Bangor Daily News* explained the game's outcome. On May 6th, Irv bested Christy Mathewson in a 2-1 cliffhanger. The Giants managed but 7 hits off the Boston southpaw. Irv picked up his second shutout on May 11th, scattering ten Chicago hits in a 5-0 match. South Bridgton native Virgin "Rip" Cannell - who was to play all 154 games in the outfield for the Beaneaters that year - got the game's only extra base hit, a double.

Other highlights in Cy the Second's steady march toward becoming Maine's only 20-game winner this century include:

May 15th - Beats Reds, 2-1, on a nine-hitter

May 23rd - Tosses a five-hit shutout over the Pirates, 1-0

May 27th - Tosses another shutout in three-hitting the Phillies, 3-0

June 3rd - Hurls yet another shutout - again a three-hitter - against John McGraw's World Champion Giants, 2-0. Writes *The New York Times,* "Young 'Cy' Young gave the champion New Yorks a sample of his pitching powers in the first game of a double header in this city to-day by allowing them only three hits during the entire nine innings."

June 24th - Loses a heartbreaker, 2-1, to the Giants in 12 innings. Again *The Times:* "Young, one of the sensational pitchers of the year, who had worsted the champions on the Polo Grounds this season, and who subsequently shut them out at Boston, proved just as effective as upon the other occasions, only two hits being made off his delivery up to the ninth inning."

July 10th - Defeats the Phillies, 3-2, in 10 innings

July 13th - Five-hits the Reds in a 6-1 Boston win

July 24th - Tosses four-hitter vs. Pittsburgh in an 8-1 win

August 21st - Allows five hits and strikes out seven in downing St. Louis, 1-0

September 1st - Tops Brooklyn, 4-2, on an eight-hitter

September 7th - Again shuts out the Giants, allowing but four hits. Highlight of the game is a catch in centerfield by Rip Cannell in the sixth inning. *The Times* terms it "astonishing."

September 13th - Six-hits the Phils in a 3-2 win (while also getting two hits and scoring a run)

September 20th - Defeats Brooklyn, 6-5, with a bases-loaded triple by fellow Mainer Rip Cannell the big blow

What's amazing is the number of games Irv Young could have - and probably should have - won in 1905. If he had come away victorious in all the games he lost by one run - mostly all by scores of 2-1 or 3-2 - he could well have been a 30-game winner. Wouldn't that have put Columbia Falls on the map!

The truth is that the Beaneaters were terrible. They won but 51 games the entire season (while dropping slightly more than twice that many, 103). Young Cy's 20 wins, therefore, constituted virtually 40% of the team's victories. With any kind of run production behind him - the team's anemic .234 batting average was the lowest in the league - Young would have easily had another eight or ten games in the win column. Ironically, Young Cy's namesake - the winningest pitcher in baseball history and the man for whom the Cy Young award is named - had a very similar season. Pitching for Boston's American League entry (then called the Puritans; now, of course, the Red Sox), he also lost one game more than he won. His record for the year was 18-19.

"Such a Deal Will Not Be Thought of"

In late September the Pirates offered to buy Irv Young for the then hefty price of $7,500. But Boston management would have none of it. *The Bangor Daily News,* in

circa 1905 photograph

IRV YOUNG

Born July 21, 1877, Columbia Falls, Maine — Died January 14, 1935, South Brewer, Maine

Batted and threw left-handed — 5′10″; 185 lbs.

MAJOR LEAGUE RECORD

Year	Team	W	L	PCT	ERA	G	GS	CG	IP	H	BB	SO	ShO	Relief Pitching W	Relief Pitching L	Relief Pitching PCT	SV	ERA
1905	BOS N	20	21	.488	2.90	43	42	41	378	337	71	156	7	0	0	-	0	4.50
1906		16	25	.390	2.91	43	41	37	358.1	349	83	151	4	0	1	.000	0	5.40
1907		10	23	.303	3.96	40	32	22	245.1	287	58	86	3	2	1	.667	1	2.55
1908	2 teams	**BOS N** (16G 4-8)			**PIT N** (16G 4-3)													
1908	total	8	11	.421	2.42	32	18	10	174.2	167	40	63	2	1	2	.333	1	3.32
1910	CHI A	4	8	.333	2.72	27	17	7	135.2	122	39	64	4	0	0	.000	0	3.00
1911		5	6	.455	4.37	24	11	3	92.2	99	25	40	2	2	0	1.000	2	3.66
6 years		63	94	.401	3.11	209	161	120	1384.2	1361	316	560	21	5	4	.556	4	3.31

A Pair of Immortals

In his short stint with the Pirates in late 1908, Irv Young played alongside a pair of the game's immortals, Honus Wagner and Fred Clarke, both shown here via the wonderful baseball card art of the day. Wagner would lead the National League in batting eight times, including 1908 when he rapped out a .354 average. Clarke would bat better than .300 eleven times, even topping the .400 plateau once. Both are enshrined in the Hall of Fame.

an article of September 29th, put the area's many Beaneater fans at ease. The paper reported Boston management as emphatically stating that "Such a deal will not be thought of." Irv was just too valuable to the team.

That the offer was not accepted, however, was most unfortunate for Cy the Second. With the Pirates he would have been with a winner. With Boston he was destined to forever pitch for a loser. In 1906 the Beaneaters were even more futile. Their batting average dropped to .226; their won-lost record to 49-102; their starting catcher batted .189; their secondbaseman hit .202; and reserve outfielder Gene Good - a sometimes actor/sometimes ballplayer who weighed in at 126 pounds - stroked a lowly .151. The team made 11 errors in one game in June. They were the doormat of the league . . . and almost nothing Irv Young did was going to change that.

In that second season in the bigs, 1906, Irv again led the National League in innings pitched (358), games started (41), and complete games (37). He was sixth in the league in strikeouts and his earned run average remained virtually unchanged at 2.91. Yet with the club worse than ever - they lost nineteen games in a row during one especially dismal stretch in May and June - our man from Down East saw his record drop to 16-25. He was one of four 20-game losers on the team! Nevertheless, John McGraw - recognizing talent when he saw it - offered $10,000 for the south-paw . . . only to also be turned down. Boston management clearly liked Irv Young. So did his teammates: when he got married in September they bought a brass bed for the new bride and groom.

Before the start of the 1907 season, the futile club's ownership changed hands. The new owners were a Pittsburgh theatrical man named John Harris and two brothers, George and John Dovey, from Kentucky. The Doveys ran the team and, in their honor, the club's nickname was changed to the Doves. It was an appropriate appellation: on the field the ballclub was almost invariably the personification of peace. They finished seventh, 47 games behind the front-running Cubs. Worse, the toll of constantly losing was having its effect on Cy the Second. His earned run average jumped to 3.96; his won-lost record fell to a most disheartening 10-23.

Irv started 1908, his last year in the National League, with the Doves. He was 4-8 for them when, on June 18th, he was traded to the Pirates for two other pitchers, Tom McCarthy and Harley Young (who, ironically, was nicknamed Cy the Third). Appearing in sixteen games for the Bucs, Young Cy was 4-3. For the entire season, then, he was 8-11 with his lowest-ever ERA, 2.42. It was not good enough. In 1909 the southpaw found himself with Minneapolis in the American Association. There he pitched well enough to earn one last shot in the bigs. Charlie Comiskey, owner of the White Sox, picked up his contract for 1910. For the Sox, Irv pitched effectively, sporting a 2.72 ERA. Again, however, he was with a weak club (although it shouldn't have been: please see page 24). The White Sox won 68, lost 85, finished sixth. Young Cy was 4-8. It is worthy of note that all four victories were shutouts.

The year 1911 was Irv Young's last in the major leagues. His record was 5-6, but his ERA leaped to a career high of 4.37. With a week left to go in the season, the Sox released him back to Minneapolis. He remained in the American Association, pitching for both Minneapolis and later Milwaukee, through mid-1916. He later played and coached in the Southern League. Later still, while living in Orrington, Maine, he played a bit and coached there, too.

Irv Young as he appeared with the White Sox, circa 1910. Poor Irv was forever with bad clubs: in the two years he toiled for the Chisox the best that can be said is that their won-lost record approached .500.

Irv "Cy the Second"/"Young Cy" Young passed away unexpectedly at the home of a nephew in South Brewer on January 14, 1935. A rather small death notice appeared toward the back of *The Bangor Daily News* two days later. One can only suspect that if Irv Young had toiled for the Giants or the Cubs or the Pirates - the powerhouse, run-scoring teams of his National League heyday - rather than the lowly Beaneaters/Doves, his passing would have instead been front page stuff.

Utility/Pinch Runner — William Alphonse "Billy" Maloney

Ballplayers of Irish descent - Hugh Duffy, Wee Willie Keeler, Big Ed Delahanty, John McGraw et al. - played a major factor in our National Pastime's surge to ever-greater popularity in the 1880s and the 1890s and the first decade of this century. According to a 1989 article in *The Irish Echo*, fully one third to one half of all major leaguers in the 1890s were of Irish ancestry. Joining those ranks in 1901 was William Alphonse Maloney. Born in Lewiston in 1878, Billy Maloney was one of the earliest "college boys" to play in the bigs. Old-time fans are likely to recall Jack Coombs (Colby), Eddie Collins (Columbia), Christy Mathewson (Bucknell), and Eddie Plank (Gettysburg) as examples of early players who went directly from college into a major league uniform. Billy Maloney had them all beat. Upon graduation from Georgetown College (now Georgetown University), he joined the American League Milwaukee team in 1901. There he batted .293 in 86 games. Surprisingly - considering what a speedster he was to become in the outfield and on the basepaths - he played 72 of those games as the team's catcher. When the Milwaukee franchise was transferred to St. Louis for the 1902 season, Billy was transferred right along with it. In St. Louis, after a weak start (he was batting .205 after 30 games), he was dealt to Cincinnati in the National League. There, playing mostly outfield, he batted a somewhat more robust .247 in 27 games.

High batting averages were not Billy's forte. Slick fielding and, especially, base stealing were where he earned his highest marks. It appeared for a while though, as if he would not get another chance to showcase them. Following his rather unsatisfying 1902 season, he was sent down to Kansas City in the Western League (1903) and then Minneapolis in the American Association (1904). His work at Minneapolis impressed Cub manager Frank Selee, however, and Billy returned to the majors - and a starting outfield berth - with the Cubbies in 1905. It would be his best year.

On Opening Day, April 14th, Billy held down right field and batted second. He had no hits but, in a hint of what was to come, he walked, stole a base, and scored a run. In May he was moved to the third slot in the Cubs' order, where he remained most of the season. He alternated between right and center, and started to loosen up . . . and to steal a base almost every game. May 21st was an especial highlight. Batting clean-up, Billy socked a three-run homer over the head of leftfielder Jimmy Sheckard (the man for whom he would be traded ten months later) in the first inning, propelling the Cubs on their way to an especially appropriate (see box) 11-2 romp over Brooklyn.

It was in June, however, that Billy really got going. He began stealing two, sometimes three, bases in many a game. In a four-game series with the Boston Bean-eaters on June 7th through the 10th he had himself an especially good time. In the first game he had two hits, stole two bases and scored three runs. In the third game he had one hit, stole three bases, and scored two runs. In the fourth and concluding encounter he had three hits, stole two bases, and scored one run. Two weeks later Billy again distinguished himself by scoring one run and driving in the other in an 18-inning 2-1 Cub victory

circa 1905 sketch

BILLY MALONEY

Born June 5, 1878, Lewiston, Maine Died September 2, 1960, Breckenridge, Texas

Batted left-handed; threw right-handed 5′10″; 177 lbs.

MAJOR LEAGUE RECORD

Year	Team	G	AB	H	2B	3B	HR	HR %	R	RBI	BB	SO	SB	BA	SA	Pinch Hit AB	Pinch Hit H	G by POS
1901	MIL A	86	290	85	3	4	0	0.0	42	22	7		11	.293	.331	5	2	C-72, OF-8
1902	2 teams	**STL A** (30G — .205)				**CIN N** (27G — .247)												
1902	total	57	201	45	7	0	1	0.5	21	18	8		8	.224	.274	3	0	OF-41, C-14
1905	CHI N	145	558	145	17	14	2	0.4	78	56	43		59	.260	.351	0	0	OF-145
1906	BKN N	151	566	125	15	7	0	0.0	71	32	49		38	.221	.272	0	0	OF-151
1907		144	502	115	7	10	0	0.0	51	32	31		25	.229	.283	0	0	OF-144
1908		113	359	70	5	7	3	0.8	31	17	24		14	.195	.273	6	1	OF-103, C-4
6 years		696	2476	585	54	42	6	0.2	294	177	162		155	.236	.299	14	3	OF-592, C-90

Doctors and Lawyers and Such

This is Georgetown's 1898 varsity baseball aggregation. After their college playing days were behind them, most of the team's members went on to become doctors and lawyers and such. Two, however, went on to play ball in the bigs. One was Charlie Moran, middle row third from the right, who played briefly for the Senators and the Browns. The other, of course, was Billy, shown here forefront (i.e., seated on the ground), left.

over St. Louis. Meanwhile, that he was playing superb outfield was attested to by the numerous plaudits *The New York Times* included in their generally rather sparse game summaries. "Maloney made two difficult running catches at centre field" (game of May 13th); "Maloney, in the third inning, made an unusually brilliant catch of Mertes's high ball to right field with his left hand and on a full run" (game of May 16th); and "A one-handed catch by Maloney, depriving Titus of an almost sure home run, shut out the visitors" (game of June 21st), were among the sterling plays singled out for praise by *The Times*.

Scoring a Run on an Out at the Plate

Other plaudits and big games - especially in terms of stolen bases - would follow. But perhaps Billy's most interesting moment came on August 9th . . . when he was the key ingredient in a scenario that the press of the day thought had never before happened (and that certainly hasn't happened very often since!). It went this way: in the seventh inning of a game against the Giants, Cub pitcher Bob Wicker led off with a single. Jimmy Slagle drew a base on balls. Billy then beat out a bunt, loading the bases with nobody out. Frank Chance hit a fly to right. Wicker and Slagle stayed close to their respective bases, ready to tag up if the Giant right-fielder, Sammy Strang, caught the ball. But Billy was off at the crack of the bat. When Strang couldn't reach the ball, Wicker trotted home while Slagle and Billy M., with not more than a step between them, hotfooted it around third and into home. The throw came in, and catcher Roger Bresnahan tagged the slid-

"Tinker to Evers to Chance"

In his banner year of 1905 Billy Maloney played outfield behind the much-heralded "Tinker to Evers to Chance" infield. How good was the storied double play combination? Not really that good is the answer on which most baseball historians agree. The trio's fame is based more on an eight-line verse that newspaper columnist Franklin P. Adams hurriedly penned on a July day in 1910. Although he wrote for the *New York Mail* - and was therefore expected to be loyal to the New York teams - Adams was a native of Chicago and had great respect for the Cubs' infield. On his way to the Polo Grounds to view a Cubs-Giants contest, he dashed off the lines that would eventually, more than anything else, land the infield trio in the Hall of Fame:

These are the saddest of possible words—
"Tinker to Evers to Chance"
Trio of Bear Cubs and fleeter than birds—
"Tinker to Evers to Chance"
Ruthlessly pricking our gonfalon bubble,
Making a Giant hit into a double,*
Words that are weighty with nothing but trouble—
"Tinker to Evers to Chance."

***as in double play**

The verse caught on, has remained with us ever since. As some have suggested, perhaps Franklin P. Adams should've been elected to the Hall rather than Tinker or Evers or Chance.

Two-thirds of the now-immortalized double play combination: firstbaseman Frank Chance and secondbaseman Johnny Evers as portrayed on a 1911 Mecca Cigarettes' double-folder baseball card.

If Only Brooklyn Had a Better Ball Club

Preaching from the pulpit the evening of May 21, 1905, the Rev. Dr. Charles Edward Locke told his congregation at the Hanson Place Methodist Episcopal Church in the Park Slope section of Brooklyn that if Brooklyn had a better ball club it wouldn't have to commit "Sabbath desecration" by playing games on Sunday. Brooklyn, at the time, was one of the few clubs in the league that did schedule home games on Sunday. Said the Reverend: "If the Brooklyn club would only get better players they would have such big crowds on weekdays that they would not have to play Sunday games."

It was that very day, the 21st, that the Cubs trounced the Superbas, 11-2, with Billy's first-inning, three-run home run the big blow.

Obviously the Cubs and the Reverend would have agreed on at least one thing: the Superbas were not very superb.

ing Slagle. But there was no way he could get to Billy . . . who slid under Slagle. After some heated discussion, Slagle was called out and our boy was called safe. Billy had scored on an out at the plate!

By season's conclusion, Billy had hung up some pretty impressive numbers. Appearing in 145 games, he batted a solid .260, scored 78 runs, drove in 56 others, and tied for the league lead (with Art Devlin of the Giants) in stolen bases with 59. In third place, with 57, was the legendary "Flying Dutchman," Honus Wagner (who, in his career, tallied 772 total steals and led the league in that category five times).

The Cubs finished a strong third in 1905. They were on the way to their 1906 success, in which they won 116 games and took the National League crown by a resounding 20-game margin over second-place New York. Unfortunately, though, Billy Maloney was not to be a part of that "Tinker to Evers to Chance" team of destiny. On December 30, 1905 he - along with outfielder Jack McCarthy, thirdsacker Doc Casey, pitcher Buttons Briggs and $2,000 - was shipped to Brooklyn in exchange for outfielder Jimmy Sheckard.

For the Superbas (as the Dodgers were known in those days), Billy put in three full years. He played in 408 games over 1906, 1907, and 1908 and, although he still patrolled the outfield with the best of them, his batting and basestealing statistics fell off. From 1909 to 1914 his love of the game - even at the minor league level - kept him in it. He, in chronological order, played for Rochester (Eastern League), Milwaukee and Toledo (American Association), Mobile (Southern League), and Fort Worth, Beaumont, and San Antonio (all in the Texas League). Texas crept into Billy Maloney's blood. After his playing days were through, he joined Gulf Oil, remaining in the Lone Star State for the rest of his long life. In Texas he traded his baseball bat for a golf club. Longtime friend and neighbor Robin Rominger of Breckenridge, Texas recalls that Billy "hit the ball about as straight as anybody I ever saw." Robin also recalls that Billy, whom he characterizes as a true gentleman, wasn't much interested in modern baseball . . . that he considered any game with more than two or three runs per team to be a "washout."

Billy Maloney passed away, at age 82, on September 2, 1960 in Breckenridge. He is buried in North Attleboro, Massachusetts, where he spent many of his formative years and where he met his wife, the former Theresa Brennan.

Manager - William Francis "Rough" Carrigan

Babe Ruth called him the best manager he ever had. The Red Sox call him the first, last, and only man to ever guide them to successive pennants (and World Championships, too!). We call him our Dream Team manager. He's Bill "Rough" Carrigan.

Carrigan was born in Lewiston in 1883. A resident of "The Spindle City" all his life, he starred in both baseball and football at Lewiston High School. There his leadership abilities surfaced early: he was captain of the baseball nine. After Lewiston High, Bill transferred his skills, both intellectual and athletic, to Holy Cross College in Worcester, Massachusetts. At Holy Cross he continued to win praise for his play on both the diamond and the gridiron. Football - he was a highly regarded halfback - almost cost him his baseball career, however. During a game, "Rough" had his leg pretty badly damaged. Bill always blamed the injury for his lack of speed on the basepaths in later years.

It was at Holy Cross that Bill became a catcher. Up until then he'd been an infielder. Coach Tommy McCarthy took note of Bill's hefty build and swift reflexes, however, and decided that Bill would do a fine job behind the plate. He was right.

Bill's performance at Holy Cross led to his being signed by the Red Sox. With the Sox he developed into one of the game's most respected catchers. He handled pitchers well, had only a fair arm but more than made up for it with the speed with which he got the ball away, and was unsurpassed at blocking the plate. It was this last skill, some of which was a throwback to his college football days, that earned him his greatest measure of fame as a player. The "Human Stone Wall," the *Boston Post* called him in 1912. White Sox outfielder and manager Jimmy "Nixie" Callahan echoed the same view: "You might as well try to move a stone wall," lamented Callahan after dropping a doubleheader to the Bosox. In fact, to the delight of fans, "Rough" would sometimes go one step further. He wouldn't just block home plate . . . he'd sit on it! Bill earned his nickname of "Rough." You didn't mess with him.

Bill was a pesky hitter, too. Although he never led the league in any offensive category, he was a feared clutch hitter. In his first shot with the Sox, in 1906, he batted a dismal .211. After a year of further seasoning with Toronto, then in the International League, the square-jawed Carrigan came up to stay. His two best years with the stick were 1909 when he hit .296, and 1911 when he had a .289 mark. Lifetime he was .258.

Manager Carrigan

Red Sox management liked, seemingly, to see managers come and go in those early years of the club's history. From 1906 until Bill took over the reins in 1913, the Bosox played under no less than nine managers. In one season, 1907, the Sox saw four men at the helm (and they still finished seventh). Even though Jake Stahl led the team, in 1912, to its first flag in eight years (and a stirring four games to three victory over the Giants in the World Series, too), he was axed before the 1913 season was out. On July 15th, with the team in fifth place with a 39-41 record, Jake was asked to vacate Fenway Park.

April, 1927 photograph

WILLIAM FRANCIS CARRIGAN

Born October 22, 1883, Lewiston, Maine Died July 8, 1969, Lewiston, Maine

MAJOR LEAGUE MANAGERIAL RECORD

Year	Team	Games	Won	Lost	Pct.	Standing
1913	**BOS A**	70	40	30	.571	4
1914		160	91	62	.595	2
1915		155	101	50	.669	1
1916		156	91	63	.591	1
1927		154	51	103	.331	8
1928		154	57	96	.373	8
1929		155	58	96	.377	8
7 years		1004	489	500	.494	

WORLD SERIES RECORD

Year	Team	Games	Won	Lost	Pct.	
1915	**BOS A**	5	4	1	.800	
1916		5	4	1	.800	
2 years		10	8	2	.800	

Selected to take his place was, of course, Lewiston Bill Carrigan. Under Bill, the club won 40, lost 30, and moved up a notch, to fourth.

In 1914, with the ballclub under Bill's leadership the entire season, the Red Sox finished a strong second to Connie Mack's powerhouse Athletics. That was the year a skinny kid by the name of George Herman Ruth made his appearance in the major leagues. The Babe arrived. And he arrived as a member of the Red Sox . . . as a left-handed pitcher. Much of his later success - which, alas, came with the Yankees - stemmed from the care and tutoring he received from Bill Carrigan. As Bill would later write in a series of articles for the *Boston Daily Record:* "Nobody could have made Ruth the great pitcher and the great hitter he was but himself. He made himself with the aid of his God-given talents. But," continued Bill, "breaking in, he had to be disciplined to save him from probably being his own worst enemy. And I saw to it that he was disciplined." Bill even went so far as to room with Babe - and the team's other irrepressible southpaw hurler, Dutch Leonard - to ensure that the fun-loving Ruth didn't overdo the fun. In short, Bill became as much a father figure as a manager. It paid off. Ruth developed into one of the game's premier lefties under squire Bill, helping the Sox take pennants - and World Championships - in both 1915 and 1916. Ruth was 18-8 in 1915; an even more dazzling 23-12, with a league-leading ERA of 1.75, in 1916.

Bill had similar success with the rest of the club. As sportswriters of the period were quick to point out, Bill was not a flashy leader, or a driver in the strict sense

"It's Bill Carrigan"

During his playing days Bill was "Rough" . . . and ready. He was second to none when it came to backstopping, and was a dangerous clutch hitter as well.

cartoon art, *Boston Post,* September 2, 1912

Titans Two

During his first managerial reign, 1913-1916, Bill Carrigan's Red Sox possessed some of the finest talent in the game's history. Two of the very finest were, bottom left, outfielder Tris Speaker, and upper right, then-pitcher Babe Ruth. Speaker, shown aboard an alligator during a break in spring training, 1913, was an ex-rodeo rider from Hubbard, Texas who played an extremely shallow center field, almost begging hitters to hit the ball over his head. Few did.

circa 1915 photograph

March, 1913 photograph

of the word. Rather, he was a hard worker himself, and his players tended to follow by example. He was also a keen student of the game, possessing an uncanny savvy for knowing what to do when. At no time was this more evident than in Bill's back-to-back World Championships. In the fall classic of 1915, his charges were matched against a strong Phillies' team that had won the National League crown by seven games. Led by the pitching of Grover Cleveland Alexander (31-10 with a miniscule 1.22 ERA) and the slugging of former Red Soxer Gavvy Cravath (24 homers and 115 RBIs, both tops in the majors), they appeared to be tough. They weren't. After the Phils took the first game, 3-1, on an eight-hitter by Alexander, the Sox swept to victory by taking the next four in a row.

It could be said, incidentally, that even the president of the United States came out to watch Bill win. On October 9th, president Woodrow Wilson was on hand as the Sox won their first game of the Series, and their first-ever for "Rough," 2-1. It was a first not only for Bill . . . it was also the first time a president ever witnessed a Series' contest.

The second of Bill's successive Cham-

What's to Do?!
Bill, right, and Red Sox owner Bob Quinn confer during the season of 1928. By then Bill's radiant smile - see page 150 - had all but disappeared. The Sox of those years were just plain awful and, sad but true, there was little Bill or anyone else could do to turn them around.

pionships was more of the same. The Red Sox faced a Brooklyn ballclub featuring the likes of Jake Daubert, Zack Wheat, and an outfielder named Casey Stengel . . . and proceeded to also polish them off four games to one. In game number four, manager Carrigan even inserted catcher Carrigan - who'd batted but 63 times all season - behind the plate . . . and with good results: he went two for three with an RBI as the Sox won, 6-2.

Bill, according to his son, Bill, Jr., remained a lifelong Red Sox fan: "He'd watch them on TV." But, adds Bill, Jr., "He never talked too much baseball."

baseball card art, 1912

The Lure of Lewiston

At age 32, riding on top of the world, "Rough" decided to call it quits after his rather remarkable 1915 and 1916 triumphs. Actually, he announced his retirement in early September, so that topping the Robins (as the Dodgers were called then) in the Series just served as an exclamation point for Bill's goodbye. He'd decided that he wanted to spend more time at home. So home to Lewiston it was, there to find considerable success in both real estate (Bill was half-owner of a string of movie theatres spread throughout New England) and banking. Also, he made no bones about being weary of the constant traveling that baseball requires. As he wrote in a series of 1943 articles entitled "My Days With the Red Sox," "I was in my thirties, was married and had an infant daughter (Ed. note: Bill would eventually add a son and another daughter to his family roster). I wanted to spend more time with my family than baseball would permit."

Back at the Helm, 1927-1929

By the mid-1920s, Bill found himself getting restless. He'd sold his movie chain shares at a hefty profit, allowing him to be a gentleman of leisure. It was a role he did not relish. The Red Sox, meanwhile, had fallen upon exceedingly hard times: in the five year period between 1922 and 1926 they finished last four times and next to last the other. They were dreadful! Bob Quinn, who'd bought the franchise in the winter of 1923-24, talked Bill out of retirement. Bill shouldn't have listened. Good manager or not, nothing he could do made much of a difference. Never one to pass the buck, Bill nevertheless would later admit that his players just didn't have it. As he penned in an article in the July, 1929 issue of *Baseball Magazine*, "Fighting spirit alone won't make a ball club into a pennant winner. You've got to have batting punch and fielding ability and steady pitching."

After three seasons of almost total frustration - and last-place finishes - Bill reluctantly tossed in the towel. He retired from the Red Sox for good. Back in Lewiston, he became a highly successful banker, eventually rising to the post of president of Peoples Savings Bank.

Bill Carrigan passed away in his beloved Lewiston on July 8, 1969. He was 85. Honest, dependable, hard-working: those were the trademarks of "Old Rough." When, in 1946, he was told that he'd been named to baseball's Honor Roll - a supplement to the Hall of Fame established to pay tribute to outstanding managers, sportswriters and club executives - he responded: "Well, well, that's fine, thank you. I've got to get back to the bank."

THE DREAM TEAM'S DREAM YEAR

When it comes to all-time great teams some may sing the praises of the 1927 Yankees, the powerhouse Philadelphia Athletics of 1929-1931, or the exploits of the Gas House Gang Cardinals of the 1930s. More recent fans will ooh and ah over the Dodgers of the 1950s, the Yankees of 1961, or the several dynasties of the Oakland A's. Let them ooh and ah all they want: here's a team that won't be beat. It's the Maine Dream Team's Dream Year: each of our players in his very best year.

Player	Pos.	Year	AB	H	HR	R	RBIs	SB	BA
George Gore	CF	1880	322	116	0	43	32	*	.360
Harry Lord	3B	1911	561	180	3	103	61	43	.321
Freddy Parent	SS	1903	560	170	4	83	80	24	.304
Del Bissonette	1B	1930	572	192	16	102	113	4	.336
Louis Sockalexis	RF	1897	278	94	3	43	42	16	.338
Clyde Sukeforth	C	1929	237	84	1	31	33	8	.354
Walter Thornton	LF	1897	265	85	0	39	55	13	.321
Topsy Magoon	2B	1901	460	116	1	47	53	15	.252
									.319

			IP	GS	CG	SO	BB	ShO	W	L	ERA
Irv "Cy the Second" Young	P	1905	378	42	41	156	71	7	20	21	2.90

*information not available

It's a team that makes you want to shout "Wow!" . . . featuring a combined batting average of .319 and a starting pitcher with 20 wins, an ERA of 2.90, and a better-than-two-to-one strikeouts to walks ratio.

Eat your heart out, Dodger, Yankee, Oakland, et al. fans!

THEY ALSO PLAYED

Since the beginning of time there have been close to 14,000 players who have appeared in a major league baseball game at one time or another. Of this total, sixty-eight have been native-born Mainers. That works out to a scant one-half of 1%.*

Now, one-half of 1% is not a heck of a lot. It just means, however, that each and every one of our sixty-eight is that much more important.

Fourteen of the sixty-eight have been featured on our Maine Dream Team. That leaves fifty-four for the They Also Played section that follows over the next twenty-one pages.

While a hefty number of the players included here enjoyed substantial careers, some were in and out of the majors almost before friends and relatives even knew they'd arrived. Regardless, they all made at least one appearance in a big league uniform . . . which is one appearance more than I suspect I'll ever make.

* Plus we've lost a couple. Older editions of THE BASEBALL ENCYCLOPEDIA show Charlie "Dutch" Bold - who appeared in a pair of games for the 1914 St. Louis Browns - as having been born in Paris, Maine. Newer editions, however, show his birthplace as Karlskrong, Sweden. Likewise with Joe Knotts, who played in three games as a catcher with the Boston Braves in 1907: old records show him as having been born in Biddeford; new records list his birthplace as Greensboro, Pennsylvania.

- ***Roland "Cuke" Barrows - Outfielder***

Born October 20, 1883, Gray (some sources say Raymond or East Raymond), Maine...batted right-handed, threw left-handed...5′8″, 158 lbs...nickname "Cuke" came from ability to remain calm and collected - i.e., cool as a *cucumber* - under any and all circumstances...also nicknamed "Kid" and "Shorty," both stemming from his small frame...graduated from Pennell Institute, Gray...moved to Westbrook to work in S.D. Warren mill...discovered by Pop Williams (see page 177), he got start on Williams' Pine Tree club...was crackerjack lefty pitcher for strong (Harry Lord played third!) amateur Portland club, 1905, but was too good a hitter to not play every day...played for Biddeford, 1906, and then Portland Blue Sox, 1907, in Maine State League...was with New Bedford in New England League, 1908-1909... batted .283 in 123 games for New Bedford, 1909, and signed by Chicago White Sox at end of NEL season...saw limited action for White Sox, 1909, getting 3 hits in 20 at bats for average of .150 ...was with White Sox for parts of next 3 seasons, 1910-1912, but seldom used...highlight was most likely going 2 for 3 against legendary Walter Johnson and successor Ewart Walker in Sox 10-3 rout of Washington, May 10, 1910...major league totals are 19 hits in 99 at bats for .192 average... played for various minor league clubs, 1913-1917, including Rochester (New York), Lowell (for which club he batted .332 in 114 games in 1915), and Portland...also managed Lowell club, 1915, until June 21st when resigned - though remaining as player - because of team's disappointing record...badly injured ankle in spring of 1913 and never fully up to par thereafter...after release from Portland, New England League, in late June, 1917, joined wife Marietta in operating greenhouse on Main Street in Gorham that yet bears Barrows' name...died in Gorham, Maine, February 10, 1955.

Cool As a Cucumber

A nicely whimsical piece of cartoon art from 1905, when cool-as-a-cucumber Roland "Cuke" Barrows was knocking the cover off the ball and doing some fancy moundwork, too, for Portland's crackerjack amateur nine.

- ***Clarence Waldo "Climax" Blethen - Pitcher***

Born July 11, 1893, Dover (now part of Dover-Foxcroft), Maine...batted left-handed, threw right-handed...5′11″, 170 lbs...began pro career with Frederick (Maryland) in Blue Ridge League in 1920 ...appeared in 5 games for Red Sox in 1923, posting 0-0 record and 7.13 ERA...bounced around minors, with stops in San Antonio, Greenville, Little Rock, Mobile, Macon...had second shot at majors with Dodgers in 1929 and was again 0-0, with an ERA of 9.00...major league totals are 0-0 with .732 ERA...spent almost all of 1930s again bouncing around minors, mostly with Atlanta Crackers, twice winning 20 games for them...managed Leaksville (North Carolina) and Savannah in late '30s...lived latter part of his life in Frederick, where he coached Little League until, at age 72, hurt his arm showing players how to slide...died in Frederick, Maryland, April 11, 1973.

• ***Ralph Wayne Botting - Pitcher***

Born May 12, 1955, Houlton, Maine...batted and threw left-handed...6′, 195 lbs...moved to Burbank, California when 6 years old...selected by California Angels in 7th round of free agent draft, June, 1974 ...progressed through minors, 1974-1979, beginning with Idaho Falls, Pioneer League, and ending with Salt Lake City, Pacific Coast League...struck out 125 in 115 innings while posting 2.58 ERA for Quad Cities, Midwest League, 1975...hurled 7-inning no-hitter for Quad Cities vs. Wausau, July 28, 1976... was 8-0 with 2.04 ERA with Salinas, California League, 1977...promoted to parent Angels, 1979. and responded with 2-0 mark in spite of high 8.70 ERA...split 1980 between AAA Salt Lake City, where was 15-8, and Angels, for whom was 0-3...hurt arm while with Salt Lake City, where was 3-5 with 7.29 ERA, 1981...underwent elbow surgery, 1981...hurt arm again in spring training, 1982, and, after going 0-1 with 9.00 ERA at Omaha, decided was time to call it quits...major league totals are 2-3 with 7.39 ERA...is currently supervisor of produce department for supermarket chain...resides in Mission Viejo, California with wife Tracy, daughter Lindsey, son Matthew.

Two of Thirty-Two

Ralph Botting, left, on the mound for the Angels, 1979, and Don Brennan getting set to chuck one in for the Newark Bears, 1932. Although they pitched almost five decades apart the two share the rather wonderful distinction of being native-born Mainers who pitched in the majors, one of a group of but 32 players who can claim that honor.

• ***James Donald "Don" Brennan - Pitcher*** (please also see pages 44-47)

Born December 2, 1903, Augusta, Maine...batted and threw right-handed...6′, 210 lbs...nicknamed "The Icicle" because of composure on mound...grew up in Augusta...lettered in 4 sports - baseball, basketball, football and track - at Augusta's Cony High School...graduated Cony, 1923, and entered Georgetown University, Washington, D.C. ...signed by New York Yankees, 1925, but sore arm kept him inactive for most of 1925-1926...began comeback with fine 11-5 record with Lewiston, New England League, late 1926...Yankees sent him to Newark, International League, for 1927-1928...1929 saw him with Atlanta in Southern Association, and saw more misfortune: he dislocated shoulder late in season...came back with Atlanta in 1930 before moving up to Newark again, 1931-1932...had most successful season, 1932, going 26-8 with 2.79 ERA for Bears and then winning 2 games against Minneapolis Millers as Newark took Little World Series...finally got shot in majors, 1933, and went 5-1 with 4.98 ERA in 18 games for Yankees...was purchased by Cincinnati Reds, 1934, spending 3+ seasons on the banks of the Ohio...was 4-3, 5-5, and 5-2, 1934-1936, in 107 games as both starter and reliever...was sent back in minors, late 1936, hooking up with Toronto and then Jersey City...had last stay in majors, 1937, starting with Reds and ending with New York Giants...was 2-1 overall in 16 games, all in relief...appeared in 2 games in 1937 World Series vs. Yankees, hurling 3 innings of shutout ball and setting Lou Gehrig down on strikes...major league totals are 21-12 with 4.19 ERA in

141 games over 5 years...finished pro career with Atlanta, 1938, and Toronto, 1939...returned to Augusta where played semi-pro on and off for years...was instrumental in development of Little League ball in Augusta and Junior American Legion ball throughout Maine...was longtime liquor salesman as well as part-time scout for Boston Braves...died in Boston, Massachusetts, April 26, 1953.

- ***Virgin Wirt "Rip" Cannell - Outfielder***

Born January 23, 1880, South Bridgton, Maine...batted left-handed, threw right-handed...5′10½″, 180 lbs...graduated from North Bridgton Academy, 1901...attended Tufts College...appeared in an even 100 games for Boston Nationals in 1904, batting .234 in 346 at bats...played outfield, usually center field, in all 154 games for Boston Nationals in 1905, hitting .247 in 567 at bats...dropped by Boston before start of 1906 season...over 111 games...died in Bridgton, Maine, August 26, 1948.

- ***Chester James "Chet"/"Pop" Chadbourne - Outfielder***

Born October 26, 1884, Parkman, Maine...batted left-handed, threw right-handed...began pro career as outfielder/infielder with Worcester in New England League, 1906, batting .327 in 114 games...was paid $125 a month...brought up by Boston, American League, in late 1906, and hit .302 in 11 games at second and short...split 1907 between Boston and Providence in Eastern (International) League, batting .289 for Red Sox in 38 at bats; .294 for Providence in 464 at bats...at Providence became outfielder, position he would play the rest of long career...termed "one of the greatest ballplayers living" by former Boston teammate Harry Lord, May 1909...spent next 6 seasons in high minors, playing for Baltimore (1908), Indianapolis (1909-1910), Portland, Oregon (1911-1913)...was paid $250 a month at Portland, 1913...jumped to Federal League, 1914-1915, playing left field for Kansas City ...had banner year in 1914, batting solid .277 in 581 at bats, stealing 42 bases (fourth best in league), and scoring 92 runs...in 1915 dipped to .227 in 587 at bats, with 29 steals and 75 runs scored...played for Memphis in Southern Association, 1916, and Vernon (California) in Pacific Coast League, 1917-1918...had one final fling in majors with Boston Braves in late 1918, getting 27 hits in 104 at bats for .260 average...5-year major league totals are 345 hits in 1353 at bats in 347 games for .255 average... continued to play in high minors with Vernon, Wichita, Salt Lake City, and Oklahoma City through 1927...played in remarkable 12,588 games during 22-year professional career!!!...managed Salt Lake City in 1926...was umpire in Pacific Coast League, 1929-1930, and Western League, 1932...died in Los Angeles, California, June 23, 1943.

- ***Wallace Oakes "Wally" Clement - Outfielder***

Born July 21, 1881, Auburn, Maine...threw right-handed...batted .222 in 16 games and 36 at bats for 1908 Philadelphia Phillies...batted .254 with 11 stolen bases in 95 games and 343 at bats for Philadelphia and Brooklyn in 1909...lifetime major league average is .251...died in Coral Gables, Florida, November 1, 1953.

- ***Raymond Franklin "Bobby" Coombs - Pitcher*** (please also see page 48)

Born February 2, 1908, Goodwin's Mills, Maine...batted and threw right-handed...5′9½″, 160 lbs... nephew of famed Athletics' hurler Jack Coombs...moved to North Parsonsfield, Maine as infant...then moved to Kennebunk, where grew up...started as catcher at Kennebunk High but switched to mound sophomore year...struck out 26 in a row vs. Sanford High senior year, 1925...starred at Exeter Academy, Exeter, New Hampshire, 1926-1928, as both pitcher and infielder/outfielder...went to Duke University, Durham, North Carolina, 1929-1933, where was mainstay on mound for baseball nine, coached by Uncle Jack...won 19 out of 23 games pitched at Duke, ending with 3 shutouts in row... graduated Duke, 1933, and went directly to Philadelphia Athletics...first batter faced in bigs was Babe Ruth (who homered on 3-2 count)...appeared in 21 games for A's, 1933, going 0-1 with 7.47 ERA... spent next 9 seasons in minors, going from Syracuse to Birmingham to St. Paul to Shreveport (where was 19-7) to Jersey City...finally got second shot at majors, 1943, with Giants...appeared in 9 games for Jints, again going 0-1...major league totals are 0-2 with 9.32 ERA in 30 games pitched, all in relief...always excellent with bat: was .400 (2 for 5) with A's in 1933; 10 for 13 for Syracuse Chiefs one year...drafted into Navy, fall, 1943...returned home in 1946, living in Ogunquit, Maine on and off since...coached baseball at Williams College, Williamstown, Massachusetts, 1946-1973...ballpark at Williams now named Bobby Coombs Park in his honor...resided in old farmhouse in Ogunquit, Maine with wife, Gath (Agatha), his wife of 61 years, until his death in Ogunquit, October 21, 1991.

Bobby Coombs, 1933

Danny Coombs, c. 1967

Jack Coombs, 1906

The Coombs' Connection

In the long and illustrious history of baseball there have been three men named Coombs to have ever taken the mound . . . and all three have decidedly strong Maine connections. Bobby Coombs was born and raised in Maine. Likewise with Danny Coombs. And John Wesley "Jack" Coombs, Bobby's uncle, moved to Maine at age four, grew up in Freeport, went to high school in Freeport and Waterville, graduated from Colby. At Colby his prowess on the mound led to his being nicknamed "Colby Jack" and "The Colby Carbine." It also led to an invitation to join Connie Mack's champion Philadelphia Athletics upon college graduation in 1906. Colby Jack went on to win 159 games with the A's and Brooklyn, including a superlative 31-9 mark (with 13 shutouts and a 1.30 ERA!) in 1910. He was also undefeated in World Series' play, going 5-0 with a 2.70 ERA in three Fall Classics.

- ***Daniel Bernard "Danny"/"Mr. Motion" Coombs - Pitcher***

  Born March 23, 1942, Lincoln, Maine...batted right-handed, threw left-handed...6′4″, 200 lbs..."Mr. Motion" nickname came from his height and abundance of movement in his delivery...was standout in baseball, basketball, and football for Brewer High, averaging 18 strikeouts per game his senior year in baseball, and 30 points per game his senior year in basketball...graduated Brewer High, 1960... attended Seton Hall University, South Orange, New Jersey, 1960-1962, playing baseball and basketball ...signed with Houston Colt .45s for bonus "in the neighborhood of $40,000," 1962...started 1963 with Durham (North Carolina), Carolina League, before moving up to Modesto, California League, where struck out 182 in 155 innings pitched and was 3rd in league with 3.48 ERA...finished 1963 with Houston but saw virtually no action...was 1-1 with 5.00 ERA in 7 games for Houston, 1964, after spending first 3 months of season in military...spent next 5 seasons bouncing between Houston and various minor league teams, with best year being 1967 when was 3-0 with 3.33 ERA for Astros...was sold to San Diego Padres, October, 1969...with Padres had most successful season, 1970, posting 10-14 mark and team-leading 3.30 ERA for last-place club...got off to slow start in 1971 and shipped to Hawaii, Pacific Coast League, but never given chance to pitch...major league totals are 19-27 with 4.08 ERA over 9 seasons and 144 games...was pitching coach for Padres' Alexandria (Louisiana) team in AA Texas League, 1972...went back to school, receiving phys ed degree from University of Houston...has been phys ed teacher and baseball/basketball/football coach at Houston area schools since mid-1970s...older brother Ray pitched in Chicago Cubs' organization, 1953-1955...resides in Houston with wife Donna and younger son Fred...older son Glenn is promising pitcher in Pittsburgh Pirates' farm system.

• ***John Sheldon Cumberland - Pitcher***

Born May 10, 1947, Westbrook, Maine...batted right-handed, threw left-handed...6′, 185 lbs...grew up in Westbrook and graduated from Westbrook High - where excelled in baseball, basketball and football - in 1965...hurled 2 no-hitters and, in senior year, pitched Westbrook High to state title... pitched Steven Manchester American Legion Post, Westbrook, to New England Legion championship, going 10-0 and averaging 18 strikeouts a game...signed by St. Louis Cardinals; was 4-1 with 4.91 ERA for Eugene (Oregon), Northwestern League, 1966...drafted by New York Yankees, November, 1966... was 14-12 over 2 seasons with Syracuse, AAA International League, 1967-1968, before getting brief shot with Yankees, late 1968...was 0-0 with 9.00 ERA in 1 game for Yankees, 1968...after going 12-8 with Syracuse recalled by Yankees, July, 1969, and again was 0-0...began 1970 with New York, where was 3-4 with 3.94 ERA before being traded to San Francisco Giants, July 21, for former Cy Young winner Mike McCormick...for Giants was 2-0 with sparkling 0.82 ERA in 7 appearances...had best season, 1971, winning 9 while losing 6 with 2.92 ERA...started game 2 of 1971 League Championship Series vs. Pirates...released on waivers to St. Louis Cardinals, June, 1972...totals for 1972 were 1-5 with disheartening 7.66 ERA...appeared in 17 games for California Angels, 1974, posting 0-1 mark with 3.68 ERA...major league totals for 6 years are 15-16 with 3.82 ERA ...career highlights are pitching in 1971 LCS and "playing with Mickey Mantle, Willie Mays, Willie McCovey, Juan Marichal, and Gaylord Perry"...tried running feed and grain company, and raising horses but missed baseball...joined New York Mets' organization in early 1980s and spent almost 10 years with them, including 5 as pitching coach for AAA Tidewater Tides...switched to San Diego Padres' organization, 1991...currently serving as manager of Wichita Wranglers, AA Texas League...resides with wife Pat and sons John, Jr., Chris, and Paul in Safety Harbor, Florida.

Mickey and Willie and Company

John Cumberland is shown here as he appeared on the mound for Westbrook High, 1965, and in his Cardinals' uniform, 1972. When I asked John what he's proudest of in his impressive six-year major league career, he said: "That's easy . . . playing with Mickey Mantle, Willie Mays, Willie McCovey, Juan Marichal, and Gaylord Perry." It's a pretty good answer.

• ***Harry Albert Curtis - Catcher***

Born February 19, 1883, Portland, Maine...threw right-handed...appeared in 6 games for 1907 New York Giants, getting 2 hits in 9 at bats...lucky number must have been 2: besides 2 hits had 2 walks, stole 2 bases, scored 2 runs, and batted .222...died in Evanston, Illinois, August 1, 1951.

- ***Harvey Barnes "Harv" Cushman - Pitcher***

  Born July 10, 1877, Rockland, Maine...pitched in 4 games for Pittsburgh Pirates in 1902, giving up 30 hits and 31 walks in 25⅔ innings...major league totals are 0-4 with 7.36 ERA...died in Ensworth, Pennsylvania, December 27, 1920.

- ***Chester Arthur "Chuck" Emerson - Outfielder***

  Born October 27, 1889, Stow, Maine...batted left-handed, threw right-handed...5′9″, 170 lbs... graduated from Dartmouth College in 1911...went right from Dartmouth to Philadelphia Athletics, receiving $500 in education expenses and another $500 to sign a 3-year contract...appeared in 7 games for A's in 1911, getting 4 hits in 18 at bats for average of .222...went 0 for 1 in only at bat in 1912...lifetime major league average is .211...later played in minors for Louisville, Baltimore, and Harrisburg...lived in North Conway, New Hampshire in later years...died in Augusta, Maine, July 2, 1971.

- ***Sidney Douglas "Sid" Farrar - Firstbaseman***

  Born August 10, 1859, Paris Hill (Paris), Maine...threw right-handed...5′10″...attracted attention for his baseball ability while working in a box factory in Massachusetts...accepted an offer of $1,000 a season to play for Philadelphia in the National League...was smoothfielding firstsacker for Philadelphia for 7 years, 1883-1889...best season was 1887 when batted .282 with 83 runs scored, 72 RBIs, and 24 stolen bases in 116 games...switched to Players League, still with Philadelphia, for 1890 season, batting .254 with 84 runs scored in 127 games...lifetime major league totals show 904 hits in 3,573 at bats across 943 games - all at first base - for an average of .253...in spite of considerable baseball success was probably better known as father of opera star Geraldine Farrar (1882-1967)...lived on his estate in Ridgefield, Connecticut, dubbed "Farrar's Thirty Acres," last years of his life...died in New York City, May 7, 1935.

- ***Charles Edward "Eddie" Files - Pitcher***

  Born May 19, 1883, Portland, Maine...batted and threw right-handed...starred in baseball and football and was class president at Bowdoin College...graduated from Bowdoin, 1908...joined Philadelphia Athletics same year, appearing in 2 games and striking out 6 in 9 innings pitched...ended season with 6.00 ERA and 0-0 record...later pitched for Holyoke in Connecticut League, Providence in Eastern League, and Worcester in New England League...taught French and Latin and coached at Rockridge Hall School in Wellesley Hills, Massachusetts, 1909-1911...was athletic instructor at Portland High, 1911-1912...was then longtime Portland bond and securities salesman...moved to Cornish, 1936... died in Cornish, Maine, May 10, 1954.

- ***Curtis Hooper "Curt" Fullerton - Pitcher***

  Born September 13, 1898, Ellsworth, Maine... batted left-handed, threw right-handed...6′, 175 lbs...moved to East Boston section of Boston, Massachusetts when 9 years old...was star hurler for Mechanic Arts High School, Boston, 1916-1917...worked in Brooklyn, New York shipyard, 1918-1919...played semi-pro ball in New York City, 1918-1920...signed by Red Sox in 1921 and farmed out to Toronto in International League...was 14-10 with 2.78 ERA with Maple Leafs when Sox brought him up late in season, 1921...was 0-1 with 8.80 ERA in 4 games with Sox, 1921...was with Red Sox

Dog Days

Curt Fullerton, looking less than fully chipper in this circa 1924 photo, had the misfortune to pitch for the Red Sox during their dog days of the 1920s. His lifetime record of 10-37 reflects it.

next 4 years, 1922-1925, winning 10 games while losing 34 for rock-bottom team...highlight was being but 1 of 3 pitchers in Grand Opening of Yankee Stadium, April 18, 1923...hung around minors, 1926-1932, finishing with Little Rock, Southern Association, in mid-season, 1932...rediscovered by Red Sox while playing in a Boston twilight league, 1933...appeared in 6 games for Sox in late 1933, chalking up 0-2 mark with 8.53 ERA...troubled by wildness entire career...major league totals are 10-37 with ERA of 5.11...died in Winthrop, Massachusetts, January 2, 1975.

- ***Ralph Nelson Good - Pitcher***

Born April 25, 1886, Monticello, Maine...batted and threw right-handed...6′, 165 lbs...graduated from Ricker Classical Institute, Houlton, 1906...won varsity letters in baseball, football, basketball, and track at Colby College...was captain of Colby's first undefeated football team, 1909...graduated from Colby, 1910...joined Boston Braves upon graduation, pitching 9 innings in 2 games and posting an ERA of 2.00 and a record of 0-0...later taught and coached at Malden (Massachusetts) High School; worked for Ayer-Houston Hat Co. in Portland; was employed by Brown Brothers Harriman; and, until his retirement circa 1950, was a longtime employee of Sealtest Ice Cream...died in Waterville, Maine, November 24, 1965.

A Man of Conviction

Larry Gowell, pictured here in Yankee pinstripes in 1972, was a man of conviction. He was also a Seventh Day Adventist. It was not a combination conducive to being a major league pitcher: his religion forbade work (and when you're a professional pitcher, pitching is work) from sundown Friday until sundown Saturday, and Larry honored that precept. Had he, with his blazing fastball, not honored it, who knows what numbers he might have rung up.

- ***Lawrence Clyde "Larry" Gowell - Pitcher***

Born May 2, 1948, Lewiston, Maine...batted and threw right-handed...6′2″, 190 lbs...raised in Auburn, Maine, graduating from Edward Little High School, 1967...was 16-0 for Edward Little over 3 years including 2 no-hitters his senior year...selected by New York Yankees in 4th round of amateur draft, 1967...was 3-2 with 3.21 ERA for Oneonta, New York-Penn League, 1967...after 2nd season at

Oneonta, 1968, mowed them down for Ft. Lauderdale, Florida State League, 1969...for Ft. Lauderdale led loop with 16 wins (vs. only 7 losses), 196 innings pitched, and remarkable 217 strikeouts, all wrapped around a 1.74 ERA...moved through Yankee system, 1970-1972...was 14-6 with West Haven (Connecticut), AA Eastern League, 1972, with 2.54 ERA and 171 strikeouts in 181 innings pitched... biggest strike (no pun intended!) against him was fact was a Seventh Day Adventist, prohibited from working (i.e., pitching) from sundown Friday to sundown Saturday...Yankees reluctant to carry man on roster could use only 5 days of week...finally given shot, late 1972...pitched 2 perfect innings of relief vs. Brewers in Milwaukee and then started game against Brewers in New York, October 4th, striking out 6 in 5 innings pitched...also lined solid double in only official time at bat (for lifetime major league batting average of 1.000!)...major league pitching totals are 0-1 with ERA of 1.29 and 7 strikeouts in 7 innings...career highlight was pitching in Yankee Stadium...was one of last players cut from Yankees, 1973...pitched for Syracuse Chiefs, AAA International league, 1973-1974, posting marks of 10-8 and 8-6...shipped to Mexican League in 1975, tried it for month and then decided to pack it in...has been financial planner since left organized baseball...became Baptist in 1981, and very active as song director for Auburn Baptist Church...owns and operates own firm, Gowell Financial Services, Lewiston...older brother Dick played briefly in Yankee system, 1967...resides with 2nd wife Sandy in Lewiston, Maine.

- ***George Edward "Chummy" Gray - Pitcher***

  Born July 17, 1873, Rockland, Maine...threw right-handed...5′11½″, 163 lbs...appears to have started pro career in New England League in mid 1890s...appeared in 9 games for Pittsburgh in 1899, posting 3-3 record with 3.44 ERA...along the way also pitched in minors for Buffalo, Baltimore, Hartford, and Providence...died in Rockland, Maine, August 14, 1913.

- ***Fred Irving Howard, III - Pitcher***

  Born September 2, 1956, Portland, Maine... batted and threw right-handed...6′3″, 190 lbs...progressed through various Little League and American Legion teams, South Portland...was star at both baseball and basketball for South Portland High...named captain of baseball team senior year, 1974... attended Miami-Dade South Community College, Miami, Florida, where was 7-1, 1975...was 4th-round draft pick of Chicago White Sox, January, 1976...moved through White Sox farm system, 1976-1979, with best seasons being 12-6 with 2.78 ERA for pennant-winning Knoxville (Tennessee), AA Southern League, 1978, and 4-1 with 1.65 ERA for Iowa, AAA American Association, 1979...combined with Chris Knapp to pitch no-hitter for Iowa vs. Omaha, September 1, 1977...given shot with White Sox, 1979, pitching both as starter and reliever...had disappointing 1-5 record but noteworthy 3.57 ERA...sole win was strong 7-inning outing vs. Milwaukee Brewers, June 9th,

At the Original Comiskey

After posting strong seasons at AA Knoxville and AAA Iowa, Fred Howard got his shot with the White Sox in 1979. The former South Portland Red Riot star, shown here at Comiskey Park, responded with a fine 3.57 ERA in 28 games pitched.

in which struck out 4 and gave up but 5 hits...hurled 3 scoreless innings vs. Red Sox at Fenway, August 16th...sent down to Iowa, 1980, where was 6-10 before hurting shoulder in August...was sent home to South Portland and told to "rest it"...went to spring training, 1981, but shoulder still painful... operated on, June 1981...rehabbed in Florida, 1982, and then pitched several games for Glens Falls (New York), AA Eastern League, but with same old shoulder pain...last shot was 1983 with Iowa, Mexico City Reds, and Glens Falls again...after 2 starts at Glens Falls decided to quit: "The pain was there, but the velocity wasn't," is way Fred explains it...came back to Portland where worked construction, 1983-1984...accompanied wife Linda, professional dancer, to Las Vegas, 1984-1989, working as bottled water route salesman and then mental health technician...decided to make medicine his profession...currently (September, 1991) in senior year of pre-med undergrad studies, William Jewell College, Liberty, Missouri...younger brother Mike was in organized ball 8 years as pitcher, getting as far as AAA Pawtucket Red Sox before similar shoulder ailment ended career...Fred and wife Linda and daughter Sarah currently reside in Ferrelview, Missouri.

- ***Fred John "Biddo" Iott - Outfielder***

Born July 7, 1876, Houlton, Maine...other nicknames were "Happy" and "Dimples"...played for Concord (New Hampshire) in New England League, 1902...had shot with Cleveland in September of 1903 but was released when it was discovered he'd also signed on with Boston in the National League ...in 3 games with Cleveland had 2 hits in 10 at bats for a lifetime major league average of .200 ...later played in Pennsylvania in Tri-State League, for Bangor in Maine State League, and in New Brunswick and Maine League...coached both league and Houlton High teams after playing career was through... in later life was a guide for sportsmen...died in Island Falls (some sources say Oakfield), Maine, February 17, 1941.

- ***Raymond Willis "Lanky"/"Rip" Jordan - Pitcher***

Born September 28, 1889, South Portland, Maine...batted left-handed, threw right-handed...6′, 172 lbs...grew up in Portland, gaining early fame as pitcher on Butler Grammar School team...was star hurler for Fryeburg Academy, Fryeburg, during high school years...played amateur and semi-pro ball in and around Portland before breaking into organized ball with Lynn in New England League circa 1910...played for independent club in New London, Connecticut in 1911, winning amazing 36 games... signed by Chicago White Sox and farmed out to Wichita, Western League, 1912...was impressive at Wichita and called up by Chicago, 1912, but broke leg sliding into third and had opportunity to get into but 3 games, posting 0-0 mark with 6.10 ERA...back in Western League, hurled successfully for Lincoln (Nebraska) and Denver...in 1915 showed his stuff - primarily a spitter that broke every which way and could, as 1926 article recalled, cause batter to "dance the Charleston" - to his home town folks, pitching for Portland in New England League...next came stint with Elmira, New York State League, in 1916, followed by a year in the service, then 2 years with Buffalo, International League, 1918-1919... with the Bisons in 1919 he tossed 2 no-hitters, one against Jersey City, the other against Toronto, and a 1-hitter against Baltimore...earned another shot at bigs: got to start 1 game for Washington Senators, late 1919, but tagged for 6 hits and 2 walks in 4 innings...major league totals over 2 seasons 7 years apart are 0-0 with ERA of 7.53...was sent down to minors again for 1920 season and became victim of banning of spitball in 1920: ban provided that no pitcher who used it could advance to higher-level league...thus Lanky either gave up best pitch or doomed to be in minors remainder of career...chose latter, hurling for various teams through at least 1928, including fantastic 21-2 record for Columbia (South Carolina), South Atlantic League, 1921...managed Portland Gulls, New England League, 1946...died in Meriden, Connecticut, June 5, 1960.

- ***Richard Edward "Dick" Joyce - Pitcher***

Born November 18, 1943, Portland, Maine...batted and threw left-handed...6′4½″, 225 lbs...son of Joseph "Jabber" Joyce, pitcher in Yankees' and Braves' systems prior to WWII...was teenage phenom for both Cheverus High, Portland, and Harold T. Andrews American Legion Post, also Portland... tossed 3 no-hitters in 4 games in Legion ball, 1960 (and the 4th game was a 1-hitter!)...struck out close to 2 of every 3 batters faced in Legion ball, 1960...led Cheverus to 3 straight Telegram League championships, 1959-1961...scouted by 14 of then-18 major league teams...offered a reported $100,000 bonus/salary by Red Sox and others, 1961...turned offer down in favor of college education... attended Holy Cross College, Worcester, Massachusetts, 1961-1965...signed with Kansas City Athletics

"No Regrets"

Dick Joyce as he appeared in his Andrews American Legion Post uniform, circa 1960, left, and in a publicity photo after he turned down the $100,000 bonus and salary package in 1961.

I spoke with Dick via phone in September of 1991, thirty years since his much publicized refusal. Asked if he had any regrets regarding the $100,000, he laughed and said, "Only when it came to paying last month's bills." Then he gave me a serious answer. It was a simple "No regrets."

after junior year at Holy Cross, 1965, for $40,000 bonus/salary/education expenses package...began season of 1965 with Lewiston (Idaho), Northwest League, where was 8-3 with 2.59 ERA and 143 strikeouts in 118 innings pitched...next stop, 1965, was Birmingham (Alabama), Southern League, where was 5-3 with 3.00 ERA and 58 strikeouts in 72 innings pitched...last stop, still 1965, was Kansas City itself, where was 0-1 with 2.77 ERA and 7 strikeouts in 13 innings pitched over 5 games for A's...strongest outing for A's was against Angels, September 8th, in which started and went 6 innings, giving up but 5 hits and 1 unearned run...began 1966 with Vancouver, Pacific Coast League, but hurt shoulder...sent to warmer climate, Mobile, Southern League, for remainder of season, 1966...was 5-9 with 3.82 ERA for Vancouver, Pacific Coast League, 1967...dropped to 3-8 with 3.83 ERA for Birmingham, Southern League, 1968...finished degree work at Holy Cross and decided it was time to move on to new endeavors, 1968...is currently Director of Telemarketing for IBM Corp., Dayton, New Jersey...resides in Upper Saddle River, New Jersey, with wife Jeanne (his sweetheart since 7th grade days at St. Joseph's School, Portland!), sons Tyler and Brandon, daughter Danielle.

- ***Peter Linwood "Pete"/"Big Foot" Ladd - Pitcher***

Born July 17, 1956, Portland, Maine...batted and threw right-handed...6′3″, 240 lbs...nickname "Big Foot" came from huge 15EEE foot size...son of Bill Ladd, star baseball and football player for Deering High, Portland, 1940-1944, and star semi-pro hurler in and around Portland through 1950s...spent formative years, through 8th grade, in Portland before moving south...graduated from Henderson High School, Atlanta, Georgia, 1974...attended University of Mississippi where, as sophomore, led Southeastern Conference with 1.74 ERA...selected by Boston Red Sox in 25th round of free agent draft, June, 1977...was 4-1 with 1.67 ERA in 19 games for Winter Haven (Florida), Florida State League, 1977...led Florida State League in saves with 18 while posting 8-2 mark, 1978...started 1979 with Bristol (Connecticut) Red Sox, Eastern League, and was 3-1 with 0.62 ERA when traded with Bobby Sprowl to Houston Astros for firstbaseman Bob Watson, June 13th...was 6-1 with Columbus (Georgia), Southern League, before called up by Astros in late 1979...was 1-1 with 3.00 ERA in 10 relief appearances for

Houston, 1979...sent back to minors, 1980-1982...traded to Milwaukee Brewers for pitcher Buster Keeton, October 23, 1981...strong 10-2 mark with 2.91 ERA for Vancouver, AAA Pacific Coast League, earned chance with Brewers, July, 1982...was 8-16 with 33 saves for Brewers, 1982-1985...highlight was saving 2 of Milwaukee's 3 wins in 1982 American League Championship victory over California Angels, striking out 5 and allowing no hits in $3\frac{1}{3}$ innings pitched...pitched $\frac{2}{3}$ of inning in World Series, 1982...released by Brewers, November 25, 1985, and signed by Seattle Mariners, January 18, 1986... was 8-6 with 3.82 ERA for Mariners, 1986...major league totals are 17-23 with 39 saves and an ERA of 4.14 over 6 years and 205 games...trained in social work, was off-season deputy sheriff/probation and parole officer at Cumberland County Jail, Portland, the winter before his 1982 LCS heroics...brother Mike was in Minnesota Twins' organization, 1970-1971...works as service rep for auto sales firm...resides with wife Eve and daughter Lindsey in Tucson, Arizona.

- ***Otis Carroll "Rabbit" Lawry - Secondbaseman***

Born November 1, 1893, Fairfield, Maine...batted left-handed, threw right handed...5′8″, 133 lbs...got nickname of "Rabbit" from his speed: supposedly could make it safely to first if ball took 2 hops to shortstop...was star athlete at Lawrence High School, Fairfield, and University of Maine, Orono... captained 1916 UMaine baseball team and also won state intercollegiate 100-yard dash...received five major league offers upon graduation from UMaine, 1916...at the time considered by many to be best-ever Maine college baseball prospect...selected Connie Mack's offer, joining Philadelphia Athletics in summer, 1916...played 71 games for A's, 1916-1917, getting 34 hits in 178 at bats for average of .191... broke ribs during spring training, 1918, and released to Baltimore Orioles, then in International League...played 11 years in International League, batting well over .300 most seasons and helping Orioles take International League crown record-breaking 7 seasons in row, 1919-1925...finished out with Toronto, 1926, Rochester, 1927, and Jersey City, 1928...was later longtime employee of State of Maine Bureau of Taxation, retiring in 1961...died in Waterville, Maine, October 23, 1965.

They Called Him "Rabbit"

Fairfield's Otis Lawry was nicknamed "Rabbit," the story goes, because he was so fleet of foot he could beat out a grounder if it took so much as two hops to short. After his days in the majors with the Philadelphia Athletics, 1916-1917, he starred in the International League with Baltimore, Toronto, Rochester, and Jersey City for a solid eleven years. Here he is in his Maple Leaf uniform, 1926.

The Milwaukee Monster?

With his size 15EEE shoes, his 6′3″, 240-pound frame, and his more-than-generous beard and crop of hair, Pete "Big Foot" Ladd must have appeared for all the world like the Milwaukee Monster as he wound up and threw. Ask Rod Carew, Reggie Jackson, Freddie Lynn, Doug DeCinces and the rest of the California Angels in the 1982 American League Championship Series: they'll tell you.

- ***Stephen Augustus "Steve" Libby - Firstbaseman***

  Born December 8, 1853, Scarborough, Maine...6½′, 168 lbs...moved to Portland at age 10...played first for local Portland club, the Resolutes, in late 1860s and early 1870s...played for Chelsea Club of Boston in 1875...was star for Fall River (Massachusetts) nine, 1876-1877...appeared in 1 game for Buffalo (then in National League) in 1879, going 0 for 2...lifetime major league average is .000...later worked as telegraph operator for New Haven Railroad...died in Milford, Connecticut, March 31, 1935.

- ***Abel Lizotte - Firstbaseman/Outfielder***

  Born April 13, 1870, Lewiston, Maine...last name was also often spelled "Lezotte"...appears to have grown up and attended schools in Lewiston...along with brother Joe, helped power Lewiston to 3rd-place finish in New England League, 1892, batting clean-up and playing either center or right field... while leading Eastern League in batting with Wilkes-Barre (Pennsylvania) was purchased for $1,000 by Pittsburgh Pirates, September, 1896...played in 7 games at first base for Bucs, getting 3 hits in 29 at bats...made hits count as also scored 3 runs and drove in 3 runs...lifetime major league average is .103 ...died in Wilkes-Barre, Pennsylvania, December 4, 1926.

- ***James Royal "Jim"/"Bud" Mains - Pitcher***

  Born June 12, 1922, Bridgton, Maine...son of ex-major league pitcher Willard "Willie" Mains...batted and threw right-handed...6′2″, 190 lbs...pitched for Bridgton High and also preparatory schools in New York and New Jersey...pitched freshman ball for Harvard College in 1942...joined pro ranks with Utica in Eastern League, 1943...had trial with Philadelphia Athletics, 1943, starting and losing only game pitched...lifetime major league record is 0-1 with ERA of 5.63...later hurled in minors for Toledo, Elmira, Little Rock, and San Antonio...graduated from Harvard, 1945...while under contract to St. Louis Browns quit organized ball to found James R. Mains Co., manufacturer of baseball bats and other wood products, 1946...died in Portland, Maine, March 17, 1969.

Like Father, Like Son
Both Willie Mains and his son Jim went into the bat manufacturing business after their pitching days were over. Here's a sample of Jim's wares.

- ***Willard Eben "Willie"/"Grasshopper" Mains - Pitcher***

  Born July 7, 1868, North Windham, Maine...threw right-handed...6′2″, 190 lbs...also known as "The Windham Wonder"...played locally with North Windham Club, 1884-1885, and South Windham Club, 1886...in 1887 turned pro, joining Portland in New England League...in 1888 was with Davenport (Iowa) in Interstate League, winning 21 of 25 games pitched...in August, 1888, signed with Chicago White Stockings and appeared in 2 games for them, winning 1 and

"The Windham Wonder"
Willie Mains, "The Windham Wonder," stole the show with St. Paul in the American Association the year this sketch was made. He recorded a remarkable 38 victories on the mound, while at the same time pounding out a lusty .323 batting average.

losing 1...won 38 games for St. Paul in Western Association, 1889, while being among loop's top 10 hitters with .323 batting average...was also with St. Paul in 1890, batting .315 and pitching well for poor club...signed by manager King Kelly and played for Cincinnati-Milwaukee (franchise was transferred in mid-season) in American Association (then a major league), 1891...enjoyed best year in bigs, 1891, with 12-14 mark and 3.07 ERA...it was then back to New England League, 1892-1896, pitching, variously, for Portland, Lewiston, and Bangor...had short trial with Boston Beaneaters (later the Braves), 1896, winning 3, losing 2, and compiling 5.48 ERA...major league totals are 16-17 with 3.53 ERA over 3 years and 42 games...because of his height which was considerable for the time was dubbed "Elevator Bill" while twirling for Springfield (Massachusetts) in Eastern League, 1897...in 1897 began to experience heart problems and retired from game...produced baseball bats in Sandy Creek section of Bridgton, 1908-1923...father of future major leaguer Jim "Bud" Mains...died in Bridgton, Maine, May 23, 1923.

- ***Charles Walter "Bobby" Messinger - Outfielder***

Born March 19, 1884, Bangor, Maine...batted left-handed, threw right-handed...5′10½″, 165 lbs... graduated from Gardiner High School...entered Bates College but left to join Toronto in the International League...played in 53 games for the White Sox over 3 seasons, 1909-1911...appeared in 1 game for the St. Louis Browns in 1914...lifetime major league average is .172...later coached baseball and football at Edward Little High School, Auburn...appointed Sagadahoc County deputy sheriff in 1924...was elected sheriff in 1936...served Sagadahoc County as sheriff the rest of his life...died in Bath, Maine, July 10, 1951.

- ***Simeon Augustus "Simmy" Murch - Infielder***

Born November 21, 1880, Castine, Maine...batted and threw right-handed...6′4″, 220 lbs...moved to Jamaica Plain, Boston as youngster...played amateur ball for numerous teams in Massachusetts in very early 1900s...was with Haverhill in New England League in 1902; Lawrence, also in NEL, in 1903...played 13 games at third, second, and short for St. Louis Cardinals, 1904, hitting .137 in 51 at bats...started 1905 with Cards, but injured arm and returned to New England League, holding down first base for Nashua...was captain, firstbaseman and outstanding player for Manchester in NEL in 1906...began 1907 with Brockton in NEL but given short shot by Brooklyn, going 2 for 11 in 6 games...lifetime major league totals are 10 hits in 71 at bats for average of .141...returned to minors, playing for Lawrence (1908), Brockton (1909), Indianapolis (1910), Chattanooga (1911), Lynn (1912), and Thomasville, Georgia of short-lived Empire State League (1913)...was baseball, basketball, and assistant football coach at Middlebury College, 1913-1917...involved in war and government work, 1917-1921...was baseball coach and physical education instructor at Phillips Exeter Academy, 1923-1939...died in Exeter, New Hampshire, June 6, 1939.

He Got Around

Simmy Murch in his Cardinals' uniform, 1904. Simmy didn't play much - 22 games total - in his major league career. But he did get around: he held down all four infield positions at one time or another.

- ***William Allenwood "Bill"/"Dasher" Murray - Secondbaseman***

Born September 6, 1893, Vinalhaven, Maine...batted and threw right-handed...5′11″, 165 lbs... presumably moved from Vinalhaven at early age as not listed in 1900 census...nickname "Dasher" may have had Vinalhaven origins: one of first recorded games on the island, dating to 1885, was between two local teams, one named the "Splashers" and the other the "Dashers"...attended Brown University where played second and short on varsity baseball team...joined Washington Senators in late June,

1917...played in 8 games, getting 3 hits (and 4 RBIs) in 21 at bats for average of .143...sold to Toronto of the International League in early August...batted .202 in 47 games for Toronto to close out season... died in Boston, Massachusetts, September 14, 1943.

- ***John W. "Candy" Nelson - Shortstop***

Born March 12, 1854, Portland, Maine...batted left-handed, threw right-handed...5′6″, 145 lbs... appears to have moved to Brooklyn, New York at early age...was playing for the Eckfords, a strong Brooklyn semi-pro nine, before he was 15, shortstopping for them or the Mutuals from 1867 to 1875... played semi-pro in Philadelphia and Allegheny, Pennsylvania in 1876-1877...joined Indianapolis, then in National League, in 1878, batting .131 in 19 games...in 1879 was with Troy, also in National League, hitting .264 in 28 games...after another year of semi-pro in Brooklyn in 1880, joined Worcester, also then in National League, 1881, posting a .282 average in 24 games...was regular shortstop for New York in American Association (a major league at the time) from 1883 through early 1887...had 127 hits in 417 at bats, a .305 average, for New Yorkers in 1883...finished big league career with Brooklyn-Baltimore (the franchise moved in mid-season) in 1890, hitting .251 in 60 games...nine year major league totals are 624 hits in 624 games and 2,457 at bats, good for a .254 average...died in Brooklyn, New York, September 4, 1910.

"Candy" Nelson: the Short Shortstop Who Averaged Exactly a Hit a Game

John "Candy" Nelson as sketched for a periodical entitled *The New York Clipper*, October 8, 1881. Candy was one of the very first diminutive shortstops. At 5′6″ he was, if you will, a short shortstop.

What's truly amazing is that Candy Nelson averaged *exactly* a hit a game over his rather lengthy big league career. Six hundred twenty-four games. Six hundred twenty-four hits. Is there any other player in the history of the game who can make the same claim? I doubt it!

- ***Patrick H. "Pat" O'Connell - Outfielder***

Born June 10, 1861, Lewiston (some records show Bangor), Maine...batted left-handed, threw right-handed...5′10″, 174 lbs...after amateur ball in Lewiston began pro career with Biddeford in New England League in 1885...started 1886 with Lawrence in NEL but drafted by Baltimore in American Association (then a major league) in mid-season...appeared in 42 games for Baltimores, getting 30 hits in 166 trips to the plate for a .181 average...also pitched part of a game, allowing 4 hits and 2 runs in 3 innings...after short stint in majors played in minors at Portland, Maine, Omaha, and Burlington, Iowa...returned to Lewiston in 1890 and became member of police force...later employed at Lewiston Bleachery...retired in 1935...died in Lewiston, Maine, January 24, 1943.

- ***Patrick "Pat" O'Connell - Thirdbaseman***

Born in 1862, Lewiston, Maine...5′10″, 175 lbs...played 11 games for Brooklyn-Baltimore (franchise was moved in mid-season) in American Association (then a major league)...had 9 hits in 40 at bats for .225 average...also drew 7 walks and stole 3 bases...died May 5, 1892.

- ***Marvin Warren "Marv" Peasley - Pitcher***

Born July 16, 1889 (some records show 1888), Jonesport, Maine...batted and threw left-handed...6′1″, 175 lbs...appeared in 2 games for 1910 Detroit Tigers, giving up 13 hits and 11 walks in 10 innings pitched...lifetime major league record is 0-1, with an 8.10 ERA...later served as Water Tender 1st Class in Navy...died in San Francisco, California, December 27, 1948.

• ***Irving Burton "Stubby" Ray - Shortstop/Outfielder***

Born January 22, 1864, Harrington, Maine...threw left-handed...5′6″...graduated from University of Maine...became one of first "college boys" to play in majors when joined Boston Beaneaters (later the Braves) in 1888...batted .248 in 206 at bats, 1888...split season with Beaneaters and Baltimore in American Association (then a major league) in 1889, batting a combined .331 in 139 at bats...played for Brooklyn-Baltimore (franchise was moved in mid-season) in 1890, batting .360, again in 139 at bats...closed out major league career with Baltimore, American Association in 1891, getting 116 hits in 418 at bats for average of .278...also stole 28 bases, scored 72 runs, and hit 17 triples (5th in league)... lifetime major league average is .292 in 902 at bats in 226 games...died in Harrington, Maine, February 21, 1948.

• ***Bertrand Roland "Bert" Roberge - Pitcher***

Born October 3, 1954, Lewiston, Maine...batted and threw right-handed...6′4″, 190 lbs...grew up in Auburn, Maine...graduated from Edward Little High School, Auburn, 1972...graduated from University of Maine, Orono, 1976, with BS zoology degree in pre-dental program...was most impressive 21-5 with 2.00 ERA in 4 years at UMO, helping lead team to College World Series in Omaha senior year...drafted

Firing One In at Fenway
One of Bert Roberge's proudest major league memories is pitching at Fenway Park, July 25, 1984. Here he is firing one in during the two perfect innings he hurled for the Sox vs. the Sox that grand and glorious day.

in 17th round by Houston Astros, 1976, and sent to Covington (Virginia), Appalachian League, where was 2-2 with 3.25 ERA...moved through Astros' farm system, 1977-1979...got call from Houston while pitching for AA Columbus (Georgia), Southern League, May 24, 1979...was 3-0 with tidy 1.69 ERA for Astros, 1979...shuttled between Houston and AAA Tucson, 1980-1983, compiling combined 3-2 mark for Astros...used primarily as middle reliever...two best pitches were slider and forkball...became free agent, October, 1983, and signed by White Sox...split 1984 between Chicago, where was 3-3 with 3.76 ERA, and AAA Denver, where was 5-1 with 1.95 ERA...traded to Montreal Expos, along with Vance Law, for Bob James and Bryan Little, December 7, 1984...split both 1985 and 1986 between Montreal and AAA Indianapolis, compiling overall 3-7 mark with Expos...released by Expos, October 7, 1986... major league totals are 12-12 with 3.99 ERA...highlights include pitching in Fenway Park (Bert is lifelong Red Sox fan and father used to take him to Fenway as a kid) on July 25, 1984 (responding with 2 perfect innings of relief vs. Boggs, Rice, Evans, et al.), and striking out Johnny Bench with bases loaded to save 1-run game for Expos, 1985...is now treasurer of family firm, Curran's Beansprout Co., Auburn... keeps in shape via golf, candlepin bowling, playing ball with his kids, jogging...does some baseball coaching and has worked with Rangers' top prospect, Mark O'Brien of Portland...resides in Auburn, Maine with wife Mary and 3 children, Jennifer, Gregory, and David.

- ***Harland Stimson "Hypie" Rowe - Thirdbaseman***

Born April 20, 1896, Springvale, Maine...batted left-handed, threw right-handed...6′1″, 170 lbs...sent to Hebron Academy by his father to prevent the pursuit of athletics ("You're going up there to get a good education, not to become an athlete," Dad reputedly said.)...fooled father, for awhile, anyway, by playing on Hebron nine under the nom de baseball "H. Stimson"...graduated from Hebron Academy, 1914...starred in baseball and track at University of Maine, 1915-1916...went directly from Orono to Philadelphia Athletics in 1916...played in 17 games for Connie Mack's assemblage, getting 5 hits in 36 at bats for an average of .139...went to spring training with Athletics in 1917 but retired from professional ball when assigned to A's minor league system...enlisted in Army in summer, 1917; wounded in action in France, 1918...played third (with Freddy Parent at short) for powerful Sanford Goodall Textile semi-pro team from 1920 into the 1930s...employee of Springvale National Bank for almost 5 decades, rising to positions of treasurer and chief teller...died in Springvale, Maine, May 26, 1969.

- ***Richard Edward "Dickie" Scott - Infielder***

Born July 19, 1962, Ellsworth, Maine...batted and threw right-handed...6′1″, 170 lbs...17th round selection of Yankees in June, 1981 draft...spent 8 years in Yankee organization, playing at every level except major league...batted .270 with Columbus in 1986...joined Oakland organization in 1989, playing at AAA Tacoma (Washington)...had 2-week stay with parent Athletics in 1989, appearing in 3 games at short...went 0 for 2 at the plate...lifetime major league average is .000...hit .308 as player/coach for Tacoma in 1990...managed Scottsdale A's in rookie Arizona League in 1991.

- ***John Henry Sharrot - Outfielder/Pitcher***

Born August 13, 1869, Bangor, Maine...batted and threw left-handed...5′9″, 165 lbs...appeared in 36 games for New York Giants, 1890-1892, both pitching and playing outfield...as pitcher was 11-10 with 2.89 ERA in 1890...traded to Phillies in 1893, batting .250 in 152 at bats...lifetime major league pitching record is 19-17 with 3.12 ERA...lifetime major league batting record is 71 hits in 299 at bats for average of .237...later played in minors for Worcester, Wilkes-Barre, Bangor, and Brockton...batted .317 with 113 runs scored for Bangor in New England League, 1896...later longtime coach and scout... died in Los Angeles, California, December, 31, 1927.

From Bangor to the Bigs

Bangor-born John Sharrott could hit. And he could pitch, too. Result: he did a bit of both in his four-year stay in the big leagues.

- ***Charles Albert "Charlie" Small - Outfielder***

Born October 24, 1905, Auburn, Maine...batted left-handed, threw right-handed...5′11″, 186 lbs... moved to New Gloucester as a child...attended Pennell Institute in Gray and New Gloucester High before transferring to Edward Little High, Auburn...starred in baseball and basketball at Edward Little ...graduated from Edward Little, 1923...captained baseball team his senior year at Bates College... graduated from Bates, 1927...signed by Red Sox as pitcher but arm injury plus hitting ability caused switch to outfield...burned up Eastern League, 1928-1930, batting .328, .322, and .331 for Pittsfield (Massachusetts)...brought up to parent Red Sox in 1930, hit disappointing .167 in 25 games ...played on and off in Albany, Des Moines, Wilkes-Barre and other minor league stops, 1931-1946... managed Geneva (New York) in Border League, 1947-1950...died in Auburn, Maine, January 14, 1953.

• ***William Charles "Bill"/"Billy" Swift - Pitcher***

Born October 27, 1961, Portland, Maine...bats and throws right-handed...6′, 180 lbs...son of Herb Swift, successful amateur twirler in and around Portland in 1940s...2nd youngest of 15 siblings...grew up in South Portland...standout at University of Maine, Orono, 1980-1984, as helped lead Black Bears into 4 straight College World Series...1st round pick, and 2nd in nation, of Seattle Mariners, free agent draft, June, 1984...received reported $100,000 for signing with Mariners...was member of 1984 U.S. Olympic team...began pro career with Chattanooga (Tennessee), AA Southern League, 1985, where was 2-1 with 3.69 ERA when Seattle called him up in early June...in 23 games, mostly as starter, was 6-10 with 4.77 ERA for Mariners, 1985...split 1986 between Seattle, where was 2-9 with 5.46 ERA, and Calgary, AAA Pacific Coast League, where was 4-4 with 3.95 ERA...began 1987 with Calgary where was 0-0 with 8.84 ERA when underwent surgery for removal of bone spurs in elbow of pitching arm, June 11th...was out for rest of season, 1987...after months of rehabilitation came back and made Mariners' roster, 1988... was 8-12 with 4.59 ERA with Seattle, 1988...recorded best won-lost mark to date, 1989, when was 7-3, with 4.43 ERA...was 6-4 with nifty 2.39 ERA for Mariners, 1990...was 1-2 with even more nifty 1.99 ERA and 17 saves for Mariners, 1991...major league totals through 1991 season are 30-40 with 24 saves...resides in Redmond, Washington with wife Michelle and daughter Aubrey.*

Mr. Mariner

Billy Swift jumped directly from the AA Chattanooga Lookouts to the Seattle Mariners in 1985, the year this photo was taken. Six seasons later, 1991, he's still with the Mariners and has just completed quite possibly his finest effort, racking up a career-high 17 saves and a career-low 1.99 ERA.

• ***George Edward Taylor - Outfielder***

Born February 3, 1855, Belfast, Maine...played 41 games for Pittsburgh in American Association (then a major league) in 1884...had 32 hits in 152 at bats for average of .211...died in San Francisco, California, February 19, 1888.

• ***Edward L. "Ed" Thayer - Secondbaseman***

Born in Mechanic Falls, Maine...played 1 game for New York Giants in 1876, going hitless in 4 trips to the plate...lifetime major league average is .000...deceased.

• ***Stanley Brown "Stan" Thomas - Pitcher***

Born July 11, 1949, Rumford, Maine...batted and threw right-handed...6′2″, 185 lbs...was named "Stanley" in honor of Stan Musial: father grew up in Oklahoma in 1940s when only team one could pick up on radio was Cardinals...raised in Mexico, Maine...graduated from Mexico High, 1967, and University of New Haven (Connecticut), 1971...was 14-3 with U/New Haven...signed by Washington Senators and appeared in 12 games with an 8-5 record and 1.63 ERA for Geneva (New York), New York-Penn League, 1971...was with Burlington (North Carolina), Carolina League, 1972, Pittsfield (Massachusetts), Eastern League, 1973, and Spokane (Washington), Pacific Coast League, 1974 before getting shot with Texas Rangers, June, 1974...was 0-0 with Rangers, 1974, but 4-4 with 3.10 ERA for them in 1975...traded to Cleveland Indians on December 9, 1975, along with Ron Pruitt, for Johnny Ellis...responded with best season, 1976, winning 4, losing 4, and posting crisp 2.29 ERA in 37 games

*(Ed. note: on December 11, 1991 just as WAS BASEBALL was about to go to press, Billy Swift and two other Seattle pitchers were traded to the San Francisco Giants for former MVP Kevin Mitchell and pitcher Mike Remlinger. Billy's reaction: "It should be fun. It's a new league and the hitters haven't seen me and I haven't seen them.").

as both starter and reliever...underwent knee surgery, October, 1976...pitched for Seattle Mariners and New York Yankees, 1977, with combined record of 3-6 and disappointing 6.12 ERA...major league totals are 11-14 with 3.69 ERA in 111 games...highlights were striking out side - Lee May, Tony Muser, and Reggie Jackson - in 9th inning to protect a Dennis Eckersley 1-hitter, and hurling 8-hit complete game, 6-1, July 18, against Rod Carew, Lyman Bostock and Minnesota Twins, both 1976 with Indians... wound down career with Tucson, Pacific Coast League, 1978, Maracaibo (Venezuela), Inter-American League, 1979, and Mexico City, Mexican League, 1980...after baseball career sold insurance by night and drove truck by day for a time...("I learned I was a better baseball pitcher than truck driver": Stan Thomas)...has been in sporting goods business since early 1980s; now owns own rep agency...resides with wife Jayne and daughter Jayne Leigh in Redmond, Washington.

The Man From Mexico

Stan Thomas, shown here as he appeared with Cleveland in 1976, came out of Mexico High to pitch for the Rangers, Indians, Mariners, and Yankees. Ironically, he also finished his career in Mexico . . . with the Mexico City Tigers in the Mexican League in 1980.

- ***Ronald Irving "Ron" Tingley - Catcher***

Born May 27, 1959, Presque Isle, Maine...bats and throws right-handed...6′2″, 180 lbs...moved to Riverside, California at age 5...selected by San Diego Padres in 10th round of free agent draft, June, 1977...began pro career with Walla Walla (Washington), Northwest League, 1977...moved through Padres' system, 1977-1982...batted solid .288 with 13 homers and league-leading 10 triples for Amarillo, AA Texas League, 1981...after going .262 in 115 games for Hawaii, Pacific Coast League, 1982, called up to San Diego where hit .100 in 8 games behind plate...batted .282 with 10 homers for Las Vegas, Pacific Coast League, 1983...granted free agency by Padres, October, 1984...signed by Seattle Mariners' organization, January, 1985...played for Calgary, Pacific Coast League, 1985, batting .253 with 11 homers...signed by Maine, International League, June, 1986...appeared in 49 games for Guides, hitting .205...after successful seasons, batting .269 and .285, at Buffalo and Colorado Springs, 1987 and 1988, appeared in 9 games for Cleveland Indians late in season, 1988, hitting .167...highlight of career to date was clouting 2-run home run against Orioles in first-ever American League at bat, August 3, 1988...traded to California Angels for Mark McLemore, September 6, 1989...called up by Angels from Colorado Springs immediately, appearing in 1st game as Angel that same day, September 6th...went 1 for 3 for average of .333 in 4 games for Angels, 1989...spent first part of 1990 with Angels' AAA Edmonton team in Pacific Coast League, hitting .267 in 172 at bats...recalled by Angels, July 17th, and spent rest of season there, getting into but 5 games and batting .000...with Angels all of 1991, batting .200 in 45 games...highlight undoubtedly was going 2 for 4 with 2 RBIs and run scored in Angels' 10-9 win over Toronto in heat of Red Sox/Blue Jays' pennant race, September 23rd...major league totals through 1991 season are 30 hits in 165 at bats for .182 average over 71 games...resides with wife Robin and sons Sean and Tyler in Riverside, California.

- ***Ledell "Del"/"Cannonball" Titcomb - Pitcher***

  Born August 21, 1866, West Baldwin, Maine...batted and threw left-handed...5′6″, 157 lbs...grew up in Haverhill, Massachusetts...began as firstbaseman but had fastball reported to "split planks," so switched to mound...starred for Haverhill in New England League's inaugural year, 1885...defeated Philadelphia Phillies, 2-1, in exhibition game in Haverhill in late 1885...offered contract by Philadelphia for 1886 season...was 0-5 but with respectable 3.73 ERA for 1886 Phils...began 1887 with Philadelphia in American Association (then a major league) but went to New York Giants in mid-season...was 5-5 total for two teams...had best season in 1888, winning 14 and losing 8 and sporting sparkling 2.24 ERA as Giants took National League crown...struck out 129 vs. but 46 walks that year...started 1889 with Jints but sent down to Toronto in International League early in season...last year in majors was with Rochester in American Association in 1890...was 10-9, including a no-hitter, in which he faced but 28 men, against Syracuse on September 15th...major league totals are 30 wins, including 5 shutouts, against 29 losses, with an ERA of 3.47...remained with Rochester when became minor league club in 1891...hurt arm circa 1892 and retired from organized baseball... was traveling salesman for United Shoe Machinery Co., Haverhill, in later life...died in Exeter, New Hampshire, June 9, 1950.

- ***Robert Garfield "Doc" Vail - Pitcher***

  Born September 24, 1881, Linneus, Maine...batted and threw right-handed...5′10″, 165 lbs...graduated from Ricker Classical Institute in Houlton... attended Colby College for 1 year, 1902-1903...appeared in 4 games for Pirates in 1908, winning 1 game while losing 2...lifetime major league ERA is 6.00...died in Philadelphia, Pennsylvania, March 22, 1942.

And Then He Was Gone

Bob "Doc" Vail, shown here in a circa 1910 photo portrait, is one of a number of our "They Also Played" squad who didn't play much. At least not in the big leagues. He arrived on the scene in 1908, pitched in four games for the Pirates, and then he was gone.

Bryson & Son. Houlton, Me.

Out at the Plate

Ron Tingley, shown here tagging out Milwaukee's Greg Brock at Anaheim Stadium early in the 1991 season, has been in pro ball since 1977; in and out of the majors since 1982. In 1991 he had his most productive season in the bigs, appearing in 45 games for the Angels and batting an even .200 in 115 at bats.

- ***Charles C. "Charlie" Waitt - Outfielder***

Born October 14, 1853, Hallowell, Maine...5′11″, 165 lbs...appears to have moved to Philadelphia, Pennsylvania early in life...played amateur ball for various Philadelphia teams, 1870-1873...was outfielder/firstbaseman for semi-pro Easton (Pennsylvania) Club, 1873-1875...played in New Haven (Connecticut), 1876...saw limited action for Chicago White Stockings in 1877, getting 4 hits in 41 at bats...played semi-pro in New Bedford, Philadelphia, Easton, and Rochester, 1878-1881...appeared in 72 games for Baltimore in American Association (then a major league) in 1882, batting .156...went 1 for 3 in 1 game for Philadelphia Phillies in 1883...lifetime major league batting average is .150 in 83 games... managed the Quickstep Club, Wilmington, Delaware, 1883...deceased.

Honest and Hard-Working Was He

From Hallowell to Philadelphia to the big leagues: that was the story of Charlie Waitt, represented here in a sketch from the December 16, 1882 issue of the periodical, *The New York Clipper. The Clipper*'s scribe wrote that, in addition to Waitt's considerable playing abilities, "a more honest and harder-working player it would be difficult to find."

- ***George Edward Washburn - Pitcher***

Born October 6, 1914, Solon, Maine...batted left-handed, threw right-handed...6′1″, 175 lbs...pitching for Newark, led International League in strikeouts in 1940...brought up to Yankees in 1941...started 1 game but was wild, walking 5 and being charged with a wild pitch in 2 innings worked...lifetime major league record was 0-1 with 13.50 ERA...finished 1941 with Newark where was 9-7...considered a top Yankee prospect for several years but always troubled by control problems...died in Baton Rouge, Louisiana, January 5, 1979.

- ***William Franklin "Bill"/"Roy" Weir - Pitcher***

Born February 25, 1911, Portland, Maine...batted and threw left-handed...5′8½″, 170 lbs...spent much of youth in Portland area before moving to Melrose, Massachusetts...graduated from Melrose High... then on to the Holderness School, Holderness, New Hampshire, where was captain of both baseball and hockey teams...won baseball scholarship to University of New Hampshire, Durham, New Hampshire...won 11 in row for New Hampshire...was signed immediately upon graduation from UNH by Boston Bees (Braves), 1936...was 4-3 with 2 shutouts and masterful 2.83 ERA in debut with Bees, 1936...pitched infrequently for Bees, 1937-1939, with total 2-1 mark...major league totals are 6-4 with 3.55 ERA...pitched effectively for Toronto, 1939, including no-hitter against Rogers Hornsby's Baltimore club on May 16th...sore arm ended career, 1940...worked for Horace Partridge Sporting Goods, Malden, Massachusetts, until enlisted in Navy as gunnery officer in WWII...after war joined AT&T and was executive for them, primarily in Chicago area, 1946-1973...was head of public relations for Lake Shore Club, Chicago, 1973-1976...moved to southern California, 1976...died in Anaheim, California, September 30, 1989.

- ***Walter Merrill "Pop" Williams - Pitcher***

Born May 19, 1874, Bowdoinham, Maine...batted and threw right-handed...5′11″, 190 lbs...moved to Topsham as an infant...graduated from Brunswick High, 1892...attended Bowdoin College, where pitched so well was induced to go pro with Lewiston, New England League, 1895...was 13-5 with Lewiston, 1895...after 2nd year with Lewiston, 1896, moved up to Toronto, Eastern (later International) League...was with Toronto, 1897-1901, with brief interlude in majors with Washington (then in National League) in 1898...for Washington was 0-2 with robust 8.47 ERA...finally got real shot at bigs with Chicago Cubs, 1902, and made most of it...was 12-16 with nifty 2.51 ERA for mediocre club...started 31 games and finished 26 of them...broke little finger on pitching hand covering first on close play and never quite the same again...took mound for 3 clubs, 1903, being sold by Cubs to Phillies in April, and then sold by Phillies to Boston Nationals (Braves) 2 months later in June...record for season, with all 3, was 5-7 with 3.99 ERA...major league totals are 17-25, a 3.20 ERA, and 40 games completed out of 46 started...after season of semi-pro in St. Albans, Vermont, 1904, headed home to Maine where was key cog in baseball in Portland/South Portland for years thereafter...pitched for and managed crack Pine Tree (South Portland) club, 1905-circa 1912...entered politics/civic service in 1912, serving as Topsham selectman almost continuously until 1957...Walter Merrill Williams School, Topsham, is named in his honor...died in Topsham, Maine, August 4, 1959.

- ***George Frank "Squanto" Wilson - Catcher/Firstbaseman***

Born March 29, 1989, Old Town, Maine...batted both left and right-handed, threw right-handed... 5′9½″, 170 lbs...nickname "Squanto" came from his swarthy complexion and dark and piercing eyes... starred as catcher for Bowdoin College in junior year, 1911...signed by Detroit Tigers and appeared in 5 games for them in summer of 1911, getting 3 hits in 16 at bats for .188 average...returned to Bowdoin and graduated, 1912...played for Toronto in International League, 1912...severely damaged arm in collision with opposing thirdbaseman, 1912, and never able to throw properly again...switched to first base and played for Lynn (Massachusetts) in New England League, 1913, leading loop with .365 average...drafted by Red Sox, but appeared in but 1 game for them, 1914, and only for defensive purposes...lifetime major league totals are 3 hits in 16 trips to plate for average of .188...played two more years of minor league ball before ending pro playing career...managed Hanover (Pennsylvania) in Blue Ridge League, 1923...played semi-pro ball in Maine through 1920s...was high school teacher, Reading, Massachusetts, 1914...was principal and teacher, Winthrop (Maine) High School, 1915-1924... was proprietor of Wilson's Dollar Stores, located in Winthrop, Livermore Falls, Auburn, Norway, and Lewiston, beginning in 1915...served as vice-president of Lewiston, Greene and Monmouth Telephone Co. in later years...died in Winthrop, Maine, March 26, 1967.

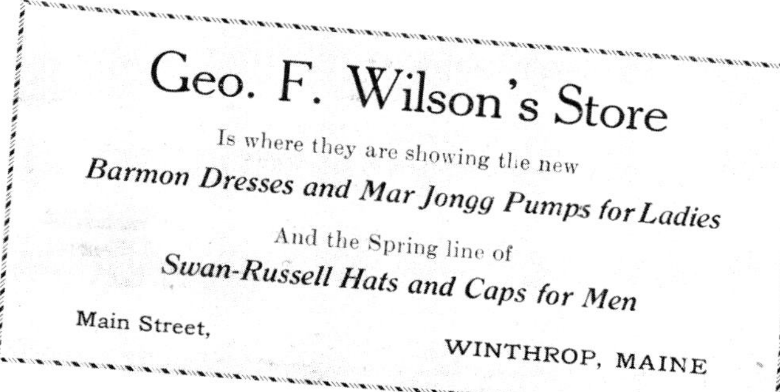

Ladies' and Gents' Attire

After his playing days were over, George "Squanto" Wilson eventually turned to retail. Here's an ad from the June, 1924 issue of *The Winthrop Winner*, Winthrop High's annual student publication.

Bees, Please

Discovered by Bees' GM Bob Quinn, stylish southpaw Bill Weir inked a contract immediately upon graduation from UNH in 1936; soon found himself enjoying his most productive season in the majors.

PHOTOGRAPH/GRAPHIC CREDITS

Page	Description	Courtesy
cover	Portland pitcher and fan	National Baseball Library, Cooperstown, N.Y.
cover	Carlton Willey	Carlton Willey, Cherryfield, Me.
cover	Bert Roberge	Joe Gromelski, Lewiston, Me.
7	1881 Chicago White Stockings	National Baseball Library, Cooperstown, N.Y.
9	Dan Brouthers	National Baseball Library, Cooperstown, N.Y.
11	Michael "Kid" Madden card	National Baseball Library, Cooperstown, N.Y.
15	Napoleon Lajoie	National Baseball Library, Cooperstown, N.Y.
18	Louis Sockalexis sketch	The Hug Collection, Lorain, Ohio
20	Freddy Parent	National Baseball Library, Cooperstown, N.Y.
21	Fans standing behind rope	Boston Public Library, Print Department, Boston, Mass.
21	Fans climbing over fence	National Baseball Library, Cooperstown, N.Y.
21	Rooter's souvenir card	Boston Public Library, Print Department, Boston, Mass.
22	Pine Tree score card and advertisement	Maine Baseball Hall of Fame, S. Portland, Me.
25	Harry Lord card	National Baseball Library, Cooperstown, N.Y.
26	Maine Central Railroad broadside	Maine Baseball Hall of Fame, S. Portland, Me.
28-29	Cleveland Indians' cartoon art	The Hug Collection, Lorain, Ohio
31	Hugh Duffy cartoon art	Maine Baseball Hall of Fame, S. Portland, Me.
31	Hugh Duffy	National Baseball Library, Cooperstown, N.Y.
37	Augusta Millionaires	Maine Baseball Hall of Fame, S. Portland, Me.
40	Jesse Burkett	National Baseball Library, Cooperstown, N.Y.
40	Duffy Lewis/Bud Cornish	Maine Baseball Hall of Fame, S. Portland, Me.
42	Hack Wilson and Bill Terry photos	National Baseball Library, Cooperstown, N.Y.
43	Del Bissonette	Tom Knight, Brooklyn, N.Y.
45	Don Brennan/BIW	Maine Baseball Hall of Fame, S. Portland, Me.
48	both Bobby Coombs photos	Agatha and Bobby Coombs, Ogunquit, Me.
49	Clyde Sukeforth/Billy Southworth	Clyde Sukeforth, Waldoboro, Me.
49	Jackie Robinson	Clyde Sukeforth, Waldoboro, Me.
51	Portland Pilots	Maine Baseball Hall of Fame, S. Portland, Me.
52	all three photos	Maine Baseball Hall of Fame, S. Portland, Me.
53	Charlie Dyke/unidentified fan	Maine Baseball Hall of Fame, S. Portland, Me.
56	Roy Campanella	National Baseball Library, Cooperstown, N.Y.
58	Bobby Thomson	National Baseball Library, Cooperstown, N.Y.
59	Carlton Willey	National Baseball Library, Cooperstown, N.Y.
60	Hank Aaron/Carlton Willey	National Baseball Library, Cooperstown, N.Y.
62	Carlton Willey	National Baseball Library, Cooperstown, N.Y.
63	Casey Stengel, Carlton Willey et al.	National Baseball Library, Cooperstown, N.Y.
65	all photos except John Cumberland	National Baseball Library, Cooperstown, N.Y.
65	John Cumberland	St. Louis Cardinals, St. Louis, Mo.
68	Cecil Fielder	Detroit Tigers, Detroit, Mich.
68	Mike Greenwell	Boston Red Sox, Boston, Mass.
68	Kelly Gruber and Fred McGriff	Toronto Blue Jays, Toronto, Ont.
77	Ron Tingley	California Angels, Anaheim, Cal.
77	Stump Merrill hitting ball	Joe Gromelski, Lewiston, Me.
80	Del Bissonette	Laura Bissonette, Winthrop, Me.
81	Del Bissonette	Laura Bissonette, Winthrop, Me.
84	both photos	Laura Bissonette, Winthrop, Me.
85	photo and ad	Laura Bissonette, Winthrop, Me.
86	all cartoon art	Laura Bissonette, Winthrop, Me.
87	cartoon art	Laura Bissonette, Winthrop, Me.
88	Del Bissonette	National Baseball Library, Cooperstown, N.Y.
91	Topsy Magoon	National Baseball Library, Cooperstown, N.Y.
92	John McGraw photo and Sam Crawford baseball card	National Baseball Library, Cooperstown, N.Y.
96	Buffalo Buffeds	National Baseball Library, Cooperstown, N.Y.
97	Ed Walsh	National Baseball Library, Cooperstown, N.Y.
98	Harry Lord Day souvenir program	Maine Baseball Hall of Fame, S. Portland, Me.

Page	Description	Courtesy
101	Freddy Parent	National Baseball Library, Cooperstown, N.Y.
102	Cy Young	National Baseball Library, Cooperstown, N.Y.
108	Clark Griffith	National Baseball Library, Cooperstown, N.Y.
110	Clark Griffith	National Baseball Library, Cooperstown, N.Y.
111	Holy Cross threesome	National Baseball Library, Cooperstown, N.Y.
112	Louis Sockalexis	National Baseball Library, Cooperstown, N.Y.
113	Cleveland Ball Club letterhead	The Hug Collection, Lorain, Ohio
116	George Gore	National Baseball Library, Cooperstown, N.Y.
117	White Stockings	National Baseball Library, Cooperstown, N.Y.
118	drawing of Polo Grounds	National Baseball Library, Cooperstown, N.Y.
121	Clyde Sukeforth	National Baseball Library, Cooperstown, N.Y.
122	Reds' and Dodgers' photos	National Baseball Library, Cooperstown, N.Y.
122	Great Northern and jumping photos	Clyde Sukeforth, Waldoboro, Me.
123	Cuba and with-daughter photos	Clyde Sukeforth, Waldoboro, Me.
125	Clyde, Branch Rickey, and Leo Durocher	National Baseball Library, Cooperstown, N.Y.
127	Kid Madden	National Baseball Library, Cooperstown, N.Y.
129	Boston team	National Baseball Library, Cooperstown, N.Y.
130	Wilbert Robinson	National Baseball Library, Cooperstown, N.Y.
133	Bob Stanley	National Baseball Library, Cooperstown, N.Y.
134	Bob Stanley	Boston Red Sox, Boston, Mass.
137	Carlton Willey	Carlton Willey, Cherryfield, Me.
138	Carlton and Jesse Gonder photo	National Baseball Library, Cooperstown, N.Y.
141	Irv Young	National Baseball Library, Cooperstown, N.Y.
142	Honus Wagner and Fred Clarke cards	National Baseball Library, Cooperstown, N.Y.
143	Irv Young	National Baseball Library, Cooperstown, N.Y.
146	Georgetown team	Georgetown University, Washington, D.C.
150	Bill Carrigan	Boston Public Library, Print Department, Boston, Mass.
152	Babe Ruth	National Baseball Library, Cooperstown, N.Y.
152	Tris Speaker	Boston Public Library, Print Department, Boston, Mass.
153	Bill Carrigan and Bob Quinn	National Baseball Library, Cooperstown, N.Y.
158	Ralph Botting	Ralph Botting, Mission Viejo, Cal.
158	Don Brennan	National Baseball Library, Cooperstown, N.Y.
160	Bobby Coombs	Agatha and Bobby Coombs, Ogunquit, Me.
160	Danny Coombs	National Baseball Library, Cooperstown, N.Y.
160	Jack Coombs	Special Collections, Colby College, Waterville, Me.
161	John Cumberland/Westbrook	Maine Baseball Hall of Fame, S. Portland, Me.
161	John Cumberland/Cardinals	St. Louis Cardinals, St. Louis, Mo.
162	Curt Fullerton	National Baseball Library, Cooperstown, N.Y.
163	Larry Gowell	National Baseball Library, Cooperstown, N.Y.
164	Fred Howard	Maine Baseball Hall of Fame, S. Portland, Me.
166	Dick Joyce/Andrews	Maine Baseball Hall of Fame, S. Portland, Me.
166	Dick Joyce/Holy Cross	National Baseball Library, Cooperstown, N.Y.
167	Pete Ladd	Milwaukee Brewers, Milwaukee, Wis.
169	Simmy Murch	National Baseball Library, Cooperstown, N.Y.
171	Bert Roberge	Joe Gromelski, Lewiston, Me.
172	John Sharrott	National Baseball Library, Cooperstown, N.Y.
173	Billy Swift	The Sun-Journal, Lewiston, Me.
174	Stan Thomas	Stan Thomas, Redmond, Wash.
175	Bob Vail	National Baseball Library, Cooperstown, N.Y.
175	Ron Tingley	Robin and Ron Tingley, Riverside, Cal.
177	both Bill Weir photos	Nela Weir, Anaheim, Cal.
back cover	author photos	Sharon Packer, Auburn, Me.

All graphic material not listed above is from the author's collection.

Index